MW01182000

ANY QUESTIONS?

A LEADERSHIP PRIMER FOR SUSTAINABILITY, DRIVEN BY LEAN SIX SIGMA

Ralph W. Jarvis

*Create A High-Performance Organization
with a Customer-Centric Culture, Link Strategies to Behavior,
Leverage Supplier Expertise, and Create Tangible Value*

"What is the major differentiator in your marketplace? Quality!
It must be Customer driven, it is a shared Leadership Value and
your Products and Services reflect it!"

ISBN: 1461072824
ISBN-13: 9781461072829
LCCN: 2011905755

Dedications

I may not be there yet, but I'm closer than I was yesterday.

~ Unknown Author

Two of the greatest loves of my life have encouraged me to take a journey less traveled:

Writing a book is journey and I have a wonderful traveling companion. I dedicate this book to my wife, Margaret Jarvis, who is my advocate and inspiration. She has witnessed my discoveries and those "kool" moments that added clarity to my vision. I am so blessed to have such a patient and special partner who encouraged me when that new journey seemed unending.

I also want to dedicate this book to my wonderful aunt, Thelma Porter, who is 101 and has always inspired me to learn and grow richer with knowledge. As an author of a western book and published writer, I can see how her journey has helped me blaze my own path. I would not have grown into who I became without her encouragement and love. Thank you for your blessings and sowing those seeds of thought.

Fellows

It is not enough to do your best; you must know what to do, and then do your best.

~Dr. W. Edwards Deming

Quality Management has almost 100 years of solid concepts and theories that are substantiated by statistical analysis and decades of producing tangible benefits. Those prudent underpinnings effectively implement Lean Six Sigma tools and methodology. Studying this body of knowledge is essential to understanding proper Transformation. I believe it is fitting to recognize the genius and original thought that created this body of knowledge:

Dr. Walter A. Shewhart was an American physicist, engineer, statistician and due to his direct involvement in the first quality program, is oftentimes referred to as the "Father of Statistical Quality Control".

Dr. William Edwards Deming was an American statistician, professor, author, lecturer, and consultant. Dr. Deming conducted a thriving consulting practice for more than 40 years. He is perhaps best known for his work in Japan. In recognition to Dr. Deming's contributions, the Japanese Union of Science and Engineering award annual Deming prizes for quality and product dependability.

Josef Juran was arguably the first quality expert to emphasize that no Quality Management system works unless people are empowered and committed to take responsibility for quality - as an ongoing process -

effectively for quality to become part of part of people's behavior and attitudes - an ethos.

Taiichi Ohno is considered the father of the Toyota Production System, which later became known in the United States as the Lean Manufacturing methodology.

Dr. Kaoru Ishikawa ("Ishikawa Kaoru") was a Japanese University professor and influential Quality Management innovator best known in North America for the Ishikawa or cause and effect diagram (also known as Fishbone Diagram) that are used in the analysis of industrial process.

Dr. Gen'ichi Taguchi is a Japanese engineer and renown statistician. He has been a vanguard of statistical prowess and was admired by Deming and others as direct contributor to Quality Management.

Philip Bayard "Phil" Crosby, was a businessman and author who contributed to management theory and Quality Management practices. He focused on zero defects, similar to Lean and modern Six Sigma.

Bill Smith is the "Father of Six Sigma". After working for nearly 35 years in engineering and quality assurance, he joined Motorola, serving as vice president and senior quality assurance manager for the Land Mobile Products Sector.

Acknowledgements

Life is partly what we make it, and partly what it is made by the friends we choose.

~ Tennessee Williams

To my friends, a village raises the children and maybe we all think along these lines, especially when we call our supporters and contributors, "friends". For their knowledge and their relationships forge tremendous insight based on openness, honesty and condor. Perhaps without knowing, they give us the special encouragement to take the opportunity to explore and go through that door down an unknown path, stretch and seek what is over the next horizon. If you are open to advice and new ways of thinking, then you will begin that journey with that first step.

Along this journey, I suddenly recognized that a tremendous resource was under my nose. I consider myself extremely fortunate to have such good friends who were willing to share their experience, knowledge, and expertise. Each of you were truly my change agents. Many thanks to my very special friends:

Traci Bernard, thank you for helping me with this book. You are a great example how business would be so much richer if all executives had your Customer-centric mind-set.
Thank you, Traci.

John Brownlow, the waves of change will continually beat down the shores of tranquility, but you have often shown me the silver lining in the storm. You are a skipper of innovation. John, thanks for being open to providing sound opinions and other ideas that I needed to consider. A sincere, thanks mate!

Walt Casey, your shared thoughts from your experience with Dr. Deming were very helpful and insightful for me. Thank you for your suggestions and approach to researching Quality Management. Your advice, experience and insight have always been greatly appreciated.

Raul Colon, you showed me how construction technology addresses sustainability strategies and converts prudent use of energy, water and other resources into tangible benefits. You have always been ahead of the curve. Mil gracias por su ayuda, Raul.

Johnny Lopez, your perspectives gave me other avenues to explore, especially in real life instances. Thank you for sharing your thoughts, Johnny.

David Sutherland, you are a born leader and good friend. Understanding your timing, I can not thank you enough for helping me better understand key executive issues. Thanks for the help, David.

Jim Whorton, you always listen to my issues and encourage me to continue that path to see the journey's end. Thanks Jim, for listening and giving me encouragement.

Letter to the Leaders

It is not necessary to change. Survival is not mandatory.

~Deming

Dear Owner or Executive Leadership:

We are now faced with the realization that our planetary resources are finite and our stewardship will indeed dictate our Quality of Life in the 21st century. In 1987, the Brundtland Commission created the concept of Sustainability to identify "forms of progress that meet the needs of the present without compromising the ability of future generations to meet their needs." As Americans, we have that heritage reflected in what Theodore Roosevelt said over a century ago; "To waste, to destroy our natural resources, to skin and exhaust the land instead of using it so as to increase its usefulness, will result in undermining in the days of our children the very prosperity which we ought by right to hand down to them amplified and developed."

Why is Sustainability so important? Today's Executives recognize that what has been a common practice is not a sustainable practice now. Since the Industrial Revolution, beginning in the 18th century, countries began their industrial growth rapidly, based on their resources, and at the expense their environment. Conservation practices were never considered, nor seldom applied. Today, many Third World countries do not have a sustainable existence for their current population let alone the next generation (i.e., Haiti). Lacking recognition of our ecosystem's degradation, endangered species, contemporary potable water issues, air pollution, Sustainability holistically recognizes commercial transformation within the constraints of limited and finite resources.

How can a Sustainability Initiative help your core business? It provides your company a Transformation model with bedrock foundations for Economic, Environmental, Social and Technological quadrants. Resources are finite. Your success will be measured by satisfying your Customer's needs, having a high performance organization to address those needs, recognizing how Sustainability will impact your products and services, and leveraging the strength of your Supplier's expertise. We are in a global marketplace where waste is no longer acceptable and its costs affect your operation's survivability.

Today, most companies are not fully optimized and retain inefficiencies in day-to-day operations of doing business. A Quality initiative provides leadership to learn from past experiences and avoid repeating poor practices or failures. By institutionalizing Continuous Improvement processes, your organization will have a higher chance of long-term success. Lean Six Sigma reigns in that change cycle and installs a framework that can manage Change into a Value proposition and Brand enhancement for your concern.

Combining Sustainability and Lean Six Sigma is a synergistic approach that will promote your initiative's success. From one focused initiative, crossover benefits would almost assuredly provide significant Tangible Benefits by understanding how to retain your progress. Recognize that your organization has different needs, approaches must be tailored to fit the stage of growth for the company, and solutions should be fitted to your company's maturity level, as well as, those bothersome elements you want help to reduce or eliminate.

This journey will build a better relationship with your Customers, Employees and Suppliers. Business and IT strategies will be linked to key processes in your organization that will have the most impact on your bottom line. Suppliers will be closer aligned to your business models and Quality standards. Specifically, Lean Six Sigma is chosen most often to provide paths to build closer Customer relations, to fulfill Customer needs, to improve internal Efficiencies, to define Supplier roles and provide flexibility for future Sustainability.

This book is focused on making that Transformation a positive effort in improving your culture, policies and procedures, but more importantly, creating an empowered culture of performance, quality growth, savings, while potentially improving your brand. Any change will have a cascading effect on your organization; however, that change can be successfully managed to transform what you now have to what you would like the organization be in the future.

As a Leader, read this primer for that journey to prepare and transform your Vision and organization into a Customer focused Quality driven Culture. Like any other business catalyst, candid one-on-one discussions and walking through the content will provide understanding and clarity. Sir Winston Churchill said; "The price of greatness is responsibility." Any Questions? Let's collaborate and discuss our Next Steps ...

Best regards,

Ralph Jarvis, Global MBA, MM, LSS BB
Jarvis Business Solutions, LLC
Ralph.Jarvis@JarvisBusinessSolutions.com
www.JarvisBusinessSolutions.com
Phone: +1-888-743-3128

Quick Topic Discovery

"Know where to find the information and how to use it - That's the secret of success"

~Albert Einstein

Book Organization: Recognizing that your time is valuable, this book has been tailored to fit your time constraints, ease of access to information and summary of every chapter. To begin, I recommend that you read these few sections, first:

- Executive Overview [first chapter]
- Your Customers, Your Company
- Opt for Change [last chapter]

For clarity, the following examples are provided to illustrate what to expect while reading each chapter:

Chapter Summary: Business Transformation is a top-down approach to making an organization into a Customer serving, competitive tool. By nature, ...

Key Points:
- Business Transformation

Special Note: More information is available in Appendix: DMADV Descriptions.

Each chapter has a short summary and list of key topics. It is suitable for Executives, advisors, facilitators, and implementation staff, as well as, external consultants. For example:

Drivers for Change: Specific drivers found in separate layers of your business planning infrastructure, include:

Customer
Direct impact of the Customer...

Financial
Country risks [economic stability, exchange rates...

Internal
Management long distance distractions impacts leader responsibilities...

Learning
Corporate staff will need to interface effectively in a global organization

Special note: Key Points that are designated in each chapter prepare the reader to anticipate specific subsections and topics. This is another feature to help the reader discover information in this book. The chapter headings and key points are also utilized in the Appendix: Key Points (found in the appendix).

Table of Contents

1.0: Executive Overview

The obscure we see eventually. The completely obvious, it seems, takes longer.

~ Edward R. Murrow

Chapter Summary: Your Customers are your focus. Ultimately, you need to understand that pushing decision making and responsibility to the front line of workers will enhance effectiveness. They work with your Customers. In reality, are they not your Subject Matter Experts?

Key Points:
- Think Quality, Think Lean
- How Do We Begin?
- Understand the Obvious
- It's the Approach
- Accountability
- Lean Accounting
- Susatianability Accounting
- A System Approach
- Integrated Transformation Solutions

Think Quality, Think Lean:[1] Why wouldn't a company embrace Quality? After all, it's virtually free. It enhances the products and servic-

---

1   Taiichi Ohno, Shigeo Shingo and Eiji Toyoda developed the system between 1948 and 1975.

es that are sold to the public. It improves the brand image of the company (and mitigates warranty, safety, and Quality issues). It can save money on removing defects, improve Customer Satisfaction, improve clarity of goals and objectives, Improve delivery of products and services in terms of time to market, enhance your production processes, and provide a structure for ongoing improvement that enhances and perpetuates your Quality effort, through the discipline of Lean Six Sigma.

How Do We Begin? As the Owner or CEO, you should recognize the Customer is foremost in the formula of success. But the picture is not complete without seeing the Business, Marketing, and IT models you have to drive that success. Additionally, you probably already think your Process and IT infrastructure may not be optimized. This is your starting point to identify points of alignment and integration. Now how do we begin?

The first major step is to understand how big the problem is. Generate ideas, but generate those ideas in a structured environment. Based on the Voice of the Client, your company's Sustainability vision, and Lean Six Sigma expertise, collaboratively scope the problem, look at possible scenarios, consider Business Influencers and where they cause impacts, identify key resources, select a champion and create a Business Transformation Plan. It is best if the senior leadership team prioritizes the Quality Initiative against their collective strategies. The initiative must be integrated into current strategies and senior leadership team must accept ownership. Commitment and buy-in from top management is the primary factor in Business Transformation success.

Why should Sustainability be included in this initiative? The marketplace is more globalized than in the previous century. Children raised in the 1960s are now an integral part of the workforce, globally, and their environmental values are now being integrated into business Plans. Outsourcing and right sourcing are now highly emotional domestic issues in the US and have become political issues. So, what are some of the current drivers for Sustainability?

- At many corporations, the Sustainability movement has a simple premise: Saving the planet can save big bucks through frugal use of resources, new technology and business practices.
- Continued volatile price swings in plastic packaging, fuel, cotton, food ingredients such as corn, and a host of other raw materials have added urgency to businesses' efforts to shave costs to keep prices competitive.
- Adoption of Sustainability efforts in this decade could have a real impact on their shareholder value. Initiatives will become as transformative for business as the earlier Quality and Information Technology revolutions.
- "Sustainability has emerged as a factor in determining which companies win in the marketplace.
- Knowledgeable enterprises see brand and corporate identity opportunities.

Sustainability Maturity			Quality Maturity		
Renewable Resources Consumption	State Of The Environment	Sustainability Level	Product Or Service	Process	Quality Level
More than nature's ability to replenish	Environmental degradation	Not sustainable	Poor Products Poor Services Poor Customer Satisfaction	Defects Variations Waiting No Control	No Quality Poor Brand
Equal to nature's ability to replenish	Environmental equilibrium	Steady state economy	Improved Products Improved Services Improved Customer Satisfaction	Reduced defects Reduced variation Process control	Implemented Quality Program Improved Brand
Less than nature's ability to replenish	Environmental renewal	Environmentally sustainable	Customer centric Customer driven Innovation Align to Customers Align Marketing	Customer centric Business driven Innovation Align Suppliers Align IT	Optimizing Enterprise Quality and Brand

Understand the Obvious: The bottom line: Long a cause célèbre of the eco crowd, sustainable business practices are yielding big savings at companies like PepsiCo and Wal-Mart. Long the subject of green

3

marketing campaigns, sustainable business practices are now yielding big savings and winning over CEOs.[2]

The 21st century will reveal a new paradigm in which business is no longer separate from society. Realizing the new "business-as-society" paradigm will require the efforts and ingenuity of organizations across the sectors and industries. It will challenge the current generation of business leaders to apply their hard-won knowledge to novel problems, and the next generation to cut their teeth on issues of unprecedented importance and complexity.[3]

To evolve from a punitive and coerced marketplace, to raise above market constraints and recognize that sustainability and quality initiatives are important roles to tailor fit transformation and service a catalyst for progress.

In the formative stages of a non-sustainable environment, many executives will view the role of government as a taskmaster who forces corporate behavior to align to laws, rules, and regulations. Compulsory requirements are often perceived by Executives as additional bureaucratic costs; therefore, sustainability is considered a cost increase and a threat to profitability.

Sustainability, when accepted by the executives, will recognize that corporate immersion will provide a long term maturity model that is flexible, driven by market needs, and will provide for prudent resource utilization. Globally, all corporations will be competing for the same limited resources. From this perspective, corporations will recognize the contributions from its Suppliers, Partners, and measure effectiveness of the internal organization.

---

2   Stanford, Duane; Why Sustainability Is Winning Over CEOs; Bloomberg Businessweek Companies & Industries; March 31, 2011; Retrieved: 14 May 2011
3   Laughland, Pamela and Bansal, Tima; The Top Ten Reasons Why Businesses Aren't More Sustainable; Ivey Business Journal; Retrieved: 4 April 2011

Not Sustainable: This is the current state in most countries and corporations. Resources are harvested faster than nature's ability to replenish. In this phase, companies become aware of how they are using resources like air, carbon, water, and electricity in order to run their businesses in compliance with government regulations. Basic recycling, energy conservation policies and cost reduction programs are usually the first steps of sustainable change. Additionally, little or no understanding is given to process improvement and Quality initiatives.

Steady State Economy: In this phase, countries and corporations establish strategies and policies that promote nature's ability to replenish and reach a state of equilibrium between supply and demand. At this plateau, companies apply increased awareness and apply systems thinking to optimize their processes, reap financial benefits, increase performance and productivity. In this phase, companies leverage sustainability to differentiate their offerings to the market and improve brand image. At this phase, companies may simply announce a separate "sustainability or green" strategy that is not necessarily integrated into other business strategies.

Environmental Sustainability: Ultimately, this is the summit for all Sustainability and Quality initiatives. Countries may pass protective laws covering regulation of land, sea, air, and endangered creatures in their domain. Whereas; Companies would weave Sustainability and Quality philosophies into their overall Corporate Strategy, Brand Name, Customer Products and Services, Supplier relationships and Corporate Culture.

Understanding your Sustainability and Quality maturity levels is a beginning to clearly understand the depth and breadth of your Transformation Initiative. Recognition of potential areas for push-back from stakeholders, either internal or external, is a wise exercise in prudence. Top 10 hurdles for Business Sustainability in 2011, include:

- There are too many metrics that claim to measure sustainability—and they're too confusing.
- Government policies need to incent outcomes and be more clearly connected to sustainability.
- Consumers do not consistently factor sustainability into their purchase decisions.
- Companies do not know how best to motivate employees to undertake sustainability initiatives.
- Sustainability still does not fit neatly into the business case.
- Companies have difficulty discriminating between the most important opportunities and threats on the horizon.
- Organizations have trouble communicating their good deeds credibly, and avoid being perceived as green washing.
- Better guidelines are needed for engaging key stakeholders, such as aboriginal communities.
- There is no common set of rules for sourcing sustainably.
- Those companies that try leading the sustainability frontier often end up losing.[4]

What are some examples of benefits from sustainability initiatives of the corporations? There's a wide variety of examples that show tangible benefits that can impact the bottom line of any corporation. In a recent interview, Graf laid out four stages that most companies move through as they use sustainability principles as a lens to better understand operations and improve efficiency and productivity.

- First, companies become more aware of how they are using resources like carbon, water, electricity in order to run their businesses in compliance with regulations.

---

4   Ibid, Laughland, Pamela and Bansal, Tima;

- Second, companies use the increased awareness to optimize their processes, reaping financial benefits through cost savings and increased productivity.

- Third, companies leverage sustainability to differentiate their offerings to the market.

- Fourth, companies weave sustainability into their overall corporate strategy, as opposed to simply trumpeting a separate "sustainability strategy." [5]

Ray Anderson (1934 - 2011) was the founder of Interface, a manufacturer of commercial carpet tile. He recognized the way we have traditionally created, operated and planned our enterprises in a short sighted method, often without regarded to the impact on our planet, was not the best approach. He wrote: "The industrial system takes too much, extracting and frittering away Earth's natural capital on wants, not needs, ... It wastes too much. It abuses too much. It takes stuff and makes stuff that very quickly ends up in landfills or incinerators— more waste, more abuse, more pollution ... I believe that a sustainable society depends totally and absolutely on a new mind-set to deeply embrace ethical values. Values that, along with an enlightened self-interest, drive us to make new and better decisions. I also believe that it doesn't happen quickly ... it happens one mind at a time, one organization at a time, one building, one company, one community, one region, one new, clean technology, one industry, one supply chain at a time ... until the entire industrial system has been transformed into a sustainable system, existing ethically in balance with Earth's natural systems, upon which every living thing is utterly dependent."

Mr. Anderson incorporated his philosophy and concern for sustainability into the day-to-day operations of Interface. During his tenure as founder and CEO, Mr. Anderson improved his company and his corporate web touted their continued progress:

---

5   Graff, Peter, Chief Sustainability Officer, SAP, Four Steps to Improving Profits through Sustainability, Forbes: CIO Network: Retrieved 31 March 2011, Forbes: CIO Network: Retrieved Forbes: CIO Network: Retrieved 31 March 2011

- Interface has a goal to be powered by 100% renewable energy. As of 2010, eight of nine factories operated with 100% renewable electricity, and 30% of our total energy use was from renewable sources.
- We reduced our greenhouse gas emissions from our global manufacturing operations by 35% from our 1996 baseline through diverse strategies including process efficiencies, energy efficiencies (such as lighting and equipment replacement), fuel switching, and use of renewable energy.
- Our waste reduction efforts have resulted in a 76% decrease in total waste to landfills from our carpet factories since 1996.
- Interface has several facilities around the world certified by U.S. Green Building Council's (USGBC) Leadership in Energy and Environmental Design (LEED) certification system, a third-party certification program that awards recognition for high performance green buildings.
- Quality Utilizing Employee Suggestions and Teamwork (QUEST) began in 1995 as a program to drive waste reduction efforts at our factories. It's an employee-led system to define and eliminate waste. This allows for more optimal yarn usage and significantly less waste. It is estimated that the portable creels reduce scrap yarn up to 54%.
- All of our global factories have been certified to conform to ISO 14001, the international standard for environmental management systems. ISO 14001 helps us minimize the environmental impacts of our operations while working toward continuous improvement.
- Trees for Travel™ – Program designed to track and neutralize the carbon emissions from employee business air travel. Interface has planted more than 118,000 trees to neutralize the carbon emissions from business related air travel since this program started in 1997.
- Cool Fuel™ – Program to track and offset carbon emissions from company cars. Using money received from corporate fuel card rebates, Interface purchases certified carbon offsets to balance the carbon emissions of our corporate fleet. Interface has purchased 2.4 million gallons of Cool Fuel and retired over 27,000 metric tons of certified carbon offsets as a result of this program.

- Cool CO_2mmute™ – Program offering Interface employees the opportunity to neutralize the emissions from their daily commutes and personal travel. Interface matches employee contributions to purchase tree plantings that neutralize carbon emissions from their commutes. Nearly 45,000 trees have been planted since this program began in 2002.

Mr. Anderson recognized that Sustainability was a change in leadership and the corporate culture. Since business models were none existent during the late 20th century, experimentation with ideas, methodologies and empowering his employees to become engrained in that philosophy was based on hard earned lessons learned. The message was embraced by everyone.

Business Roundtable (BRT)is an association of chief executive officers of leading US companies with nearly $6 trillion in annual revenues and more than 13 million employees. BART member companies comprise nearly 1/3 of the total value of theUS stock market best more than $114 billion annually in research and development - nearly half of all private US R&D spending. Those companies pay more than $179 billion in dividends to shareholders. The BRT companies get nearly $9 billion a year in combined her contributions.[6] These corporations who have embraced sustainability have garnered tangible benefits from their efforts and include:

Healthcare industry:
McKesson: McKesson has existed for more than 178 years. So, Sustainability goes hand-in-hand with their goal of building healthier organization that delivers better care to patients. They owe their success to by accuracy, efficiency and continual improvement. With web based analytics technology, they are able to minimize carbon dioxide emissions and related distribution costs. Through data center consolidation, they have reduced annual energy consumption by more than 1.58 million kilowatt hours and reduced carbon dioxide emissions by 1,160 metric tons.

---

6   Business Roundtable, 2011, the BRT Sustainability Report

Abbott: Abbott has 123 year history of sustaining their enterprise and continuing to deliver value to their stockholders. As a worldwide corporation, it's focus has been on for strategic citizenship and sustainability priorities: innovation, enhancing access, protecting patients and customers, while safeguarding the environment.

In 2010, Abbott invested $3.7 billion in research and development and partnering with 75 leading universities and research institutions. Their focus is on critical global challenges like cancer, heart disease, diabetes and neurological disorders.

Also in 2010, Abbott and the Abbott Fund invested more than $625 million in grants, private donations and projects to increase health system capacity and infrastructure. Also during that time, Abbott remains deeply committed to providing safe, effective products that patients and consumers can depend on. They conducted more than 1,200 site quality audits of key suppliers to ensure safety of their products ingredients.

Information Technology industry:
IBM: In 2011, IBM's Sustainability strategies are a reflection of societal, and environmental objectives that are fused into IBM's business approach. That focus is centered on four segments: energy-efficient buildings, next-generation data centers, Smarter Cities, and Smarter Computing.

CA Technologies: CA Technologies believe today's world requires more than a sustainable business model and it's smart business that counts: good for people, good for the planet, and good for company. They believe doing the right thing attracts the best people, builds brand value, and deepens relationships with our customers in parts.

Some of the most significant technology innovations have been inspired by sustainability objectives. They consider themselves a leader in software that monitors and manages corporate sustainability. The new products and services were also critical for future growth. Their innovations are applied to reducing energy consumption, increase operating efficiency, and addressing concerns about climate change.

Insurance industry:

The Hartford Financial Group: the Hartford is celebrating their 200th birthday in 2010. The company has implemented innovation Sustainability strategies that have reduced greenhouse gas emissions, brought "green" products to the market, adopted an environmental investment policy and invested in electric vehicle technology. It has committed to reducing greenhouse as emissions by 15 percent from 2007 to 2017. Hartford's most recent building was built to LEED Silver standard. Since 2009, they have saved a billion sheets of paper from their usage in 2009. They are also the first company to cover electric vehicle charging stations under its homeowner policies.

Aetna: Aetna is a healthcare company that provides insurance and other services. One of its major strategic initiatives is focused on reducing delays that accounts for up to one third of a healthcare spending.

In 2010, Aetna reached important milestone in reaching her goal of decreasing energy consumption in all of their largest own facilities. This decline safe 6.4 million kilowatt hours across the enterprise over three years. Their sustainability program applied newer more energy-efficient technology and implemented a plate frame eating exchange technology that is typically used for office buildings, however they applied it in a 24/7 data center environment, using outside air.

Aetna also reduced their carbon footprint. They invested in infrastructure and cultural changes to need to expand their telework program. Currently, 38% of their total workforce works from home, safe and estimated 79,000,000 miles of driving, 3.3 million gallons of gas, and more than 20,000 metric tons of carbon dioxide emissions each year.

Manufacturing industry:

Motorola: Has successfully reduced their carbon footprint by 35 percent and their energy use by 28 percent since 2005. They have also increased their purchase of renewable energy by 21 percent worldwide. In addition, Motorola has incorporated their Sustainability strategies into existing business strategies to apply their technologies to reduce Customers run supply chains, logistics and energy grids more efficiently.

Alcoa: 2010, Alcoa aggressively restructured their cost base and re-shaped their portfolio and applied efficient and disciplined operating procedures to enable sustainability, profitable growth, and sharing long-term survivability.

These criteria necessitated the adoption of both innovated operational and financial initiatives. Whether the marketplaces were centered on aerospace, transportation, defense, packaging, construction, or con-sumer electronics, Alcoa recognized their customers new realities in sustainability challenges.

Sustainability is not a foreign concept in Alcoa. Aluminum has been a clear choice for recyclable, light eight, strong, conductive, and sustain-able. Approximately 75% of all aluminum ever produced is still used today.

Alcoa continues to reduce greenhouse footprints of their operations while replenishing the land. In 2010, they reduced greenhouse gases by 18% below 2005 levels. Their goal for 2020 it is a 20% reduction in those pollutants and they appear to be on track.

Alcoa also leads in recycling innovation. Currently there processes save 90% of the energy used to make aluminum from ore. Their recy-cling efforts, leads the industry, and insurers that aluminum cans are back on store shelves within 60 days.

Service industry:
Accenture: Skills to Succeed is a strategy to equip 250,000 people globally by 2015. Accenture is also using their Telepresence services to provide 60 international locations to avoid more than 10,000 tons of carbon dioxide from air travel. They have also extended the scope of current strategies to recognize Sustainability, like their global supply chain that reviews the environmental, social, and ethical performance of key suppliers.

FedEx: FedEx flies about half million miles and drives almost 12 million miles daily in order to deliver 7 million packages to 220 countries. FedEx recognizes the power it well in his prime products. In 2009, petroleum contributed 43% of US carbon emissions.

Phoenix is considering one alternative, under development, for their cargo planes to use biojet fuel. FedEx is working with the Federal Aviation Administration, Department of Energy, and Commercial Aviation Alternate Fuel Initiative to develop certification standards for biofuels.

Another new energy alternatives is electric vehicles in the last 31 in service by mid-2011. Operational management costs are much lower than those gas engines, in some cases 70-80% lower.

Transportation industry:
Union Pacific: : Union Pacific has almost reached its 150 anniversary and prides itself owning core resources to connect a nation. In 2010 alone, it reduced diesel fuel by 27 million gallons that improved fuel efficiency by 3 percent. During that time, it increased gross ton freight miles by 8 percent, while reducing fuel emissions. Compared to 2009, it delivered 13 percent more carloads per day while using only 8 percent more train miles.

BNSF: BNSF believes that their transformation model is more fuel-efficient, has less emissions, and contributes to sustainability innovation more than land-based tracking. It provides its customers with customized analysis of total real carbon footprint and savings compared to alternative freight lines. In 2010, the NFS services reduced emissions by about 30 million metric tons of carbon dioxide by moving freight via rail instead over the road. This is equivalent to reducing consumption by approximately 3 billion gallons of diesel fuel compared to truck only choices.

BNSF continues their effort to improve fuel efficiency and sustainability through technology by: installing energy management systems that offer tremendous fuel savings, investigating alternative fuels and rail lubrication technologies, establishing training and incentive programs to implement fuel efficient train handling practices.

In 2011, BNSF is committing $3.5 billion in capital expenditures to improve their network, facilities and operations. Having acquired for than 1,100 new locomotives last four years, a BNSF training can now move each turn they have 100 miles on a single gallon of diesel fuel.

If you are considering Quality Management, chances are you have an organization that is structured and recognizes the need to align your organization to better serve your Customers. You holistically see your organization's need to increase its effectiveness and profitability. Lessons Learned promote improvement and creativity to solve problems and improve Control.

However, there are many companies that will not choose Quality methodologies mainly because they do not see potential benefits, but rather see problems in changing their organization, not willing to invest time, money, and effort to better Service their Customers or feel that Quality Management is too complicated. These organizations are usually in the first phase of most Maturity models. They are in a niche that has no interest to increase their performance other than "fight fires" more often in their stressful fast-paced environment to meet their Customer demands.

Unfortunately, this business philosophy ignores how to retain their current Customers, promotes excessive costs to create new Customers for Customer replacements, does not understand Product or Service attributes, and probably does not acknowledge its competition. They sorely need a Business Transformation initiative to ensure better chances of survival. But, a journey begins with the first step. In this case, that initial step is recognizing the Customer. Lean Six Sigma can be applied in this case to better align to Customer needs, encourage repeatability, and meet Customer Satisfaction.

For those who want to better understand the value of Lean Six Sigma and how their organization could benefit from its methodology, answers to five business questions will reveal interests and direction. Additional Quality questions will help you focus on the specifics and where LSS methodology can be engaged.

In 2008, Leader-to-Leader Institute published a book that focused on the five most important business questions that should be asked:

- What is our Mission?
- Who is our Customer?
- What does the Customer Value?
- What are our Results?
- What is our Plan?[7]

Why is the examination important? Business leaders are always asking the questions: "Where are we now?" and "Where do we want to be?" These five important questions drive home critical issues of Mission, Customer, Customer value, Results, and a plan to improve the situation. Each of these questions will drive the focus of the Business Transformation and how it will be integrated into your organization. The gap between strengths and weaknesses is an opportunity for improvement with the potential benefits for your organization.

However, the core of those five initial questions will focus on your enterprise understanding. For those questions will be central to your effort and importance to that understanding, as well as, awareness of potential consequences. Additional principles work around these next seven process-oriented concepts:

- What is an Input?
- What is a Process?
- What is an Output?
- Who is our Supplier?
- What is the Supplier's Value?

---

7   Drucker, Peter; The Five Most Important Questions You Will Ever Ask About Your Organization; Leader to Leader Institute, 2008

- What is a System?
- What is the System's Value?

It's the Approach: As Dr. W. Edwards Deming, the father of Quality Management, pointed out, focus on your how your resources are applied, so, Quality Management can provide gains in many areas:

- Quality up...
- Production of good Product up...
- Capacity up...
- Lower cost per unit of good product...
- Profit improved...
- Customer happier...
- Everybody happier...

These gains were immediate (seven weeks), cost zero, used the same work force, created the same burden, and required no investment in new machinery. This is an example of a gain in productivity accomplished by a change in the System, namely, improvement in definitions, effected by management, to help people work smarter, not harder.[8]

Accountability: The president of a company wrote: "Our people and the plants are responsible for their own Product and for its Quality."

Deming strongly disagreed, saying, "They are not. They can only try to do their jobs. The man that wrote the article, the president of the company, is the one that is responsible for Quality."

The management of another company put the following dictum in the hands of all employees. They can only be described as pitiful. "Our Customers expect Quality. The Quality of our products is the primary responsibility of the operator in that he must make it correctly. Inspectors share this responsibility."

---

8   W. Edwards Deming, Out of the Crisis (1986).

Deming was dismayed by this example and said, "Again, the operator is not responsible for the Product nor its Quality. He can only try to do his job. Moreover, responsibility divided between operator and inspector, as it is in the quotation, assures mistakes and trouble.... the Quality of the Product is the responsibility of management, working with the Customer."[9]

"The problem is at the top; management is the problem." Dr. Deming emphasized that the top-level management had to change to produce significant differences, in a long-term, continuous manner.

Lean Accounting: There are both positive and negative reasons why Lean Accounting is important. The positive reasons are that Lean Accounting

- Provides information for better lean decision making. These better decisions lead to improved revenue and profitability.
- Reduces time, cost, and waste by eliminating wasteful transactions and systems.
- Identifies the potential financial benefits of lean improvement initiatives and focuses on the strategies required to realize those benefits.
- Motivates long-term lean improvement by providing lean-focused information and statistics.
- Addresses customer value directly by linking performance measurements to the drivers of value creation and driving changes to maximize this value.

All the negative reasons relate to the shortcomings of traditional accounting, control, and measurement systems. Traditional systems do not work for companies pursuing lean thinking; indeed they are actively harmful. Traditional systems are not the wrong way to work, but they are designed to support mass production. Lean manufacturing and

---

9   W. Edwards Deming, The New Economics – For Industry, Government, Education; Second Edition; page 16, MIT press, 1994

other lean methods violate the rules of mass production. When you try to use traditional accounting systems and lean manufacturing, you will find they conflict with each other.

Problems caused by traditional accounting, control, and measurement systems include the following:

- They motivate people to use non-lean procedures, such as running large batches and building inventory.
- Traditional systems are wasteful. They require huge amounts of unnecessary work, gathering and analyzing data, producing unhelpful reports, and generating additional non-value-adding tasks.
- Standard costs can harm lean companies because they are based on premises grounded in mass production methods. Lean manufacturing violates all the assumptions of mass production. Whereas mass production is based on achieving economies of scale through long production runs, lean focuses on making products one at a time. It is no wonder, then, that these accounting methods lead people to do the wrong things, such as out-source items that should be in-sourced. In addition, the methods are complex and confusing to generate, they provide a misleading understanding of cost, and they lead to wrong management decisions on important issues, such as make/buy, profitability of sales orders, rationalization of products or customers, and so forth.

Lean Accounting provides:

- Lean performance measurements, which replace traditional measurements.
- Methods to identify the financial impact of lean manufacturing improvements.
- A better way to understand costs, product costs and value stream costs.
- Methods to eliminate large amounts of waste from the accounting, control, and measurement systems.
- Time freed up for finance people to work on lean improvement.

18

- New ways to make management decisions relating to pricing, profitability, make/buy, product/customer rationalization, etc.
- A way to focus the business around the value created for customers.[10]

Sustainability Accounting: Implicit in the development of social accounting is a recognition that the activities of an organization have effects not just upon the organization but also upon its wider environment. Thus social accounting shows a concern with the effects of the actions of an organization on this external environment. This is based upon the recognition that it is not just the owners of the organization who have a concern with the activities of that organization. Additionally, there are a wide variety of other stakeholders who justifiably have a concern with those activities, and are affected by those activities. Indeed those other stakeholders have not just an interest in the activities of the firm but also a degree of influence over the shaping of those activities. Such stakeholders can include:

- suppliers of raw materials and other resources;
- customers for the organization's products or services;
- employees;
- the local community;
- society at large;
- the government of the countries in which the organization is based or conducts its activities.

This influence is so significant that it has been argued that the power and influence of these stakeholders is such that it amounts to quasi-ownership of the organization. Indeed the traditional role of accounting in reporting results has been challenged. This challenge argues that accountability should be based upon a stakeholder approach, recognizing the whole stakeholder community rather than an ownership approach. The benefits of incorporating stakeholders into a model of performance measurement and accountability have, however, been

---

10   Maskell, Brian H. and Baggaley, Bruce; Chapter 1 - Why Is Lean Accounting Important?, Practical Lean Accounting: A Proven System for Measuring and Managing the Lean Enterprise, Productivity Press copyright 2004 Citation

extensively criticized. Thus different schools of thought exist, however, as to whether there is any benefit in taking into account the needs of all stakeholders in the management of a company. Thus, for example, the techniques of value based management are based upon the premise that the way to maximize the performance of a company, for the ultimate benefit of all stakeholders, is by focusing upon the creation and maximization of shareholder wealth. On the other hand, the stakeholder management school of thought disagrees and argues that performance for an organization can only be maximized when the organization addresses directly the needs of all stakeholders.

Social accounting first came to prominence during the 1970s when the performance of businesses in a wider arena than the stock market, and its value to shareholders, tended to become of increasing concern. This concern was first expressed through a concern with social accounting. This can be considered to be an approach to reporting a firm's activities which stresses the need for identification of socially relevant behavior, the determination of those to whom the company is accountable for its social performance and the development of appropriate measures and reporting techniques. Thus, social accounting considers a wide range of aspects of corporate performance and encompasses a recognition that different aspects of performance are of interest to different stakeholder groupings. These aspects can include:

- the concerns of investors;
- a focus upon community relations;
- a concern with ecology.

Measuring performance in terms of these aspects will include, in addition to the traditional profit-based measures, such things as:

- consumer surplus;
- economic rent;
- environmental impact;
- non-monetary values.

Many writers consider, by implication, that measuring social performance is important without giving reasons for believing so. Solomons (1974), however, considered the reasons for measuring objectively the social performance of a business. He suggests that while one reason is to aid rational decision-making, another reason is of a defensive nature.[11]

A System Approach: In 1993, Deming observed, "It would be better if everyone would work together as a System, with the aim for everybody to win." It was apparent to him in the early 1990s a Corporation was more than a collection of processes, it was a framework that included top management's involvement, Process standardization and Transformation, Quality Evaluation and Improvement, and dependent on effective Continuous Improvement.

Then, what is a System? A System is a network of interdependent components that work together to try to accomplish the aim of the System. A System must have an aim. Without an aim, there is no System. The aim of the System must be clear to everyone in the System. The aim must include plans for the future. The aim is a value judgment. (We are, of course, talking here about a created System.)

A System is a network of interdependent components that work together to try to accomplish the aim of the System. A System must have an aim. Without an aim, there is no System.[12]

A System must be managed. It will not manage itself. Left to themselves in the Western world, components become selfish, competitive. We cannot afford the destructive effect of competition.

By investing money, people, and time into a Quality Transformation initiative, you are addressing concerns that impact your strategies, processes, effectiveness and how those components are institutionalized.

---

11   Aras, Guler and Crowther, David; The Durable Corporation, Chapter 7 - External Verification—Audit and Rating Systems, Gower Publishing Limited © 2009
12   W. Edwards Deming, The New Economics – For Industry, Government, Education; Second Edition; pages to 95-96, MIT press, 1994

You are "tuning" your "change engine" in your company to better reflect the marketplace. How? By relying on what can be discovered, measured, analyzed, and managed. Lean Six Sigma methodology scrutinizes costs, develops in-house expertise in performance areas, effectively utilizes resources and enhances your corporate culture to focus on controlling your entire organization to produce Quality products and services you know will satisfy your Customers. Business Transformation should recognize and provide:

- *Executive Quality Commitment* – is focused long-term strategies that focus on Customers' needs and Satisfaction of those needs. This commitment is based on a Quality vision for products and services and how that vision can be effectively implemented. Commitment should be focused on the Products, Processes and Services that can be measured through these five points:

  o   Lower cost of production
  o   Continuous Improvement
  o   Process cycle time
  o   Fixed asset utilization
  o   Working capital efficiency[13]

- *Meta Planning* – is based on the enterprise landscape and the Quality vision. It addresses business alignment, business concepts, and addresses the need for innovation of Products, Services, and Processes.
- *Transformation* – is accomplished through integrated solutions based on Lean Six Sigma methodology. Those components include Quality Strategies, Process Transformation, Quality Evaluation, and Learning Transformation throughout the Business Transformation initiative. Management must recognize that Business Transformation will affect the corporate culture, begin accumulating information

---

13   Robert S. Kaplan and David P. Norton, Strategy Maps, Harvard Business School Press, 2004, page 67.

on corporate effectiveness (Profound Knowledge), and provide a mind-set for management and employees alike.

- *Realization* – is the phase that recognizes the tracking of efforts and translating those efforts into tangible benefits for the Corporation. This is done through the institutionalization of best practices; the periodic review of Products, Services and Processes; the integration and application of any systematic approach to two fundamental strategies, Continuous Improvement; and the cultural integration of Lean Six Sigma principles and developing an environment for learning.

Any existing organization, whether a business, a church, a labor union, or a hospital, goes down fast if it does not innovate. Conversely, any new organization, whether a business, a church, a labor union, or a hospital, collapses if it does not manage. Not to innovate is the single largest reason for the decline of existing organizations. Not to know how to manage is the single largest reason for the failure a new venture.[14]

To successfully respond to the myriad of changes that shake the world, Transformation into a new style of management is required. The route to take is what I call Profound Knowledge—knowledge for Leadership of Transformation.

The worker is not the problem. The problem is at the top! It is Management's job. It is management's job to direct the efforts of all components toward the aim of the System. The first step is clarification: everyone in the organization must understand the aim of the System, and how to direct his efforts toward it. Everyone must understand the damage and loss to the whole organization from a team that seeks to become a selfish, independent, profit center.[15]

---

14   Drucker, Peter F.; The New Realities, first edition, Harper and Row publishers, 1989, page 226

15   Deming, W. Edwards. 1993. The New Economics for Industry, Government, Education, second edition.

Lean Six Sigma provides Business and IT solutions to enhance efficiency, productivity, and profitability based on your Customers' needs, through Business Transformation, to establish holistic principles that provide a necessary structure for visibility through integrated analytical and problem solving, collaboration to establish objectives for efficiency, productivity, profitability, and address areas of improvement:

- Address Customers' needs and problems
- Relationship between sales, operational, technical and financial metrics
- Transformation Methodology
- Customer-Related Processes
- Supplier-Related Processes
- Customer orientation of IT applications
- Supplier orientation of IT applications
- Internal orientation of IT applications and Processes
- Systems Integration
- Business readiness of Customers and Suppliers
- Relationship Between Drivers and Operational Excellence

Integrated Transformation Solutions: Why do successful companies remain so? They transform waste, inefficiencies and risks into tangible benefits. They refine their strategies and incorporate Quality into their products or services and eliminate defects. By using Lean Six Sigma methodology, new solutions become a daily routine to improve efficiency, productivity, enhance profitability, and translate those solutions into tools and other competitive instruments.

Lean Six Sigma initiatives should be designed to address needs based on Strategic Services, Tactical Services, and utilization of Resources. Again, collaboration is a key communication model to define the scope, depth, and breath of your Quality initiative. Holistically, top management should consider the Four Corners of Lean Six Sigma integration, which include:

- Strategic services address the conceptualization of your Quality initiative and address the underlying components needed for a firm **Quality Strategy**.
- Processes are fundamental keystone in the support and delivery of Quality products, services, and other internal processes. These **Process Transformation** services provide two different Roadmaps: the first Roadmap addresses legacy processes and refinement of those processes to remove defects, cycle time, and other wastes that may be present; and, the second Roadmap addresses the need for designing effective and efficient new processes.
- **Quality Evaluation** is essential in measuring and identifying tangible benefits from the Business Transformation. These business performance services address the current activity, compare to your targets for a future state, and verify those benefits extracted from your organization.
- Finally, **Learning Transformation** provides Continuous Improvement techniques that are applied to your resources (human resources, IT resources, and other business resources). Again, these services are based on Deming's Cycle (PDSA: Plan, Do, Study, Act).

2.0: Your Customers, Your Company

Quality is the result of a carefully constructed cultural environment. It has to be the fabric of the organization, not part of the fabric.

~ Philip Crosby

Chapter Summary: Fundamental building blocks of a successful Transformation initiative is based on the understanding of the business environment and how those components could impact your success or failure.

Key Points:
- Understand Your Culture
- Generic Catalysts
- Applying Quality (Frequently Asked Questions)
- Maturity Knowledge
- Future Transformation Pressures
- Corporate Drivers for Change

Understand Your Culture: "Company cultures are like country cultures. Never try to change one. Try, instead, to work with what you've got." was the mantra of Peter Drucker. Organizations not prepared to address the internal culture will meet stiff resistance and "push back" against the change. Understand how communication with employees can be enhanced by empathizing, creating a business case, providing a vision for the future, and enlisting employee-led changes to improve procedures and processes.

Lean Six Sigma will instill a "measured" culture; one that quantifies a problem, investigates the root cause, and applies solutions that should mitigate the problem. One of Lean Six Sigma's goals is to attain Process stability and efficiency.

Why would your company's philosophy and management style be important to the adaptation and adoption of Quality programs? First, are you self-motivated to improve your financial opportunities through Business Transformation? You are most likely to succeed, primarily since you believe it is the right path and you are self-motivated and willing to "adapt and adopt." These are critical elements of the Transformation. Management's openness and ability to convey the desire to work smarter—not harder—will influence the workforce to improve, take pride in their accomplishments, and channel that energy into measurable progress.

Are you pursuing this course in order to garner future business and be perceived as a "Quality" company? In this scenario, if you are driven by "certification" rather than qualifications, you will ultimately fail due to lack of understanding and commitment to any Quality program. Brand recognition is important, but you need substance behind the façade. Build the infrastructure you want in terms of Business, Marketing, and IT models, and then you will succeed.

Last, are you in a crisis due to the constraints of the Great Recession and fear failure is near? A company in dire straits with its back up against the wall may be looking for a silver bullet. Any Quality program is not a quick fix. It is a long-term commitment that is in the corporate fabric. To be obliged to accept this change, under duress, could very well distract your true need to focus on survival. You can begin that Transformation with cost-effective Lean techniques that are both quick to implement and cost effective.

Generic Catalysts: Proactive, focused businesses are generally the winners. Businesses move into a proactive mode, but what inspires the business Owner to take such a step? Ten of the most frequent reasons for change within a business are:

- *Third Party Intervention* – A financial institution that has supported the business may seek improvements in business performance to reduce a potential risk to their investment. This may prompt the business leaders to take improvement actions that were previously alien to satisfy the institution and reduce the risk to their own assets that may be held as a guarantee against the investment.
- *Sales Decline* – There may be a serious decline in sales. Competition, new technologies, a failure to meet the Customer needs and expectations, a history of poor Product development and introduction or poor marketing may all contribute to reduced sales and be the catalyst for the business Owner to change the approach to the business development.
- *Management Buyout* – Other directors remove the Owner or CEO through a buyout and change business policies; therefore, a Transformation approach ensues.
- *Takeover* – The business is acquired and the policies and practices of the acquiring business are adopted and introduce a proactive approach to the business. This may follow the appointment of new executive directors.
- *Lack of Internal Skills* – The dearth of management skills within the business may trigger the appointment of an external senior executive who brings new methodologies, planning and enterprise to the business.
- *Family Business 'Turmoil'* – The autocratic Control of an Owner may at times be changed only through the realization that permanent family divisions are undesirable. It may well be the opportunity for perhaps the "university-educated next generation of family" to demonstrate their abilities in setting and achieving sustainable growth strategies and managing the culture change.
- *Raise Capital* – The success of raising new funding may be dependent upon the appointment of an executive or non executive

director to oversee the business on behalf of the provider. Such an appointment will add new skills to the management team as well as promote improved business practices.

- *Exit Strategy* – A business Owner may realize that in order to optimize business value at the expected time of his or her exit, changes in the way the business is run will be necessary. The delegation of responsibilities, training of staff, and implementation of strategic plans may be areas exploited to reduce the dependence of the Owner on the business.

- *Delegation or Renegade Action* – When the business Owner does not have the skills necessary to effectively manage the organization, authorities may be delegated to or seized by an opportunist director to manage the business. A weak, unskilled business Owner may be relieved that some responsibilities have been reassigned; however, should the delegate or opportunist fail to match expectations, more severe difficulties may arise for the business.

- *Project-Based Change* – Should implementation of an improvement project be planned without sufficient internal resources or the capability to manage the change, it may be desirable to appoint a consultant or interim manager for a fixed term. Change can be implemented with less interruption of staff conducting their normal duties.

The business Owner should always Control the business and this is easier to achieve if change is planned, well managed, and is aligned to the goals of the organization.[16] A bridge to better understand your Customers' needs should include at least these three principles:

- Lower cost to serve
- Responsive delivery time
- Enhance Quality[17]

---

16   Willetts, David; Retrieved: 23 July 2010
17   Robert S. Kaplan and David P. Norton, Strategy Maps, Harvard Business School Press, 2004, page 67.

Applying Quality (Frequently Asked Questions): How can Lean Six Sigma help a small or medium-size business? Here are a few key issues that typically lead a medium or small CEO or Business Owner to decide to exit the business, usually through a sale, at less than desirable financial results:

Question: The company is overly dependent on short-term debt. No cash reserves have been established to meet short-term cash situations. Also, cash shortages preclude funding essential business growth strategies. Serious cash needs can cause shortsighted actions.

Answer: Lean Six Sigma elimination of waste, defects, and cycle times can have an immediate impact on cash flow and reduce cash needs by becoming more efficient and productive.

Question: Management structure is too thin. The Owner or CEO is so tied to the business that there are no resources for the Owner or CEO to share management responsibilities. Thus decision making, sales, marketing, operations, and growth are restricted to the Owner's or CEO's abilities and available time.

Answer: Lean Six Sigma empowers employees to become more responsible for their actions. Additionally, the concept of a "Process owner" also instills better management and control at each Process level providing visibility and control that may not currently exist.

Question: A specific business strategy is lacking. There is no strategic business plan to focus resources effectively toward goals and to increase profits. This is critical and rarely done consistently in small business today.

Answer: Lean Six Sigma is a business strategy that drives Continuous Improvement and retains the gains of your Quality program. The methodology focuses on efficiency and addresses cost effectiveness. Also, Lean Six Sigma provides a holistic approach, from a strategic level to mitigating variation at your Product and Service levels. Incentives and bonus plans can be linked to support required efficiency, productivity and utilization of resources based on their area of responsibility.

Question: The Owner or CEO dies or is disabled. Being prepared for the calamities that can ruin a business is a responsibility that many business Owners do not take seriously enough. Insufficient financial and management preparation for the death or disability of the Owner or CEO can create chaos for those left to sort out the issues.

Answer: Lean Six Sigma provides a framework that focuses on consistency and structure. In the event that an Owner or CEO is disabled or dies, Lean Six Sigma provides architecture to continue day-to-day operations; monitors areas of weakness; and assigns "Process owners" and links to ongoing strategies.

Question: The assets of the Owner or CEO or business Owner are unbalanced. Most personal assets are in the value of the business. Little independent retirement savings have been established for the Owner or CEO/major shareholders in the event of a business downturn. In the absence of a strategic exit, the sale of the business is required as a retirement alternative. (CEO Advisor Blog n.d.)[18]

Answer: A Lean Six Sigma disciplined culture adds a tremendous level of professionalism in your organization. Management practices that are currently absent would be injected into the concern. Lean Six Sigma is a respected Quality methodology that should add value to your organization and its culture.

Maturity Knowledge: So, what business knowledge should be used in Business Transformation? Not all change is homogenous and the Maturity of the concern will also be a qualifier. That means that every company has a unique set of variables, assets, and needs, which are dictated by various influencers (i.e., marketplace, product, service, strategic vision, etc.). So, those needs and required changes to incorporate

---

18   CEO Advisor Blog, This entry was posted on October 6, 2010. This source provides the original ten key issues that motivate change in a business. LSS remarks were not included. Retrieved: 30 November 2010.

solutions in your everyday business Process will require openness, critical thinking, and adaptation based on your Quality definition, commercial needs, and recognition of your corporate culture.

To manage, one must lead. To lead, one must understand the work that a leader and his or her people are responsible for. Who is the Customer (the next stage), and how can we serve better the Customer?[19] If we are to understand Deming's point, we must understand that work includes effective usage of resources (Human, Information and Organization capital), a keen understanding of the processes, and a clear identification of the Customer(s).

If the Customer is satisfied and your team meets or exceeds expectations, then a manager will naturally focus on Quality, cost, timeliness, and effectiveness of resources to meet goals. If the Customer is not satisfied, are you sacrificing Quality, cost, timeliness, and effectiveness of resources due to urgency, expediency, or fear? Are you recognizing that a Customer issue or problem is an opportunity to Improve your processes to ensure that Quality; cost, timeliness, and effectiveness of resources are not sacrificed?

Future Transformation Pressures: Within the next five years, there will be significant global trends that will impact your organization. Some of these are market forces, substantial in Asia, and illustrate the fundamental growth of the world market and the consequences of globalization. Another key point is the continued use of outsourcing rather than looking at Quality alternatives. Last but not least, is the realization of limited resources. Many strategic resources will become apparent during this time frame, especially water. The following five points elaborate on the importance of these global trends:

• Continued rise of economic influence in Asia, especially in China, which is now the second-largest economy, after only the United States. The Indian economy is also growing significantly. Future

---

19 Deming, W. Edwards; Out of the Crisis (1986).

anticipated growth is expected to come from four major countries: Brazil, Russia, India, and China.

- Use of outsourcing as a cost-cutting strategy will continue in most Western countries until reduction of costs will no longer be beneficial.
- Banks and other financial institutions will increase rates to increase their revenue. Future trends after the Great Recession will reflect a stable financial environment and foster increased competition.
- Scarcity of rare earth resources will continue. Current resource tensions between China and its major trading partners (i.e., Japan, United States) will expand in the future.
- Potable water will continue to be a limited resource. Other countries will face similar water problems should trends continue. Increased demand due to population increase is currently pitting water rights against industries and people in both India and China.
- Increased terrorism and piracy along with military and economic instability in the Indian Ocean region will continue to grow.

From a US perspective, within the same time frame, corporate America is faced with strategic opportunities in the form of current environmental considerations, Sustainability, health care, and international relations that develop increased trade for the United States. Within this five-year time frame, US trends will have a significant impact on the direction and business philosophies that promote Quality Processes products, and services. The following key trends are of the utmost importance in developing a holistic approach to the marketplace:

- Increased attention to a "green" environment will increase the cost of this energy alternative, unless technological breakthroughs reduce production costs. Also, current carbon-based energy sources will increase energy costs.
- Health care costs in the United States will climb in spite of current health reform legislation.
- US trading will need to increase substantially to help move the US out of the Great Recession. European limited cooperation will con-

tinue. Latin American countries have looked for trading policies for decades with little or no resolution.

- Environmental and natural disasters, combined, could have a significant impact on the environment due to pollution, flooding, drought, and high summer temperatures on agricultural products.

Corporate Drivers for Change: Beware of losing Quality and acquiring waste. Specific drivers found in separate layers of your business planning infrastructure, include:

Customer
- Direct impact of the Customer
- Corporate dependence on International Suppliers
- Recertification/rework of goods and services
- Reintroduction of defects, waste, and variation
- Communication pitfalls (language various English definitions, slang, lack of corporate lexicon, lack of industry vocabulary)

Financial
- Country risks (economic stability, exchange rates, crime levels, type of crimes—drug/weapon/terrorism/kidnapping)
- Home office to outsourced location—travel costs
- Retraining for policy and procedures
- Loss of Intellectual capital by theft or corporate espionage
- Obligation to create contingency and risk-mitigation planning for outsourcing
- Expat costs to ensure Quality of products and service; policy and procedures; protect corporate assets

Internal
- Management of long distance distractions impacts leader responsibilities
- Technology transfer without Control
- Technological differences (electricity stability, reliable communications, IT standards, and protection could be jeopardized, data risk)
- Loss of processes and possible strategic processes

- Communication pitfalls (language, various English definitions, slang, lack of corporate lexicon, lack of industry vocabulary)

Learning
- Corporate staff will need to interface effectively in a global organization
- Understood trust between management and employees may be different culturally
- Knowledge, in-house, may be depleted in outsourcing project
- Knowledge levels and expertise (a degree in country X may not be comparable to US college degree, technical expertise by certification is critical, need for testing to validate skills)
- Cultural differences in the outsource host country may have castes systems, ethnic cliques, or other societal divides that may be contentious.
- Cultural differences (holidays, work ethic, work schedule different than your office, corporate rethink of timing and expectations, learn to approach topics with several examples—always validate understanding)

2.1: Barriers to Change

It's the only program I've seen where customers win, employees are engaged and satisfied, and shareholders are rewarded.

~ Jack Welch, former Chairman and CEO, GE

Chapter Summary: Whether you are a small, medium, or large business, your corporate culture, team and individual behaviors are barriers to change. Recognize their characteristics and begin to mitigate those barriers to change.

Key Points:
- Transformation Is
- Understand Cultural Concerns
- Underlying Factors for Failure
- Early Warnings
- Behaviors Encouraging Failure
- Your Culture as a Competitive Tool
- Understanding The Power Of Empathy
- Making Sense By Making The Business Case
- A New Look Toward The Future
- Progress By Establishing New Procedures

Transformation Is: Remember what Andy Grove, CEO of Intel, said about Transformation? That shedding Process helps your organization transform almost immediately, in the short run and continues to transform in the long term, depending on Executive Quality Commitment. For the remainder of the book, store that definition and understand the details and their implications as we unfold the layers of complexity and present a structured path to successful Business Transformation.

65

Six Sigma initiatives focus on improving profitability and Customer Satisfaction, rather than simply improving Quality. Six Sigma initiatives are for companies that want to be profitable and achieve world-class performance.[20]

Looking at Six Sigma through the lens of a Systems approach, we can begin to understand why GE has been so successful in its implementation. In their 2000 annual report, we see that Six Sigma is one of four strategies for success (included with Globalization, Services, and Digitization) and is used as the fundamental way in which all GE employees run their processes.[21]

As mentioned earlier, Leadership is key to driving values and guidelines throughout the organization. Lack of Leadership or an unwillingness to demonstrate discipline or a sense of purpose will impact your System of Quality. "Work-arounds" or methods that circumvent your processes are indications that your leadership and processes are broken and probably cost your corporation in resources, time, or information.

Understand Cultural Concerns: Why the resistance to change? Would top executives not consider anticipating resistance in their organization? Change must be taken in context. The last twenty years have witnessed significant changes in almost all industries in the United States and impacted trading partners worldwide. There has been downsizing, restructuring, takeovers, bankruptcies, and significant economic instability. So, from an employee's point of view, the last thing that many

---

20   Adams, Cary; Praveen Gupta and Charlie Wilson; Six Sigma Deployment; Butterworth-Heinemann © 2003 (311 pages) Citation ISBN:9780750675239.
21   Ibid; Adams, Cary; Praveen Gupta and Charlie Wilson; Six Sigma Deployment ISBN:9780750675239.

l. g. Dupree /computers

want is more change. In many cases, employees are stressed, angry, and distrustful of management.

The risk of change is seen as greater than the risk of standing still. – Making a change requires a kind of leap of faith. Making a change is all about managing risk. But if you sell your idea of change based only on idealistic, unseen promises of reward, you won't be nearly as effective in moving people to action. The power of the human fight-or-flight response can be activated to fight for change, but that begins with the perception of risk.

People feel connected to other people who are identified with the old way. – We are a social species. As you craft your change message, you should make statements that honor the work and contributions of those who brought such success to the organization in the past, because on a very human but seldom articulated level, your audience will feel asked to betray their former mentors (whether those people remain in the organization or not). A little good diplomacy at the outset can stave off a lot of resistance.

People have no role models for the new activity. – Get some people on board with your idea, so that you or they can demonstrate how the new way can work. Operationally, this can mean setting up effective pilot programs that model a change and work out the kinks before taking your innovation "on the road." For most people, "seeing is believing". Less rhetoric and more demonstration can go a long way toward overcoming resistance, changing people's objections from the "It can't be done!" variety to the "How can we get it done?" category.

People fear they lack the competence to change. – Change in organizations necessitates changes in skills, and some people will feel that they won't be able to make the transition very well. They don't think they, as individuals, can do it. The hard part is that some of them may be right, and that's why part of moving people toward change requires you to be an effective motivator. You can minimize the initial fear of a

38

lack of personal competence for change by showing how people will be brought to competence throughout the change process.

People feel overloaded and overwhelmed. – Fatigue can really kill a change effort, for an individual or for an organization. You've got to motivate and praise accomplishments as well, and be patient enough to let people vent (without getting too caught up in attending to unproductive negativity).

People have a healthy skepticism and want to be sure new ideas are sound. – It's important to remember that few worthwhile changes are conceived in their final, best form at the outset. Healthy skeptics perform an important social function: to vet the change idea or Process so that it can be improved upon along the road to becoming reality. So listen to your skeptics, and pay attention, because some percentage of what they have to say will prompt genuine improvements to your change idea.

People fear hidden agendas among would-be reformers. – Reformers, as a group, share a blemished past...if your change project will imply reductions in workforce, then be open about that and create an orderly Process for outplacement and in-house retraining. Get as much information out there as fast as you can and create a Process to allow everyone to move on and stay focused on the change effort.

People feel the proposed change threatens their notions of themselves. – Sometimes change on the job gets right to a person's sense of identity. When resistance springs from these identity-related roots, it is deep and powerful, and to minimize its force, change leaders must be able to understand it and then address it, acknowledging that change does have costs, but also (hopefully) larger benefits.

People anticipate a loss of status or Quality of life. – Some people will, in part, be aligned against change because they will clearly, and in some cases correctly, view the change as being contrary to their interests.

People genuinely believe that the proposed change is a bad idea. – To win people's commitment for change, you must engage them on both a rational level and an emotional level.

Underlying Factors for Failure: No executive plans to fail, but failure to address barriers in your organization can promote failure from the onset. Here are seven critical areas that every Executive or Owner should be aware of:

- Failure begins with lack of Executive Quality Commitment (Owner/CEO)
- You do not address reluctance, since you were burned in the past
- Top Management does not value the upfront investment in planning time
- Most organizations do not know how or have the skill set to implement change in an organization
- Senior Executives and Managers think Transformation is voluntary, not obligatory
- IT Executives and Managers think Transformation is a software tool
- Organization are not aligned to your Business effort (i.e., Accounting, IT, etc.)

Early Warnings: There are many signs of failure. Some are based on the Strategic Transformation Plan, others are based on employees' fears and still others are obvious behaviors evident from management. Pay attention to these insights and anticipate their consequences. Improve your success possibilities by mitigating behaviors, early:

- No Incentives to Change Behavior or Motivation
- Lack of Personal Ownership
- Poor Communications from Management
- No Plan Behind the Concept
- Passive Management
- Reluctant Leadership
- Lack of diverse thinking or collaboration

Behaviors Encouraging Failure: Dr. Peter Drucker was said: "Most of what we call management consists of making it difficult for people to get their work done." Where do top executives fail in the implementation and deployment of Lean Six Sigma? Oftentimes, management is not aware of potential problems. If not incentivized to ensure the success of Lean Six Sigma implementation, executives may not agree to the selection of the projects that are candidates for improvement or they may be too politically isolated in their organization to actively participate in the methodology. For numerous reasons, Lean Six Sigma programs can fail due to inactions and behavior of top executives.

Modeling behavior starts with the Executive Team. Listed below are seven types of behaviors an Owner or CEO would want to be aware of to preempt pitfalls to your Business Transformation Initiative. For illustration purposes, the following partial list of key senior management pitfalls illustrates how management undermines potential success of Lean Six Sigma projects from inception:

- Lack of organizational alignment (horizontal or vertical)
- No visible Leadership at the executive level
- Not having a metrics in place for management participation
- Project selection process does not identify projects related to business objectives
- Business executives do not show up for review of project reviews (conveys a lack of priority)
- Believing a single initiative can or will solve all your problems
- Not having multiple projects queued up for each Master Black Belt, Black Belt, or Green Belt (so when they complete a project, the next one has already been selected)[22]

Executives are not the only ones who must be diligent that their actions do not impact efforts to complete the initiative. Middle management behaviors related to failure are another weakness that needs to be highlighted:

---

22   Wurtzel, Marvin; "Reasons for Six Sigma Deployment Failures" Wurtzel Consulting, Inc., Posted: Friday June 13, 2008, Retrieved: 18 October 2010.

- Using Black Belts for firefighting
- Process Owners believe they have the option to not buying in to the Lean Six Sigma methodology
- Managers do not show or schedule project reviews (this conveys a lack of priority)
- Poor selection process for Black Belts (i.e., experience, education, desire, aptitude, etc.)
- Not having multiple projects queued up for each Master Black Belt, Black Belt, or Green Belt (so when they complete a project the next one has already been selected)[23]

Your Culture as a Competitive Tool: Resistance is a key element of why change fails. Resistance to change may be active or passive, overt or covert, individual or organized, aggressive or timid, and on occasions totally justified. It is prudent for senior management to anticipate a vast array of resistance. To achieve their objectives, the Leadership of these companies must first recognize that the employees need to let go of the past and move forward as quickly as possible, both emotionally and in terms of their work. Secondly, after the status quo has been weakened, support for new initiatives must be strengthened. Also, advance planning and stakeholder management will avoid some of these pitfalls. Each company approaches resistance to change differently; however, general themes communicating that change include:

Understanding The Power Of Empathy: Empathy is a powerful tool when garnering employee trust. Employees are more likely to hang on to the fear, uncertainty, resentment, and other negative emotions that big changes bring. Especially when they view management as not having a clue about their circumstances. Leaders who have knowledge of those feelings and help employees deal with them create an environment of cooperation, trust, and collaboration.

Making Sense By Making The Business Case: Connecting employees and emotional level is important, but they also need to be engaged

---

23   Wurtzel, Marvin; "Reasons for Six Sigma Deployment Failures" Wurtzel Consulting, Inc., Posted: Friday June 13, 2008, Retrieved: 18 October 2010.

at an intellectual level. Everyone in the organization must understand the business case for change and how that transition will let them improve the organization. To fully make the case for change, executives need to convince employers that it's not only necessary but achievable. This can be a hard sell, especially when employees already have been asked to do more with less.

A New Look Toward The Future: As employers begin to accept change and loosen their grip on old ways of thinking and working, and opportunity emerges, and employees begin looking at what the future may provide, it is critical for executives to recognize this transition and to get people excited about where the company is heading. They must support that effort, and become involved in redefining their roles in the journey. People can be excited about a new opportunity for the company and still be anxious about the future. Personal worries consume employee energy and impact energy from your efforts and tasks. To ease the anxiety, engage all employees as much as possible in developing new approaches to their work, in part through voluntary workshops on innovation and creativity. This will raise their self-confidence, allay concerns about the possibility of another downsizing, and restore some of their pride in the company.

Progress By Establishing New Procedures: Recognize employees also need to be involved in translating the company's vision into everyday procedures. They are truly your front line experts that make a System prevail in failing circumstances. Their involvement and empowerment bolster their commitment to the transition by helping them maintain a sense of Control. Senior Leadership's vision should first translate into Mission statements and guidelines for employees' behavior. Then managers and supervisors will be tasked to socialize Missions and guidelines in each department throughout the company. By working in groups, employees translate those Mission statements and behavior guidelines into day-to-day operating policies and procedures.

2.2: Maturity Insights

**If you have always done it that way,
it is probably wrong.**

~ Charles Kettering

Chapter Summary: *Like people, organizations reach levels of Maturity. Why is that important? Primarily because the capabilities you now have are the basis and platform for what you will become.*

Key Points:
- Business Maturity Insights
- CMMI Overview
- Measure Maturity

Business Maturity Insights: "Quality is never an accident." It is recommended that your approach is to determine where your organization currently stands, where you may have gaps, investigate whether the Business and IT organizations are aligned, and ascertain where services could be improved. The Transformation Maturity Model (TMM) outlines characteristics in each Maturity Level of your Transformation journey. The underlying linchpin for improvement is facilitated by the methodology incorporated in Lean Six Sigma and other Business and IT methodologies.

Transformation Maturity Model

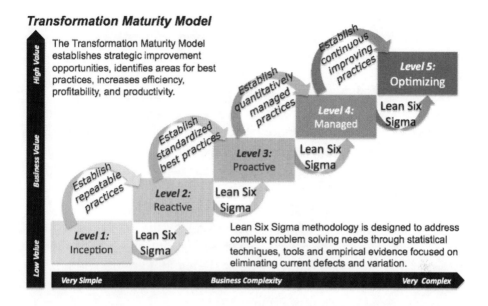

A Maturity model can be described as a structured collection of elements that describe certain aspects of Maturity in an organization. A Maturity model may provide, for example:

- Acknowledgment of your community's prior experiences
- A place to start verification and examination
- A shared vision that uses a common vocabulary and language
- A standard framework to capture and prioritize action
- A methodology to define what improvement means for your organization.

A Maturity model can be used as a benchmark for comparison and as an aid to understanding—for example, for comparative assessment of different organizations where there is something in common that can be used as a basis for comparison. Within each of these Maturity levels are Key Process Areas (KPAs), which characterize that level, and for each KPA five definitions are identified:

- Goals
- Commitment by the Client

- Ability to accept the Transformation
- Monitoring the Transformation by Measurement
- Validation and Verification of Benefits

The TMM provides a theoretical continuum along which Process Maturity can be developed incrementally from one level to the next. Knowing each client's environment is unique; these general guidelines describe the steps your company should elect to take advantage of existing capabilities and transform your company from one level to the next.

Each stage of Maturity will demonstrate a vital theme that is focused on a particular area for growth. However, organizations may elect to include other strategies from previous stages that are deemed essential for improvement and alignment. Each level represents a level of general objectives with respect to:

- *Inception* – Select a small project for Proof of Concept (POC) demonstrating the value of Lean Six Sigma and begin training.
- *Reactive* – Stabilize processes to achieve meaningful data and broaden Lean Six Sigma training.
- *Proactive* – Standardize processes to enable organization-wide benefits from Lean Six Sigma.
- *Managed* – Statistical Process Control; Control and understand sources of variation; Vendor engagement.
- *Optimizing* – Continuous Improvement, proactive, data-driven improvement and innovation; Design of Experiments; Supplier relations.

CMMI Overview: CMMI[24] is a Process improvement approach that provides organizations with the essential elements of effective processes that ultimately improve their performance. CMMI can be used to guide Process improvement across a project, a division, or an entire orga-

---

24   CMMI V1.3 is the most recent version of CMMI, which was released November 1, 2010.

nization. It helps integrate traditionally separate organizational functions, set Process improvement goals and priorities, provide guidance for Quality Processes, and provide a point of reference for appraising current processes. The benefits you can expect from using CMMI include the following:

- Your organization's activities are explicitly linked to your business objectives.
- Your visibility into the organization's activities is increased to help you ensure that your Product or Service meets Customers' expectations.
- You learn from new areas of best practice (e.g., measurement, risk).

CMMI is being adopted worldwide, including North America, Europe, Asia, Australia, South America, and Africa. This kind of response has substantiated the SEI's commitment to CMMI. You can use CMMI in three different areas of interest:

- Product and Service acquisition (CMMI for Acquisition)
- Product and Service development (CMMI for Development)
- Service establishment, management, and delivery (CMMI for Services)

CMMI models are collections of best practices that you can compare to your organization's best practices and guide improvement to your processes. A formal comparison of a CMMI model to your processes is called an appraisal. The Standard CMMI Appraisal Method for Process Improvement (SCAMPI) incorporates the best ideas of several Process improvement appraisal methods.[25]

The following appraisal principles for CMMI are the same as those principles used in appraisals for other Process improvement models. Those principles are as follows:

---

25   CMMI, Capability Maturity Model Integration (CMMI); http://www.sei.cmu.edu/cmmi/; Software Engineering Institute, Carnegie Mellon, Retrieved: 10 March 2010.

- Senior management sponsorship[26]
- A focus on the organization's business objectives
- Confidentiality for interviewees
- Use of a documented appraisal method
- Use of a Process reference model (e.g., a CMMI model) as a base
- A collaborative team approach
- A focus on actions for Process improvement[27]

There are several misconceptions regarding Six Sigma that need to be addressed before we elaborate on its connections with CMMI. Six Sigma is not:

- Just about statistics
- Just for manufacturing
- Exclusively about defect density
- Limited to large organizations
- Equivalent to compliance with standards and models, and vice versa
- Necessarily synonymous with Level 4
- Limited to use in high-maturity organizations
- A competitor to CMMI or other Process models and standards
- Always the performance goal (From current 3 sigma to the highest feasible goal of 6 sigma.)

Three of these statements, in particular, merit elaboration. They are discussed briefly below:

- *Six* Sigma successes are not equivalent to compliance with standards and models, and vice versa. Industry models and standards frequently demand measurements, monitoring, and control. Frequently used standards include CMMI models, ISO, IEEE standards, and ISO 12207. Six Sigma can be used to achieve compliance with aspects of each of these standards. However,

---

26   Experience has shown that the most critical factor influencing successful process improvement and appraisals is senior management sponsorship.

27   CMMI: SEI Web site at http://www.sei.cmu.edu/; Retrieved: 11 March 2011.

interpreting Six Sigma usage as achievement of model compliance, and likewise assuming Six Sigma when compliance is
found, is a mistake.

• *Six Sigma is not limited to use in high maturity organizations.* In
organizations that primarily use CMMI, many people associate
Six Sigma with the high maturity Process areas. However, there
is a direct connection between Six Sigma and the generic practices, which are used for Process areas at all maturity levels.
Six Sigma enables a tactical approach to the implementation of
the generic practices, and therefore much of the intent of the
high-maturity Process areas is implemented at lower maturity
or within the continuous representation. This drastically acceler-
ates the cycle time required for the final steps to high maturity by
putting the building blocks for the high-maturity Process areas
in place.

• *Six Sigma is not a competitor to CMMI or other Process models and
standards.* There are many domain-specific models and standards.
Six Sigma is not domain specific and can be a governance model or
a tactical improvement engine. It can provide the problem definition
and statement of benefit against which a decision about adopting
a technology can be made. It can help solve specific problems and
improve specific products or processes within the larger context of
overall organizational Process improvement. Or, in more general
terms, it can serve as an enabler for the successful implementation
of domain-specific improvement models.[28]

Measure Maturity: One of the most obvious qualifiers is the Maturity
of the business. Is your business in a start-up phase? In that case,
you may not be able to afford massive investments in automated solutions, elaborate Dashboards, or time required for training. However,
you could benefit from non-structured techniques that reduce time,
waste, and costs. If your corporation is a proactive middle-matured

---

28   There are also misconceptions about CMMI. For more information, see "CMMI Myths and Realities," available at http://www.stsc.hill.af.mil/
crosstalk/2004/06/0406Heinz.html. Retrieved: 23 Oct 2008

organization, you may need to start monitoring progress through your Balanced Scorecard and supporting Dashboards to identify areas that need improvement and incorporate your Quality program (i.e., production defects, implementation for a Continuous Improvement program, etc.).

Improving enterprise Maturity revolves around four very important aspects: Executive Commitment to Quality, IT Alignment, Process Transformation, and Knowledgeable People. A Maturity model can be described as a matrix of elements that describe certain aspects of Maturity in an organization. A Maturity model may provide, for example:

- A place to start verification and examination
- Acknowledgement of a community's Maturity prior experiences
- A shared vision that uses a common vocabulary and language
- A standard framework to capture and prioritize actions
- A methodology to define what improvement means for your organization.

A Maturity model can be used as an internal benchmark for comparison and as an aid to understanding—for example, for comparative assessment of different organizations where there is something in common that can be used as a basis for comparison. Within each of these Maturity levels are Key Process Areas (KPAs), which characterize that level, and for each KPA there are five definitions identified:

- Executive Commitment to Quality
- Transformation Goals and Objectives
- Cultural Ability to Accept the Transformation
- Ability to monitor the Transformation by Measurement and Valid Metrics
- Validation and Verification of Benefits (linking Accounting with Transformation)

A Maturity model can be described as a structured collection of elements that describe certain aspects of Maturity in an organization. A Maturity model may provide, for example:

- Acknowledgment of a community's prior experiences
- A place to start verification and examination
- A shared vision that uses a common vocabulary and language
- A standard framework to capture and prioritize actions
- A methodology to define what improvement means for your organization.

2.3: Organizational Impact

Always treat your employees exactly as you want them to treat your best Customers.

~ Stephen Covey

Chapter Summary: Ultimately, you are in the people business. You have Customers, you have Suppliers, and you work with your employees each day. You will certainly need those relationships in your Transformation; before, during, and after.

Key Points:
- Executive Team Perceptions
- What Is A Process?
- Why Is It Important To Understand?
- Lean Six Sigma Searches for Inefficiencies
- Business Transformation Factors
- Quality Leadership
- Transforming Behavior
- Measurement and Evaluation
- Integrated Solutions for Change

Executive Team Perceptions: G.K. Chesterton said, "It's not that they can't see the solution...They can't see the problem." But Sir Winston Churchill looked at it from another view: "However beautiful the strategy, you should occasionally look at the results." That observation is still common in our contemporary business environment. Perhaps you have seen those examples in your organization? Have you witnessed this phenomenon of perception bias?

If you discuss a problem to an Owner or CEO, the problem might be broken down into business segments (i.e., IT, Financial, Marketing, etc.) and the Owner or CEO will suggest following up with him or her. Discuss a challenge to a CIO person, and it will be seen as a technology problem. Discuss the same issues to a CFO, and it will be seen as a financial problem. Discuss it to a marketing person and it will be seen as a branding problem. Leonardo da Vinci said, "All our knowledge is the offspring of our perceptions."

In 2010, an article appeared in the Harvard Business Review blog, The Conversation, regarding Owner or CEO personality types and overlooking key subject matter experts in their organization.

- *Conceptual* – Reads signs of coming change, sees the "big picture," recognizes new possibilities, tolerates ambiguity; integrates ideas and concepts; communicates through analogy and metaphor; inspires with visions of the future.
- *Analytical* – Gathers facts, focuses on the bottom line, maintains emotional distance, argues rationally, measures precisely, and considers financial aspects.
- *People* – Recognizes interpersonal difficulties, intuitively understands how others feel, picks up nonverbal cues, empathetic, persuades, teaches, influences. According to John Reed, this was Sandy Weill's thinking preference.
- *Operations* – Approaches problems practically, stands firm on issues, perseveres, maintains a standard of consistency and Quality, provides stable leadership and supervision, develops detailed plans and procedures, implements projects in a timely manner, keeps financial records straight. This is the preferred style of proficient Process improvers.

Few business Owners or CEOs I know have operations-focused thinking styles or backgrounds…Meanwhile, the folks who love to do Process improvement are hiding in the middle levels. They are viewed from the top as solid, reliable, good soldiers but not "leadership material." I've seen this in the organizations where I've consulted. We all have. The folks who thrive on "how" and "why" and understand the people aspects enough to actually implement the Process change once it's identified don't have the clout to be heard by the seniors. Senior executives must make a real effort to listen to the process-focused communication from below—but it's not their native tongue.[29]

The primary focus is to understand the various points of view of experts in your culture, whether they are executives or key subject matter experts, you will need their support in the Business Transformation. They will need to be engaged and contribute to the future solution. ***Remember: don't overlook your opportunities.***

What Is A Process? "Sequence of interdependent and linked procedures which, at every stage, consume one or more resources (employee time, energy, machines, money) to convert Inputs (data, material, parts, etc.) into Outputs. These Outputs then serve as Inputs for the next stage until a known goal or end result is reached."[30]

Why Is It Important To Understand? Again, this seems obvious but this is becoming a global problem throughout many corporations, worldwide. It permeates automated telephony interfaces and cascades through internet interfaces and it cripples order processing and credit systems, the problem? No one person or group understands what the process is suppose to accomplish, how it should be accomplished, and what it needs to do to complete its tasks. What is the impact? There are many areas of impact such as Customer dissatisfaction, lost business opportunities, and building barriers to Customers at additional expense.

---

29   Power, Brad; The Right CEO Personality for Process Improvement, November 23, 2010.
30   BusinessDictionary.com, ed. http://www.businessdictionary.com/definition/process.html.

Lean Six Sigma Searches for Inefficiencies: The defining of a process involves three roles (sponsor, facilitator, process definition team) and nine steps.

- First, assess the documentation of items such as Vision, Mission, Process description, Process scope, Process goals, and Customers.
- Second, hold a kick-off meeting to: discuss Process goals and scope, provide an overview of the definition task, and set up team rules and schedules.
- Third, practice team skills, using tools such as negative brainstorming, cause/effect analysis, and multivoting.
- Fourth, maintain an implementation issues list, paying special attention to human factors.
- Fifth, document global process information (such as process objectives, scope, and Process Owners), and diagram the Process flow.
- Sixth, document Process steps, Measures, and metrics. Each Process step is to be characterized by its:

  o Purpose
  o Roles
  o Responsibilities
  o Entry criteria
  o Inputs
  o Next steps
  o Exit criteria
  o Outputs
  o Work instructions
  o Tool usage,
  o Techniques
  o Other special considerations

- Seventh, acquire or develop forms, tools, standards, and examples.
- Eighth, implement a formal inspection process that examines software deliverables and documentation.
- Ninth, plan and execute the implementation issues listed earlier.

These steps serve to reduce variation, non-critical work, and rework; increase cooperation; and improve Quality, estimations, and cycle times.[31]

Business Transformation Factors: From a Client's viewpoint, success is the implementation of change with minimum impact to the outside observer (i.e., your Customers, Suppliers, regulators, etc.) that translates into tangible benefits that are measured and monitored around external or internal processes. Those four key factors include:

- *Clear Vision* – Top management needs to conceptualize their Business Transformation in tangible benefits, identify their opportunities, and convey a sense of urgency in a collaborative format. Change should not be dictated, for that approach may encourage failure. Conversely, management's perspective should encourage esprit de corps, coordination, acceptance of change, illustrate success, and permit your people to bring creative ideas to the project. Transformation is best served by empowerment of all employees and planning for its success.
- *Service Roadmaps* – Each type of Service needs to reflect what phases of change will be brought to the process. A strategic planning Service will not be comparable to a business intelligence service. Planning for change needs to be structured to anticipate what people, processes, information, and organization resources will be impacted. It should also include the milestones, time lines, and additional resources that will be needed. A formal Communication Plan should also be implemented to illustrate progress, issues, and other identified variables.
- *Utilize Portfolio Management* – Each business model will need to identify, assess, and prioritize each process into groupings of importance (e.g., strategic, critical, required, manual, etc.).

---

31   Darcie DiBasio, *"How to Define a Process,"* Series: International Conference on Software Quality, October 4-6 1999, ed. American Society for Quality, trans. http://asq.org/qic/display-item/index.html?item=13826, Vols. Vol. 9, No. 0 (Cambridge, MA, 1999).

Transformation effort should be allocated on critical processes to Quality, profitability and timeliness. By exploiting these instances, your corporation should be able to quickly impact tangible benefits early in the initiative's implementation. By capturing your processes, products, services, and other resources that support their existence and functionality you will then be able to Measure their contributions and effectiveness. This repository of corporate assets will help executives determine more cost efficient Processes and procedures when extending your Business Transformation end-to-end (Customer to Supplier).

*   *Effective Communication* – Support, conveyed in communication and action, is the primary key factor for success. The approval from top management and the selection of a Champion to facilitate the Business Transformation are demonstrative acts underling the import of the initiative. Communication of the vision is important. Feedback on the progress of the program is also important. But, what is invaluable is the reminder to your organization that Business Transformation is a serious change process.

Quality Leadership: Quality Leadership from a national perspective has changed over the past five to six decades. After the Second World War, Japan clearly recognized their economic devastation and decided to make Quality improvement a national imperative as part of rebuilding their economy, and sought the help of Shewhart, Deming, and Juran. Deming championed Shewhart's ideas in Japan from 1950 onward. He is probably best known for his management philosophy that established Quality, productivity, and competitive landscape.

He formulated his points of attention for managers, which are a high-level abstraction of many of his deep insights. They should be interpreted by learning and understanding the deeper insights and include:

*   Break down barriers between departments
*   Management should learn their responsibilities, and take on leadership
*   Improve constantly

- Institute a program of education and self-improvement
- Six Sigma relies on total commitment from the Executive Leadership Team.
- Projects and initiatives are aligned with strategic objectives of the organization.
- Six Sigma emphasizes studying, inspection, audit, and analysis.
- Empowered employees tackle issues proactively rather than reactively.

Lean Six Sigma is a problem-solving methodology using systematic and organized project management tools. Lean Six Sigma success requires:

- Strong proactive support with required resources provided by the top management.
- Acceptance and implementation of Six Sigma's basic disciplines by employees. The role of middle management has to be active and supportive for the success of a Six Sigma.
- Managers at all levels are required to be active.
- Linkage with all innovative and infrastructure activities.
- Accurate and fair evaluation of all successful Six Sigma projects with meaningful recognition and rewards for employees.

Transforming Behavior: In many small and medium-sized businesses there is little or no strategy to improve the fortunes of the organization. This may happen in good times as well as bad and may result from a belief that:

- If it is not broke don't fix it
- The business is in a niche market with no competition
- No skills are available in-house to make proposed changes
- The business Owner is retiring—it will be someone else's problem
- And other arguments against change…

The lack of a desire to continually develop and improve the business encourages a reactionary mode within the business, rather than a more desirable proactive stance. Why is this important? Generally a reactionary organization fails to take business planning seriously and is more focused on resolving current issues than establishing a mechanism to allow problems to be anticipated prior to becoming an issue. The import of this can be found when comparing organizations that: gain success on an ongoing basis, are able to more easily attract skilled staff, train staff in order to raise the skill set within the business, have set their goals, and know how they are to be achieved with those businesses that do not.

Measurement and Evaluation: Peter Drucker said: "What's measured improves." So, if you don't measure something, you can't improve it. It's even more important to realize that your choice of metrics binds your organization's future. If there is a key success factor and it's not acknowledged or tracked, that information may be a missed opportunity.

Traditionally, businesses have viewed the following financial measurements as indicators of success:

- Sales
- Profitability
- Return On Capital Employed
- Return On Assets
- Earnings Growth
- Market Share
- Stock Price

More recently, business publications have recommended using non-financial measurements as well as the more traditional accounting measures to assess, report and drive success. Most notably, the Criteria for Performance Excellence of the Malcolm Baldrige National Quality Award have always stressed:

- Customer Satisfaction
- Process Excellence
- Employee Satisfaction

When done well, measurement of these criteria can indicate whether the elements of success are in place—indicators such as fast, responsive time-to-market; a loyal Customer base; outstanding processes for Quality and timeliness; and mechanisms that ensure learning, growth, and Continual Improvement.

Sometimes organizations define their own indicators of performance in key areas. Such metrics are often useful because they try to reduce complex measurements and results to a single value that can be tracked, managed, and improved...Your business measurements must be carefully managed to make sure that they give right answers, and that the right questions are being asked.[32]

Integrated Solutions for Change: Specific LSS Services applied to your separate layers of your Business Planning infrastructure include:

Quality Strategies:
- As Juran said; "Focus on the vital Few instead of the Trivial many when setting company goals." Do the same for individual goals and incentivize behavior. Remember that rewards don't have to be monetary (education, sports events, evening dinners with a spouse, etc.).
- Foster an organization of candor. Work through a communication framework. Be transparent and honest, enable people to provide feedback about their performance, and limit the opportunity to hedge around an issue.
- Accountability begins with focused responsibility. The whole organization, including leaders, managers, and employees, should systematically work together to establish clear objectives, goals, and expectations that are linked to tangible results.
- Accountability starts at the top of the organization and works itself down. Owners, CEOs, and managers must strive to perfect their

---

32   Stein, Philip; *"Effective Measurement of Business Performance,"* ASQ Annual Quality Congress proceedings, May 1998.

own leadership skills and accountability before expecting others within the organization to do the same.

Process Transformation:
- Use Lean Six Sigma to establish clear enterprise objectives, set initiative expectations and define Quality goals. Identify areas of improvement to eliminate waste, defects, cycle time, workforce, assets and utilization of other resources.
- When Quality improvements are completed, document revised standards for performance, and put in place policies and procedures. Communicate those new Results to the Owners and responsible stakeholders in the organization.
- Inventory your business and IT processes and assign your Process Owners, who are accountable for management and control. These managers will drive the performance of other employees and their measured results.

Quality Evaluation:
- Establish group and management reviews with regular meetings that measure and track Quality, performance, and productivity to planned objectives.
- Motivate all of your people. Tutor them. Changing behavior is incremental. All individuals appreciate and are motivated by verbal praise and recognition in both private and public settings.

Learning Transformation:
- Using Lean Six Sigma methodology to define ownership, establish standards, and identify what products and services are supported for each new process and procedures you improve.
- Continuous Improvement is your refinement engine. Utilize its by-products to meet Customer needs, provide financial impact, improve internal processes, utilize resources and improve your corporate planning environment.

- Training is the catalyst for cultural change. Information and knowledge provide the linchpins for profitability, efficiency, and savings. Provide your team with tools to work smarter, not harder. Deming said; "The aim of the system must be clear to everyone in the system."

Through understanding how your business works, provide the vision, plan for its development and implementation, and provide effective communication vis-à-vis feedback on its progress. Business Transformation is the paradigm of adapting your organization, in a Continuous Improvement process, to reflect and mitigate the commercial environmental influences that affect Quality, cost, timeliness, and effective use of your business resources. It is also an opportunity to enrich and motivate your organizations.

2.4: Outsourcing vs. Quality?

One of the great mistakes is to judge policies and programs by their intentions rather than their results

~ Milton Friedman

Chapter Summary: What is the best choice for your company, outsourcing or Quality improvement? The final decision may be a turning point in your organization. Consider your options very carefully and ask whether that decision will make you more competitive in the marketplace.

Key Points:
- What is Business Process Outsourcing?
- Outsourcing Offshore Issues
- Outsourcing Risks
- Outsourcing Consequences
- Why Outsourcing Fails
- Cost Reduction Alternatives
- Investment in Quality

Outsourcing – Misunderstood Consequences ──────➤
Rethinking Outsourcing – Continued Waste? ◄ ─ ─

What is Business Process Outsourcing? Business Process Outsourcing (BPO) refers to services provided to handle business activities for your enterprise by international businesses that traditionally provide IT outsourcing services. They are usually located in Eastern Europe, India, or China.

Originally BPO outsourcing services began with payroll. Those business services grew into other areas, such as employee benefits management, but now have expanded into "non-core" functions such as financial and administration processes, human resources functions, call center and Customer Service activities, and accounting and payroll.

The "cost reduction" initiative often involves a multiyear commitment that can run into hundreds of millions of dollars. Typically, your people performing the current work internally are transferred and become employees for the Service provider. At that point, legally, how your employees are treated is no longer your company's responsibility. Sometimes outsourcing practices have backfired and reflected unfavorably on the original company. Cultural differences between your company and the outsourcing company can be significant. Outsourcing practices include: transferring personnel within a short time period, working under harsher conditions or depending on local labor laws, reducing salaries and benefits, inducing "reduction in force" with or without minimal benefits and beginning practices of attrition.

Outsourcing Offshore Issues: Many companies today are outsourcing offshore. However ramifications and bigger impacts come with this decision. This list highlights factual data gathered from real-world experiences we have encountered on client sites and from published articles relating to this subject.

Downsizing or reduction in force is the generic reduction of an employer's workforce, it is often an undetermined method, and may or may not include senior employees or staff that no longer meet business criteria. It may be a voluntary approach, such as early retirements, or maybe involuntary. The company may exert pressure on its employees to make a choice perhaps via plane and layoff or termination that would otherwise be imminent or by offering an attractive severance early retirement package.

Outsourcing is recognized worldwide as a key business strategy. However, many companies are still hesitant to join the bandwagon. It is not uncommon to hear the sentiment that "as many as half of outsourcing deals fail." And those who have chosen outsourcing may find themselves in the dilemma that the original assumptions and benefits do not materialize. In those cases, a corporation should rethink outsourcing and avoid making another costly mistake (i.e., continued waste).

Outsourcing Risks: Outsourcing offers cost reduction and reduction of capital commitment through a process of contracting employee responsibilities and liabilities to a third party. Outsourcing is often viewed as a component to promote corporate growth and that practice has increased as a subcontracting practice across national boundaries since the 1980s.

There is not an agreed upon definition of outsourcing; however, one that is commonly used refers to processes or tasks that were originally performed in-house that were contracted to an external provider. This would also include the term off shoring or sometimes called offshore outsourcing. In either case, organizations entered into a contractual agreement involving exchanges of services for specific payments, usually in US dollars.

In today's world, companies are constantly looking at improving methods of reducing cost. That focus is on outsourcing and the consequences of choosing that alternative for their Corporation. The projected cost savings are tempting more companies to refocus their internal talent on innovation and growth, using outsourcers for non-core business activities, yet consequences to making this decision still remain.

One consideration is the unexpected loss of intimacy with their Customer base as they going to amount sourcing scenario. For instance support for Customer Service may run into a language or cultural barrier when implementing this option.

No single technology or a mix of services or products will work for every corporation. You need to be specific when opting for outsourcing processes and tasks. By totally outsourcing your processes overseas, potential risks are inherent in loosing control, ownership and risk to your corporate intellectual capital.

In a geographically local area, i.e., US and Mexico, web-enabled services may be just the beginning. With the use of Lean Six Sigma methodology, CRM integration, and Customer segmentation, opportunities to enhance the Quality and cost-effectiveness of your Customer is a present-day reality.

Customers on a single point of contact value time, theirs; they don't want to call more than once for the answer. Oftentimes this is a weak link in the communication process of outsourcing. Therefore, you must consider a communication component when outsourcing for your company.

The ultimate business driver for your Customer is Satisfaction. Success is providing the right answer, at the quickest time, which can be understood the first time.

However, be aware that numerous risks must be mitigated: specifically, losing Quality, acquiring risk, and waste. The following list includes examples of those lists and does not imply these are the only risks to consider:

Outsourcing Consequences: Outsourcing is a major radical decision that is sometimes made in haste without regard to truly strategic consequences. The devil is truly in the details. This chapter approaches the topic in terms of how the decision could affect your current Quality standards and alludes to various facts to consider when contemplating outsourcing.

Customer
- Risk to Service: Gartner discovered many risk areas, including incomplete processes, ill-planned compensation structures, and lack of management.
- Call Center Alienation: Customers get frustrated when they can't understand what's being said or feel as though they themselves aren't being understood.

Executive, Financial, or Legal touch points
- Contract Execution: Clients and Service providers are not operationally prepared to work together after contract signing.
- Lack of Executive Buy-in: Lack of buy-in from senior client leaders who will be recipients of the outsourcing services.
- Poor Contractual Understanding: Client staff and Service provider teams are created without fully understanding the specific agree-

ment that has been negotiated. Languages, as a rule, and legal interpretations are sometimes barriers to a smooth transition.

- Client Governance Non-existent: There is a lack of a defined retained or governance team due to ignorance, lack of detail, or "washing their hands."
- Client Governance Implemented: Even if a client puts a team on-site to manage the implementation and ongoing operations, the team may not have the right skills required for their new roles.
- Cost Driven: Gartner determined that 80 percent of Customer Service outsourcing projects that are designed to cut costs will fail.
- Special Management Required: In order to maintain Quality and efficiency, any outsourcing program will require ongoing management from your own leadership.

Internal touch points
- Stretched Resources for Services: Due to increased Service demand, prior to an outsourcing implementation, the client may postpone large projects and spending.
- End-User Resistance: End users on the receiving end of new methods can inhibit the achievement of business objectives through lack of compliance, strategy disagreements or delays in executing their new responsibilities.
- Labor Backlash: There is a groundswell of backlash against the current trend toward exporting jobs outside the US. This backlash may cause negative publicity for your firm.

Learning touch points
- Poor Knowledge Transfer: Client staff may be temporarily engaged for knowledge transfer to the Service provider during the implementation, but elect to leave before outsource is complete.
- Key Talent Loss: Outsourcing creates uncertainty. Employees and contractors who provide existing services could look elsewhere for employment and leave before or during the outsourcing implementation.

Supplier touch points

- Infrastructure: Many offshore countries lack the network bandwidth for fast communication and many experience intermittent electrical outages.
- Security: Not all foreign countries have the high-level concern or the laws, such as those for privacy or intellectual property, to protect your company's assets.
- Skill Set/Quality: We have encountered poor or unacceptable Quality of work in test automation, regardless of the CMM level touted.
- Objectivity: Is your offshore partner performing your development and your testing? Will they keep your best interests at heart (and provide adherence to functional, performance, reliability and usability testing standards) when it conflicts with meeting their deliverable date?
- Geopolitical Climate: While recent events have proven that the US is not immune to terrorism, Asia and other underdeveloped areas experience instability caused by unstable government, political unrest, terrorism, etc.
- Culture: Cultures are different. Business conduct, greetings, forms of address, gestures, value systems, and punctuality vary widely around the globe. In terms of corporate culture, the client and Service provider may have different norms in terms of speed, style, decision making, and organizational structure.
- Language Barriers: Unquestionably many offshore resources provide communication challenges, especially over teleconferencing that does not allow you the ability to view facial expressions—and e-mail can be worse. It is possible to inadvertently insult offshore partners in simple everyday conversations.
- Time Zone Conflicts: Many of the firms in Asia have as much as a ten-hour time difference. The outsourcing firms try to spin this as a "good thing" for you. Is it good to not be able to have your team discuss issues with their team as they arise?
- Difficulty Visiting Their Site: Because of the cost and length of travel (as much as twenty hours each way), visiting your partners with any frequency becomes much more unrealistic. Also, foreign ground transportation is not like that in the US.

- Difficulty Bringing Resources Here: There are possible visa issues and heavy expenses with bringing your partners to where you do business.
- Increasing Price Trends: Many offshore providers that have been successful are increasing their prices due to fact that competition for local human resources is pushing up the cost of labor.

Why Outsourcing Fails: KPMG created a study to address this point. They found five top reasons why an outsourcing contract fails.

- *Client's Lack of Company Vision* – As an Owner or CEO, you should have a clear idea on what your core functions are and what your business is all about.
- *Lack of a Formal Strategic Measurement Framework* – Almost half of the companies who enter into an outsourcing contract do not know if their endeavor was successful. Why? They do not bother to establish a measurement framework to test it.
- *Lack of Vendor Management* – Outsourcing is a partnership between your company and your outsourcing vendor. This means that you need to manage the relationship if it has any chance to flourish.
- *Heavy SLA* – The bottom line of outsourcing is results. Sometimes, the bottom line is lost and both parties are stuck at the Service Level Agreement. This commonly leads to SLAs that are so improbable that they look like a prelude to disaster.
- *People* – You don't normally outsource something that you can already automate. Finding the right people is almost an imperative for success. It is therefore not a surprise that it tops the list of difficulties encountered in outsourcing.

Cost Reduction Alternatives: As the economic outlook remains uncertain, today's companies are pressed by both internal and outside forces to find quick cures for their fiscal woes. ... Downsizing offers an immediate reduction in payroll costs, and thus the opportunity to quickly impact the bottom line and appease investors. But layoffs are not always the best or even an appropriate solution.

Since layoffs are by their nature unpleasant for all involved, it is tempting for a business to adopt a crisis mentality at the first sign of trouble, make a snap decision to downsize, and move through the process as quickly as possible.

However, many organizations learn too late that an inadvisable or hastily conducted reduction in force can result in costs that far outweigh the benefits obtained. Negatives can include a sharp drop-off in productivity, risk-averse decision making, increased legal liability, and low employee trust, commitment, and morale.

Before planning and implementing a layoff, it is important both to assess your options to determine whether another solution may be preferable to downsizing, and to conduct an honest appraisal of whether your business can, in fact, absorb a reduction in force without serious adverse consequences.[33]

Assess your options. Many innovative companies lose their creativity, when it comes to considering the alternatives to layoffs. Usually, a thorough examination of corporate spending across the company will reveal other viable ways to cut costs. These solutions may include:

- Postponing acquisitions
- Freezing all new equipment purchasing
- Reducing operating supplies and services
- Limiting or reducing outside contractors or consultants
- Restricting business travel expenses
- Asking employees, who can be the best sources, to identify corporate waste, and surveying workers to solicit their ideas

Investment in Quality: Is Quality a better investment option for your organization? Is it a better alternative to outsourcing? Dell,™ Capital One, and JPMorgan Chase, walked away from outsourcing

---

33   Consider The Options Before Downsizing; Publication: Westchester County Business Journal; Published: 26 May 2003; Retrieved: 23 Jan 2009.

relationships, realizing that for them the disadvantages far outweighed the cost benefits.[34] Had they understood that the complexity of outsourcing and its costs could outweigh their benefits, would it not have been a better investment in improving Quality in their organizations?

By choosing outsourcing, you dismantle your organization and rely on unknown Suppliers to support your internal and Customer needs. The previous list of touch points illustrates some of the potential pitfalls. Would this impact your Customers or improve your situation? Should you consider the alternative and invest those monies into your organization and steer it to a "performance culture"?

A senior government official, who wishes to stay anonymous, said; "The federal government is a good case study for this...outsourcing was the buzz word in the late '90s...for many of the exact reasons that you cite in this chapter, it failed... the federal government is too diverse, too large, and lacked a central vision on how it would implement outsourcing... lack of oversight over contractors and lack of a vision within the smaller organizations was its death knell. The interesting perspective is that when we changed our focus back to 'in-sourcing,' it was done at a time when the economy was tanking, money was tight, we couldn't afford to hire the quality of workers we need, and now as a direct result of outsourcing, the federal government was left with a 'management class' of workers that have a higher average salary, provoking news articles that the federal government workers are overpaid..."

Concerning outsourcing and Quality investments, both of these options are long term. Both options impact your immediate short-term costs, but what benefits do you anticipate you will reap in two years, four years, or even six years in the future? As Gandhi said; "Be the change that you want to see in the world." So, what is the future state you want to see in your organization?

---

34   Pfeffer, Jeffrey; The hidden cost of outsourcing. 2006; Business 2.0. Retrieved December 29, 2008, from money.cnn.com.

3.0: Transformation Paradigm

Willingness to change is a strength, even if it means plunging part of the company into total confusion for a while.

~ Jack Welch

Chapter Summary: Business, IT, or Marketing Transformation is a Leadership decision and must rely on Long-Term Commitment. That Transformation will encourage everyone to be more knowledgeable, efficient, productive, flexible to the marketplace, and sensitive to your Customers' needs.

Key Points:
- Executive Quality Commitment
- Meta Planning
- Transformation
- Realization
- Incremental Change
- The Core – Lean Six Sigma
- Lean
- Six Sigma
- Solution-Based Roadmaps

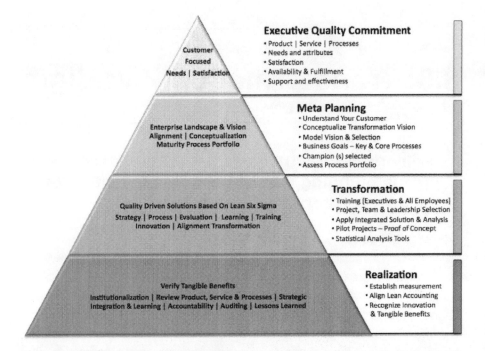

Executive Quality Commitment: This commitment is focused long-term strategies that emphasize Customers' needs and satisfaction of those needs. This commitment is based on a Quality vision for products and services and how that vision can be effectively implemented.

- Executive buy-in and commitment
- Selection of a Champion
- Selection of a pilot program (focus of pilot, set expectations, communication plan, base line metrics established, data collection approach, remediation process, selection of candidates, etc.)

Meta Planning: This is based on the enterprise landscape and a Quality Vision for the future. It addresses business alignment, business concepts and addresses the need for innovation of Products, Services, and Processes.

- Develop the business case (i.e., Business model, Marketing model, IT model)

74

- Establish participants (i.e., Executives, Champion, Process Owners, etc.)
- Selection of projects prioritized by net impact (cost versus benefits analysis, requirement, strategic priority, etc.)

Transformation: Accomplish transformation through integrated solutions based on Lean Six Sigma methodologies. Those components include strategies, Processes, Quality Evaluation, and Learning throughout the Business Transformation initiative. Management must recognize that Business Transformation will affect the corporate culture, begin accumulating information on corporate effectiveness (Profound Knowledge), and provide a mind-set for management and employees alike. The Four Corners of Integration (Quality Strategies, Process Transformation, Quality Evaluation, Learning Transformation) will be aligned with the following tools defining scope and goals:

- Voice of the Client (providing focus of project)
- Cost of Poor Quality (provide cost justification, connect the benefits, cycle time impact, etc.)
- Quality metrics (Measure areas that will change, Measure performance for ongoing improvement, address data repository needs, align reporting requirements and integration with existing Dashboards and Scorecards, etc.)
- Project scope, boundaries, constraints, resources and time line

Realization: This recognizes the tracking of efforts and translating those efforts into tangible benefits for the Corporation. This is done through the institutionalization of best practices, the periodic review of Products, Services and Processes, the integration and application of any Systematic approach to two strategies: Continuous Improvement, and the cultural integration of Lean Six Sigma principles and developing an environment for Learning.

- Institutionalization (from lessons learned, change in procedures, etc.)
- Review Impact of Results on Product, Services, and Processes
- Revise or Modifications to your Strategic Systems

- Address and mitigate collateral impact to other adjacent organizations

Incremental Change: Successful Transformation can be implemented incrementally, based on a project's focus such as efficiency, productivity, profitability, or a selected combination. Management of risk and its mitigation are key to any successful project. In a low reward scenario, a single project that is positioned to take advantage of technology could also be applied in order to streamline processes and provide efficiencies with little downside risks. At the operating or department level, productivity gains and financial rewards can be gained through streamlined processes and/or technology. In another scenario, co-Transformations between departments can produce a synergistic effect, and again the efficiency increases rewards. Last and most significant is the strategic scenario of Transformation that would encompass the whole organization providing Systematic rewards and Results.

The Core – Lean Six Sigma: Lean Six Sigma is a disciplined, accomplished methodology that promotes efficiency, increases productivity and profitability, while avoiding pitfalls. It is a Systematic approach, rather than ad hoc approach, and is an amalgamation of Lean and Six Sigma methodologies.

According to Motorola, the originator of the methodology,

> Six Sigma has evolved over the last two decades and so has its definition. Six Sigma has literal, conceptual, and practical definitions. At Motorola University (Motorola's Six Sigma training and consultancy division), we think about Six Sigma at three different levels:

> As a metric – Six Sigma as a Metric: The term "Sigma" is often used as a scale for levels of "goodness" or Quality. Using this scale, "Six Sigma" equates to 3.4 defects per one million opportunities (DPMO). Therefore, Six Sigma started as a defect reduction effort in manufacturing and was then applied to other business Processes for the same purpose.

As a methodology – Six Sigma as a Methodology: As Six Sigma has evolved, there has been less emphasis on the literal definition of 3.4 DPMO, or counting defects in products and Processes. Six Sigma is a Business Improvement methodology that focuses an organization on:

- Understanding and managing Customer requirements;
- Aligning key business processes to achieve those requirements;
- Utilizing rigorous data analysis to minimize variation in those processes, and
- Driving rapid and sustainable improvement to business processes.

At the heart of the methodology is the DMAIC model for Process improvement. DMAIC is commonly used by Six Sigma project teams and is an acronym for:

- Define opportunity;
- Measure performance;
- Analyze opportunity;
- Improve performance, and
- Control performance.

As a management system – Six Sigma Management System: Six Sigma is a business management strategy. It will identify and remove the causes of defects and errors in manufacturing and business processes. It uses a set of Quality Management methods and creates a special infrastructure of people within the company who are experts in these methods. When practiced as a management system, Six Sigma is a high performance system for executing business strategy.[35]

---

35   Motorola University; Copyright 1994-2005 Motorola, Inc., http://www.motorola.com/; Retrieved: 12 September 2010.

As a business planning system – Lean Six Sigma addresses end-to-end Quality. Lean Six Sigma does not replace your current Strategic Planning system. Rather, it is a strategic refinement that should be woven into existing strategies. Unfortunately, Quality is not a consideration in most business planning systems. This book addresses that deficit and demonstrates how Lean Six Sigma is a catalyst for long-term improvement. Using Lean Six Sigma obligates Quality objectives to be integrated across business models and organizations. It is the forward-thinking component that affects management and utilization of resources, capital, performance, addresses Customer Satisfaction, employee satisfaction, and profitability perspectives. As a key Strategic Process methodology, that can ensure Continuous Improvement; it facilitates and institutionalizes Lean Six Sigma tools for continued benefits.

Lean: Lean methodology, which includes low-cost techniques, improves your organization's effectiveness. It is a methodology to improve operations and the supply chain with an emphasis on the reduction of waste in activities like waiting, transporting, material handoffs, inventory, and overproduction. By taking this approach, it often improves productivity and performance in your organization with little or no extra costs. The five-step thought process for guiding the implementation of Lean techniques is easy to remember, but not always easy to achieve:

- Specify value from the standpoint of the end Customer by Product family.
- Identify all the steps in the value stream for each Product family, eliminating whenever possible those steps that do not create value.
- Make the value-creating steps occur in tight sequence so the Product will flow smoothly toward the Customer.
- As flow is introduced, let Customers pull value from the next upstream activity.
- As value is specified, value streams are identified, wasted steps are removed, and flow and pull are introduced, begin the process again and continue it until a state of perfection is reached in which perfect value is created with no waste.

Lean methodology is focused on the costs that are linked to the Customer Product or service. The application of "Lean" techniques is to rid your organization of those additional expenses that are being charged to the Customer. Thus, a reduction in those costs will improve your profitability, lower prices, or both. Here are seven key areas that Lean targets:

- Eliminates defects
- Reduces inventory
- Reduces labor
- Eliminates overproduction
- Reduces space requirements
- Reduces transportation costs
- Eliminates unnecessary human motion

Lean methodology is a cost-effective approach to provide your organization with various corporate benefits. The impact affects expenses, effectiveness of resources, addressing the employees through their buy-in and empowerment and elimination of waste and defects. The major areas of benefits are shown below; however, other areas may also be included that may be found in your environment. These examples include:

- Affects products or services to be more competitive in the marketplace
- Enhances overall manufacturing flexibility
- Ensures a safer work environment
- Results in improved Quality and fewer defects
- Improves employee morale
- Reduces Inventory
- Requires less space

Six Sigma: Six Sigma methodology refines current processes and molds efficiency into new ones. This accepted standard helps reduce variation that produces waste and defects in your processes and helps alignment those processes with your Quality strategies.

Six Sigma benefits should be dealt with in the same way any change initiative is approved, budgeted, and tracked. This emphasizes that Six Sigma is part of the way business is conducted and not an additional "to do." Here are some suggested categories to consider:

Cost Reduction Efforts – Take resources or other costs out of the business and provide an overall reduction of expense that falls to the bottom line. If resources are eliminated as a result of the Six Sigma project, the project receives a benefit for the cost reduction. These are reductions in cost that fall directly to the bottom line and should be measured by the amount of annualized cost eliminated from the business.

Increased Capacity – Focuses on improving the productivity of a process (process more with the same resources, thereby reducing the overall unit cost). This benefit is Measured by calculating the amount of expense retained in order to prevent future cost increases.

Cost Avoidance – Responses to competitive pressures and changing environment (such as new legislation). This benefit is Measured as the realistic cost avoided as a result of the implementation of the new process.

Revenue – Growth or increase in revenue from new business. This is measured by calculating the value of new business for the increase in revenue over a pre-defined period.

Retained revenue (profit) – Revenue retained from existing Customers at risk. This is Measured by calculating the value of existing business over a predefined period.

Improved Investment Income – The additional investment income earned due to an acceleration of the receipt of monies. The financial benefit is calculated by determining the net present value of the accelerated cash flow over a predetermined period.

Risk Management – Projects that enable more effective management of the company's risk in functional areas such as actuarial, audit, and insurance. Benefits of these types of projects are Measured by improvements in either reduced economic capital or a lower cost of capital.[36]

Lean Six Sigma seeks to improve the Quality of Process Outputs by identifying and removing the causes of defects (errors) and minimizing variability in manufacturing and business processes. It uses a set of Quality Management and statistical methods, and creates a special infrastructure of people within the organization who are experts in these methods.[37]

Solutions-Based Roadmaps: Solutions are designed to be collaborative and involve our clients through teamwork. They act as catalysts and transform those problems and issues into meaningful payback opportunities for your company. Management operates through various functions, often classified as planning, organizing, leading/motivating, and controlling. They should include checks and balances and rely on your internal expertise to validate your findings.

Does one size or type of Roadmap fit all situations? Simply stated, NO! Understand that not all Roadmaps fit all real life situations. Recognize that fact and build your solutions around unique and structured Roadmaps that are focused on the services needed to deploy the types of solutions in your Transformation. We recognize that your organization has different needs; approaches must be tailored to fit the stage of growth for the company, solutions should be fitted with your company's Maturity, and those elements help formulate your Transformation.

---

36   Carey, Bryan; Measuring Six Sigma Financial and Operational Benefits; http://www.isixsigma.com/; Retrieved: 28 Sep 2010.
37   United States Army, Office of Business Transformation, Business Transformation Plan; 1 October 2010, page 11.

Roadmaps are just that: they should provide the Client with a clear journey of the Business Transformation, which should include these fundamental points:

- *Set Enterprise Expectations* – from Top Executives to all employees involved in the Transformation.
- *Provides a Communication Platform* – A practical simple language statement of what is to be accomplished or learned that reinforces Executive Commitment and timetable.
- *Provide a Thought Process* – A description of activity to conceptualize the methodology or thought to be learned and documented.
- *Individual Steps* – Multiple steps required to complete activities.
- Required Tools – Links, references, and templates to specific tools needed to effectively do the job.
- *Profound Knowledge* – Provide a process to capture business knowledge that can be utilized by the entire corporation.

3.1: Executive Quality Commitment

It is not the strongest of the species that survive, nor the most intelligent, but the one most responsive to change.

~ Charles Darwin

Chapter Summary: Quality is an idea, goal, and concept that reflect the mind-set of a corporation and its Executive Quality Commitment. Quality brand names are recognized globally and reflect upon their corporate culture that controls that image.

Key Points:
- Executive Quality Commitment
- Demand Quality and Aligned Technology
- Integrate and Align Business Strategy
- Avoid Complexity
- Executive and Management Accountability
- Project Nomination, Size, Complexity, and Collaboration
- Track Results Rigorously and Accurately
- Change is a Constant

Executive Quality Commitment: Jack Welch, former CEO and chairman of the board at General Electric, said, "An organization's ability to learn, and translate that learning into action rapidly, is the ultimate competitive advantage." He recognized that in order to springboard that vision into reality, and he acknowledged Six Sigma's capability to translate a low-performing organization into a high-performing culture that was empowered to improve business Processes, Products, and Services.

The point of origination lies at the behest of the Chief Executive Officer or Owner of the Corporation. The Transformation Process begins after the decision is made to improve and establish a framework of Quality that relies upon accountability for those responsible. Additionally, the wise Owner or CEO will go through a consensus-building exercise and gain support from his or her Executive Team ensuring their participation and collaboration will support Transformation needs, effective communication, removal of barriers between organizations, and prepare their organization to shift to a collaborative approach in solution solving. In this phase, your key considerations should at least include:

- Executive Commitment to Business Transformation Initiative
- Strategic focus on Quality integration
- Executive Sponsor (CEO | CXO)
- Optional Steering Committee
- Optional Executive Team
- Optional Governance Committee
- Survey to identify Quality areas for improvement
- Formal Communication Plan

First, the Owner or CEO must identify a Transformation champion for the success of the initiative and outline how that success will be measured and what will be defined as successful milestones. If accountability is not institutionalized, the champion will be responsible for establishing and mentoring that program. Accountability will be for all team members, from top management to front-line employees, and include an incentivized program for savings, performance, and Quality (i.e., this should reflect measured results, not subjective assessments).

As a CEO or Owner, other variables or influences could contribute and motivate your company's Leadership to consider Business Transformation as an implement to improve your organization's capabilities. Examples of some of those factors would include:

- Owner or CEO-mandated executive management involved
- Drastic intervention for rescue of distressed companies
- Primary impact to business as usual
- New IT System implemented with no change in the Processes, organizational culture, structure, roles, and accountabilities
- Basis of competition changed
- Focus on a massive reorganization, not accompanied by changes in the way the business is run
- Overall performance enhanced, renewed, and sustained, Leadership in the marketplace
- Driven by a need to stabilize and fund the business (turn around)
- Drastic increase in market share/ market responsiveness[38]

Demand Quality and Aligned Technology: Quality is a forefront issue that will be a critical success factor for the next decade. At senior levels in all major developed and developing countries, Quality and refining existing Quality is a paramount concern. Understanding and addressing Quality methodology today will prepare you and your organization for the upcoming competitive forces of the next decade.

Lean Six Sigma has an impressive pedigree of Quality improvement that continues to manage change in the Business and IT environments today. The discipline of Quality Management includes notable individual efforts and groundbreaking ideas that include:

- *Lean Production*, which is often known simply as "Lean," is a production practice that considers the expenditure of resources for any goal other than the creation of value for the end Customer to be wasteful, and thus a target for elimination.

---

38   Infosys, "Defining Business Transformation," May 2006.

- *Just in Time* is an inventory strategy that strives to improve a business's return on investment by reducing in-process inventory and associated carrying costs.
- *Toyota Production System* is one of the most respected production systems. Although warranty repair issues have been newsworthy for the last two years, TPS is demonstrated how Lean and Just-In-Time methodologies have increased Quality to reduce costs and provided for growth of products and services.
- *Total Quality Management* is a business management strategy aimed at embedding awareness of Quality in all organizational processes. TQM has been widely used in manufacturing, education, hospitals, call centers, government, and Service industries, as well as NASA space and science programs.

Lean Six Sigma comes from a heritage of Quality Management and is a reflection of optimizing Lean and Six Sigma principles to benefit the client and his or her environment. From a Quality approach, Lean Six Sigma, melds well with Toyota Production System, Just-In-Time, and Lean Manufacturing environments. In addition, it integrates easily in other varieties of Quality Management, Total Quality Management, and Six Sigma methodologies. In many cases, either exact tools or similar tools are utilized in Lean Six Sigma processes that were previously used in other methodologies. The significant difference is the way those tools are applied in a structured environment in which they are applied. The benefits are real for the client. Being able to leverage prior experience and knowledge will be a springboard in the application and understanding of Lean Six Sigma methodology.

So how does this apply to the future? Lean Six Sigma provides Quality strategies that must be implemented in Marketing, Business, and IT models in order to reap benefits. Again, Lean Six Sigma provides a smoother transition from those disciplines considered to be an engineered approach. Lean Six Sigma provides integrated Process Architecture to align those disciplines into a collaborative Lean Six Sigma solution that leverages strengths from each. An example of the success of integrating these two approaches, Quality versus engineered, was demonstrated within General Electric when CMMI complemented Lean Six Sigma and provided a synergistic effect that produced significant savings for that corporation.

Integrate and Align Business Strategy: Lean Six Sigma techniques are powerful in reducing process variation. So what does reduced variation in your process imply? First, measuring for variation will provide Control over what your process is designed for. Second, in a manufacturing environment, production processes that can reduce variation will produce a higher Quality Product at reduced cost levels. Another example, in a Service process, variation could impact the delivery of a Product or Service to a Customer, therefore impacting Customer Satisfaction. Today, an increasing number of companies are also implementing Lean Six Sigma approaches to business excellence as part of the business strategy.

Senior management must be clear about the reasons for change in the overall objectives. Successful deployments are based on a sense of urgency where the company's business leaders have a clear understanding as to how to adopt strategies based on Lean Six Sigma principles. In many cases, management recognizes major business challenges or risks that the company can overcome only through Lean Six Sigma. Those challenges could be a need to regain market competitiveness, introduce new products or services, attract new Customers, retain existing Customers, or simply improve profitability.

Information Technology is becoming an increasingly critical part to most business solutions. The fundamental understanding is that technology supports the business and not the other way around. Therefore, this dictates using technology as a tool to speed up, automate, or remove manual time-consuming processes. Through the use of Lean Six Sigma methodology, alternatives that have not traditionally been used in the IT segment can be utilized to assist in IT strategy alignment to your Business strategy.

Avoid Complexity: When implementing a Business Transformation Initiative, avoid complexity and choose an approach that is suited for your business. Ensure that your methodology is a cookie-cutter approach that encourages replication and ease of transition. Do not layer the complexity of your Transformation by piling methodology upon methodology, program upon program. One example of an organization that included Six Sigma, Balanced Scorecard, and IIP methodology all at the same time. The results were dismal.

I encourage integrating Lean Six Sigma into your Balanced Scorecard. But use the KISS method and link to a direct path from the strategic objective to the Individual achievements that contribute to accomplish targets. Transparency is also key, so study data points that are easily communicated across the organization to convey progress. Empowering your employees, providing clear information and direction, making all employees accountable, while utilizing a decision making process that is data driven will help assure your transition.

Executive and Management Accountability: Two years into a Six Sigma deployment, one company reviewed its progress. The review included interviews with key decision makers throughout the organization. One of the more revealing interviews came from the vice president of Product development—a key player in the organization. First, the vice president said he had not been invited to attend any Six Sigma training, nor had any Champions or Black Belts asked him about his priorities. Second, he and his staff were keenly aware of all the money and effort being devoted to the Black Belts. The vice president and his staff had absolutely no reason to actively support Six Sigma, and instead had grown to view it with some resentment. By ignoring the importance of their commitment and support, the organization missed a prime opportunity to capitalize on its resources.

In another instance, senior management announced a strategic direction for their change. Then top executives remained aloof and distant, leaving the hands-on and actual change to less-motivated and incentivized people. Lack of involvement from senior Leadership is a guaranteed formula for failure.

Managers will never fully support Six Sigma if they view it as taking away from their resources rather than adding capability and helping them become more successful in achieving their goals; nor will they actively support it if they think it is eating up vital budgetary allotments rather than setting the stage for significant financial payback. To avoid such pitfalls, a company must involve all key business leaders in helping to design its Six Sigma deployment. By giving them a voice in project selection, priorities and ongoing monitoring, an organization can be assured of their commitment to the effort.

If corporate leaders are not prepared for the change, or consider the appropriate management style that is required to manage Transformation, then resistance may be formidable where change is the norm. "Change programs" fail in that they are seen as just that: "programs." When "change" becomes a cliché, then it becomes a constant, which presumably has an illusion of a start and a finish, but in reality, doesn't address the long-term change in management style. Clearly understand that a rigid management style, a poorly thought out Transformation Process and implementation will always result in resistance, poor Quality, and increased costs. Management must recognize that all organizational levels will need to accept and embrace change for clear success. Transparency, honest communication, incentives, and visible commitment to Quality will be your initiative linchpins.

Many books have been written about accountability, performance, and responsibility such as *The One Minute Manager*, *Who Moved My Cheese*, and Stephen Covey's works, especially *The Seven Habits of Highly Effective People*. However, all of those personal skills and disciplines must be exercised in a structured business environment that will reap personal and professional benefits, like a Lean Six Sigma environment. Using such skills and practicing those principles are based on personal motivation. From a corporate point of view, parallel disciplines should be institutionalized to Measure and promote performance and responsibility. This is based on the understanding of accountability and rewarding desired behavior through clear incentives.

A RASIC (Responsible | Accountable | Support | Informed | Consulted) diagram helps structure that responsibility based on the context of engagement and how each stakeholder participates. Then roles and accountability can be identified and communicated; therefore, responsibility of the participant is aligned into these tasks:

- *Responsible* – Those responsible for the performance of the task. There should be exactly one person with this assignment for each task.
- *Accountable* – Those accountable for the performance and completion of the task.
- *Support* – Resources allocated to Responsible. Unlike Consulted, who may provide Input to the task, Support will assist in completing the task.
- *Informed* – Those who are kept up-to-date on progress; and with whom there is one-way communication.
- *Consulted* – Those whose opinions are sought; and with whom there is two-way communication.

Project Nomination, Size, Complexity, and Collaboration: In the 1990s, Tom Peters said; "To build a sustaining new culture may take decades, but to get a running start—with dramatic changes in Output—takes only months." Your Quality initiative time line will vary according to your company size, complexity and organizational collaboration, and reception of outside expertise.

- Your enterprise classification will be determined by the number of sites/locations and whether they are globally dispersed.
- Depending on the use of technology and Systems implemented, their use and IT collaboration could impact your time line.
- Corporate structure and company philosophies also play a significant role in freely communicating progress and methods of refinement among dissimilar organizations.

Project nomination is contingent on engaging your managers, staff, and overall culture. This is a critical success factors. Any Process Owner can nominate a project for Lean Six Sigma remediation. However, every project nominated for deployment must meet the following eligibility requirements:

- Deployment must be a corporate-wide initiative with Lean Six Sigma ingrained in the way your company does business.
- Deployment must use Lean Six Sigma methodologies and incorporate Quality Strategies, Process Transformation, Quality Evaluation and Continuous Improvement practices.
- You will be asked to address achievements and practices around each of the following:
  Deployment return on investment (minimum 5x)
  Deployment alignment with senior Leadership's intent and goals
  Change management and corporate culture
  Accounting and Audit teams will Verify tangible benefits
- Deployment program management and infrastructure to include:
  Training program for both soft and technical skills
  Deployment plan development
  Project selection process
  Repatriation process for Black Belts
  Recognition/reward/incentive System
  Project knowledge sharing
  Talent selection and Leadership development

The most effective Six Sigma companies have a rigorous project selection process driven by an evaluation of how much shareholder value a project can generate. It can be characterized as a trade-off decision comparing value delivered to effort expended. The most effective Six Sigma companies have a rigorous project selection process driven by an evaluation of how much shareholder value a project can generate. It can be characterized as a trade-off decision comparing value delivered to effort expended.

It may seem obvious, but many times resources are not applied or applied unbalanced. Some companies start their deployments by training a handful of people and launching a few "demonstration" projects. Others ramp up for immediate corporate-wide deployment, training hundreds of Black Belts and launching dozens of projects within the first six months. Either approach is workable, but for every company there is a critical level of Six Sigma effort: Below that level, projects and focus eventually fade away. Above that level, excitement and momentum build into a sustainable advantage.

Given that most companies want to generate measurable, significant results within six months or a year, the tendency is to push as many projects into the Lean Six Sigma deployment as possible. But one of the most important lessons that Lean principles teach is that pushing excess work into a process slows down the process and dramatically increases lead times.

As Six Sigma practitioners know, reducing the amount of Work-In-Process per Black Belt can speed up results. That means controlling the number of active projects at any given time. It is better to focus on getting a few high-potential projects done right than to just flood the workplace with dozens of less-important projects. With the right resources working on the right projects, learning and results are maximized by short cycle times.

Also avoid poor decisions under time constraints. Remember, "do it right the first time." An example cited when a business "rammed" certain functions with little regard to the overall business (i.e., they had changed one part of the process and not considered the impact up or downstream). In short, they had panicked and were looking for a quick win or to declare victory too soon. This decision led to process disconnects and poor Quality that also required additional rework.

Use of Lean Six Sigma involves some technical skills—the ability to process and analyze data, for example. But good Leadership skills are even more important. This emphasis on Leadership also relates to how a company chooses people to fill Black Belt roles. Placing the most promising people in the Black Belt role is painful at first, yet it yields fast results and a rapid Transformation of the organization.

Track Results Rigorously and Accurately: Lean Six Sigma results should "pay as you go" and be confirmed by objective parties. Too many companies discount the necessity of having a reliable means to judge project results and impact, or they underestimate the difficulty in creating such a System.[39] Six Sigma results must be quantified so a company can appropriately evaluate their impact and make good decisions about whether resources are being used wisely. A senior-level finance person should participate in the development of a results-tracking rulebook. As a deployment is planned, a company must think in terms of leading measurements or key performance indicators of the potential financial results.[40] At a minimum, project cycle times and project values must be measured on a regular basis and to gain an understanding of the level of variation in these numbers.

Henry Ford was an astute industrialist who encapsulated "business truths" into succinct and often pragmatic phrases, such as; "One of the greatest discoveries a man makes, one of his great surprises, is to find he can do what he was afraid he couldn't do."[41] Mr. Ford was ahead of his time, and would probably agree that resistance to change is one of the first hurdles to climb when introducing change to an organization. The key point is to make this change work for you and become a benefit for the company, and more importantly, provide your organization with an experience that fosters a "can do" attitude.[42]

---

39   Marks, Mitchell Lee; "In With The New," Wall Street Journal, May 24, 2010, Dr. Marks is an associate professor of management at San Francisco State University's College of Business.
40   Keck, Paul R.; "Why Quality Fails?" 1995.
41   Andel, Tom; "Lean and Six Sigma Traps to Avoid," Mar 1, 2007.
42   Palmer, Jonathan; "Change Management in Practice: Why Does Change Fail?" 2008.

Change is a Constant: Your enterprise growth and Sustainability will rely on your decisions to effect strategies that pursue excellence and optimization in order to compete in the marketplace. Remember what Andy Grove articulated: "A corporation is a living organism; it has to continue to shed its skin. Methods have to change. Focus has to change. The sum total of those changes is TRANSFORMATION." Very few business scenarios develop where your entire enterprise can benefit from structured and deliberate change.

In this example, your organization has effectively assessed details to provide you and your team with information to make a decision to create a Business Transformation Initiative. Using the above example, root cause assumptions are filtered and consolidated by critical issues that require actions to achieve your goal to reduce operating expenses. In this process, your assessment would determine the cost reduction, assumptions and resources affected. In this case, it is also assumed that changes to your Customer base have also been considered in terms of Quality degradation, fulfillment, availability and Customer Satisfaction. It is also assumed that cultural considerations, both external and internal, have been identified and understood.

Your next step is to understand the alternatives and how their respective consequences will affect your bottom line, performance, Quality, production, fulfillment to the Customer, and final impact on your current Customer base. For our discussion, we will exclude any potential new Customer growth and its impact in the decision and financial position in the future. So, what do these options provide?

As an Owner or CEO, you have been in meetings and the likelihood for a short meeting will depend on your management style. Generally, selection will be based on the best potential return with the least amount of risk. In many cases, Lean Six Sigma will fall into this grouping and provide you with an empowered organization that is both Quality and performance oriented. What are other considerations? Investing in a Quality initiative that addresses strategies and processes, evaluates effectiveness, and institutionalizes the change in your company, that shedding process helps your organization transform almost immediately, in the short-run perspective and in the long term. As Deming said, "The aim of the System must be clear to everyone in the System. The aim must include plans for the future. The aim is a value judgment."

3.2: Meta Planning

It is business that can exercise the fastest degree of change by seeing the opportunity rather than the threat.

~ Christopher Hune, MP

Chapter Summary: Before Initiatives can be implemented into your core process architecture, the CEO and Executive Team must lay the foundation of change in conceptualizing where the organization needs to grow and furnish a map for that journey.

Key Points:
- Meta Planning
- Meta Planning Principles
- Meta Planning vs. MBO
- Meta Planning Governance
- Model Recognition
- Meta Planning Framework
- Flexible Transformation
- Process Interlocks
- Planning Steps
- Transformation Linkages
- Apply Lessons Learned

Meta Planning: Meta Planning does not replace other management strategies, it is a Transformation Infrastructure System that identifies the process portfolio, monitors implementation progress, orchestrates Continuous Improvement, and breakthroughs. It accomplishes that task by pinpointing the accountable business model and selects the area that needs improvement, makes sure the right people get involved, and that solutions are implemented. It leverages existing strategic planning information and tailors additional planning activities and information-gathering requirements to prepare for Business Transformation in your enterprise.

Drucker said, "The result of business is a satisfied Customer." To make that happen, you must communicate your vision, integrate Strategies, map to Strategic Processes, define Accountability, implement Continuous Improvement, and Learn to promote success. Meta Planning assessment includes, External needs, Common Values and Internal needs:

External Needs
- Infrastructure
- COTS or In-house Systems

Common Values
- Human Resources
- Corporate Culture

Internal Needs
- Skill sets
- Staffing Requirements
- Style

Implementing a Business Transformation Initiative must hinge on a well thought out solutions that are based on best practices, best-in-class models to make a company more competitive, efficient, and profitable, in addition to the conceptual tools for molding your Transformation concept.

97

- Alignment to strategy
- Alignment across cross-function areas
- May include Customers and/or Suppliers
- Prioritize project with cross functional levels
- Focus on Process
- Requirements gathering
- Process documentation and tools
- Innovation, Process simulation
- Establish Quality Evaluation – Measurement

Strategic planning is the most effective management tool for controlling change and instilling Transformation. However, external influencers often provoke obligatory modifications to your business model (i.e., laws, regulations, competition, globalization, deregulation, etc.). In some cases, change is slow and easy to digest. In others cases, such as the current energy crisis, dramatic and quick changes affect and impact your business and its organization. Proactive management anticipates this possibility and reflects that insight into their plans. An example could be the recognition of Maturity models and what should be considered for the "next step" in Transformation. Strategic planning is a mind-set to embrace change for the benefits to your concern, but this mind-set must conform to a framework in order to be repeatable and consistent.

Lean Six Sigma methodology is the foundation for excellence. The first tier of Business Transformation is based on utilizing integrated services that include: Strategy, Processes, Monitoring Progress, and Continuous Improvement. Based on your vision and approaching your Transformation as an integrated initiative, these services will be tailored for improving your organization, utilizing resources, improving effectiveness and empowering your personnel.

Additionally, what are other factors in making a Business Transformation Initiative successful? The following list provides an outline of objectives, which can be amended to include other responsibilities and guidelines for your Champion:

- Champion the vision – compelling reason(s) for change
- Motivate the teams
- Remove roadblocks
- Gain buy-in and overcome resistance
- Execute the project/program
- Link sponsorship to executive pay

Success does not hinge solely on the Owner or CEO, Executive Team, or your selected Champion for the Business Transformation Initiative. There are also a number of milestones that must be accomplished for your entire enterprise in terms of activities, roles, acceptance of the methodology and the ultimate conformance of your business culture. The following are considerations that would further integrating your organization to a performance culture:

- Defined metrics and aligned incentives
- Enterprise architecture
- Involve veteran leaders with experience in initiatives
- Involve your best people
- Set expectations for "change readiness" and how it impacts the enterprise
- Discipline and rigor
- Team structure and organization
- Communications

Meta Planning Principles: Meta Planning, which means, "plan for changing conditions," is designed to compliment your Strategic Planning and is a logical extension to Strategic Management methodology. Meta Planning, designed for Sustainability and Lean Six Sigma initiatives, applies best-in-class principles and practices to help a company turn its Quality Systems into a potent competitive tool.

It is loosely based on a concept popularized by Professor Kaoru Ishikawa when he observed that each person is the expert in his or her own job. "Top managers and middle managers must be bold enough to delegate as much authority as possible. That is the way to establish respect for humanity as your management philosophy. It is a management System in which all employees participate, from the top down and from the bottom up, and humanity is fully respected."

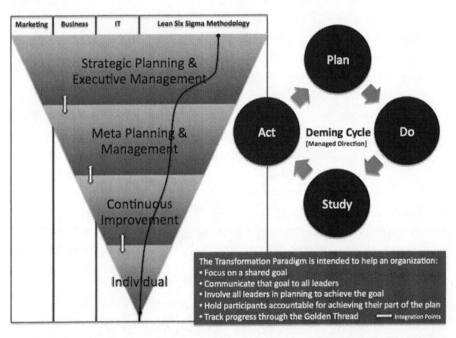

Note: *Dr. W. Edwards Deming, who is considered by many to be the father of modern Quality Management, made PDCA popular; however he always referred to it as the "Shewhart cycle". Later in Deming's career, he modified PDCA to "Plan, Do, Study, Act" (PDSA) so as to better describe his recommendations.*

So, how is the individual the expert? How can that person understand the strategy? The individual cannot link efforts in the most common ways of setting objectives, or can he or she? The answer is based on Meta Planning. The individual uses "The Golden Thread" and links to a direct path from the strategic objective to the Individual achievements that contribute to accomplish targets. Meta planning links each level of governance to agreed data that reflects effort. Six key elements that are components of Meta Planning include:

- Focus for the organization in the form of a few breakthrough goals that are vital to the organization's success.
- Commitment to Customers includes targets and means at every level of the organization that are based on meeting the needs and expectations that Customers rank as most important.
- Deployment of the organization's focus, so that employees understand their specific contributions to it. Referred to as The Golden Thread that links employees to what is important to Customers and to one another. In a broader sense, it links People, Quality, Profit and Sustainability strategies to directed efforts and actions.
- Internal experts are your specialists to develop the plan. Brainstorming is a key idea tool. Ideas are prioritized based on importance and deployment plans are aligned to those business needs.
- Tools and techniques should be helpful, clear, and easy to use. Management and planning tools (affinity charts, tree diagrams, decision matrices, process decision program chart) should clearly portray the situation.
- Ongoing evaluation of progress should facilitate learning and Continuous Improvement.

Meta Planning also addresses pitfalls that often occur in corporate planning processes. These "disconnects" are linchpins that often cause more discourse in the organization, rather than the intended goal of effective communication, aligning effort to actions and producing tangible results. These five pitfalls include:

- Incomplete Planning
- Not linking strategies to objectives to goals
- Not integrating Quality into Strategies
- Not measuring Quality and its impact on the Customer
- Missing Links To Action
- Poor Communications or poor follow-up

In order to implement a Sustainability and Quality initiative, Meta Planning principles and practices address a huge role in the planning, building, management, and improvement of Quality Systems. So, what exactly is Meta Planning? It is an enterprise architecture of business process management and improvement based on the following five steps:

- Executive Quality Commitment is reflected in the effort dedicated in each Sustainability and Quality Initiative and its harvested tangible benefits.
- Portfolio management and execution based on business model definition, that Measures key business Processes, Products and Services in conformance to Customer needs and other business requirements.
- Governance of Lean Six Sigma methodology, based on accepted Project Management standards, ensure enforced behavior that set expectations and objectives.
- Target by Survey confirms the "real" issue versus the "perceived" issue in the business environment that is directed towards Processes, Products and Services.
- Quality Evaluation links Meta Planning to specific continuous measurement actions, project by project, to reduce variation in existing business processes that cause failures to conform to Customer requirements.
- Repeating steps 1 through 4 continuously as necessary for the enterprise to remain viable and sustain shareholder value over the long term.

Meta Planning continues to perform an important role. After successful implementation of your Initiative, it is designed to be used in a post initiative state to specifically refine the "system" to meet changing Customer needs and market requirements by:

- Providing oversight of new processes for innovative Products, Processes and Services.

- Providing oversight of Silo Alignment of Products, Processes and Services.
- Providing oversight of IT Alignment with Business effort to improve strategic competitiveness for Products, Processes and Services.

Meta Planning vs. MBO: Often, stakeholders may overlook or not recognize the interdependence between process components. Therefore, failure of management to comprehend these interfaces can cause MBO programs to drive efforts improperly. The efforts of the various divisions in a company, each given a job, are not additive. Their efforts are interdependent. One division, to achieve this, left to itself, kills off another division. Drucker is clear on this point.[43] How does Meta Planning compare with Management By Objectives? Let us compare multiple levels for purpose, focus, execution responsibility, methodology, time frame, review, objectives, and decision basis:

Purpose
- Meta Planning – Organizational governance and problem solving for breakthroughs
- Management By Objective – Management of individual performance

Focus
- Meta Planning – Focus on the Remediation Capabilities in meeting Customer expectations
- Management By Objective – Individual responsibilities for achievements

Execution Responsibility
- Meta Planning – Executive Team, Champions, Process Owners and Quality Teams
- Management By Objective – Individuals

---

43   Drucker, Peter; Management Tasks, Responsibilities, Practices; Harper and Row, 1973.

Methodology
- Meta Planning – Business Model approach, Portfolio Management and Lean Six Sigma Quality principles/tools
- Management By Objective – Not specified

Time Frame
- Meta Planning – Project and Resource driven time frame, Customer alignment, Supplier alignment and alignment with long-term goals
- Management By Objective – Final reviews on Results

Review
- Meta Planning: Periodic progress reviews on Process and Results centering on Products, Processes and Services
- Management By Objective: Final reviews on Results

Objectives
- Meta Planning – Focus on the Customer needs and the "vital few" for competitive advantages that concentrate on Customer Satisfaction Results
- Management By Objective – Numerous and may not focus on the Customer

Decision Basis
- Meta Planning – Facts and data that provide a quantitative depiction of the scenario
- Management By Objective – Data not required

Meta Planning Governance: Look for an old attitude in your organization and nurture it. One of the first foreign writers to document America's experiment with democracy was Alexis de Tocqueville, a French count who visited the US in 1831 and became intrigued with what seemed to be a peculiarly American phenomenon: small groups of citizens who came together to solve problems. American problem-solvers, Tocqueville observed, were different from what he had seen on the continent. These were groups of common citizens who had decided that they had the power to determine what the problem was, that they had the power to determine how to solve the problem and, more often than not, that they, themselves, would be key actors in implementing the solution. Writing in Democracy in America, Tocqueville concluded that these problem-solving citizen groups were the foundation stones of American communities and that they constituted a uniquely powerful instrument.[44] If these assumptions hold true, you can achieve dramatic improvements:

- It's likely that your initiatives are focused on solving change from your influencers. Therefore, each initiative is probably not a clone of the other initiatives.
- Your people cannot explain what their processes accomplish.
- Your people are trainable and capable of making basic business decisions.
- You are willing to empower your workforce to execute those basic business decisions.
- Your managers are capable of utilizing their resources, effectively.
- You sometimes face diverse Customer needs and deadlines.
- Your Customer satisfaction is not important and does not need improvement.
- It is impossible to know all the requirements at the beginning of an effort.
- Resistance to Change, sometimes even minor change, is a normal part of the process improvement and "not a problem."[45]

If these assumptions reflect your organization, then the process that follows will add great value. Organizationally, alignment of management, accounting and IT will be determining resources that will affect your results. Meta Planning is a system of measuring strategy effectiveness, provides resources control, monitor tangible benefits, and retain gains while adapting your corporate culture to your Vision of a high performance organization.

---

44   de Tocqueville, Alexis "Democracy in America", 1835.
45   Strassmann, Paul; The Squandered Computer, The Information Economics Press, 1997, Retrieved: 2 February 2008.

Model Recognition: Meta Planning must recognize all aspects of Business Transformation in your enterprise. Recognize that issues and problems often cause "pain" and pressures on your organization. Express that recognition through the "Voice of the Client" to drive the direction of Transformation. Actual benefits will vary and understand that a detailed assessment will be the only method to quantify targeted benefits in each project. Meta Planning is one segment of the change paradigm and focuses on three models most enterprises are based on: *Business, Information Technology,* and *Marketing.*

Business Model – In most cases the business model incorporates all aspects of the organization, its resources, technology, innovation vision, and the overarching strategic vision of the corporation and its organization.

Information Technology Model – The IT organization often wears multiple hats and in this case the IT group must focus on the end Customers as well as internal Customers. IT managed services and commitments to Service levels are common. In many cases, there are gaps between business efforts and IT support that can be transformed and provide better alignment. In some cases this alignment can produce a strategic asset that would better fulfill existing and prospective Customers.

Marketing Model – The Customer is always the focal point in any business model, especially the Marketing Model. This model addresses the marketing effectiveness of Products, Services, and Processes that are sold to the Customer base to meet specific needs. Oftentimes, marketing and sales efforts are integrated and coordinated to provide end-to-end visibility of corporate actions and Customer behaviors.

Meta Planning Framework: In the course of examining Corporate Strategies and linking to corresponding Silo Strategies, each of these levels will drive the focus of the Transformation Initiative and how Transformation will be integrated into your organization. For weaknesses found in each of these questions, an opportunity exists in

106

transforming that weakness into strength. Earlier, I shared the five most important business questions that should be asked:

- What is our Mission?
- Who is our Customer?
- What does the Customer Value?
- What are our Results?
- What is our Plan?[46]

In the planning model, it is extremely important to integrate these questions and focus effort on the commitment, meaning, and desired outcome, acknowledgment from each question to determine the model's attributes and behavior.

It is useful to use a collaborative approach to further enrich your Visions and Missions. For breakthrough sessions, brainstorming is a tool of choice for these group discussions. It is important to select SMEs in distinct and varied disciplines from each business model. This approach brings diverse points of view that lay the foundation for idea building that fosters eventual breakthroughs.

Planning Rationalization – Meta Planning is a Business Transformation planning process designed to ensure that the Initiative's Vision, Mission, Objectives, and Goals are communicated throughout an organization, and implemented by everyone from top management to the frontline. The organization develops multiple (not more than five) Vision statements to encourage breakthrough thinking about its future direction. Then goals and work plans are developed, based on the collectively chosen Vision statement; and progress toward them is periodically monitored through performance audits.[47]

Meta Planning is based on the enterprise landscape and focus on your Quality Vision. It addresses business alignment, business

---

46   Drucker, Peter; The Five Most Important Questions You Will Ever Ask About Your Organization; Leader to Leader Institute, 2008.
47   BusinessDictionary.com; Retrieved: 10 March 2011.

concepts, and addresses the need for innovation of Products, Services, and Processes.

- Develop the business case (i.e., Business model, Marketing model, IT model)
- Establish participants (i.e., Executives, Champion, Process Owners, etc.)
- Selection of projects prioritized by net impact (cost versus benefits analysis, requirement, strategic priority, etc.)

Additionally, Meta Planning is a body of planning knowledge centered on Business Transformation that is created on core principles of Lean Six Sigma. Leadership needs to recognize traits and behaviors that will impact your initiative. Look for these positive signs for change:

- Strong Executive Commitment that is open-minded and flexible
- Committed to long-term institutionalization
- Apply Meta Planning Principles
- Program requirements based on accountability and alignment
- Program Management Office [optional]
- Process Portfolio Assessment
- Dedicated Lean Six Sigma training
- Recommended a pilot project for each Silo Model
- Matrix structure for review for multiple clients
- Matrix structure for review for multiple stakeholders
- Update Communication Plan and provide timely dissemination of progress

Project Evaluation for Meta Planning – Handing off the agreed criteria for the selection of Transformation Projects is a key linchpin in the direction of the Initiative. Use the Deming cycle (PDSA: Plan, Do, Study, Act) to ensure that your projects fit within the criteria or recognize that your criteria may have too many constraints. Also scrutinize the acceptance thresholds, prudent targets for improvement, and rationalize the time line required with the resources required. This enhanced project selection process should identify the right projects, those that will:

- Create a project nominee list, based on issues, costs or strategic direction, that will be the root directory for Process Transformation.
- Ensure that each identified project is incorporated in the Meta Plan.
- Estimate the benefits from tangible resources that could be derived from each project based on key metrics. Use tangibles that increase in revenue, decrease in costs, increase in assets turnover or changes in cycle times to Measure benefits.
- Produce the highest value in relation to business goals.
- Improve performance of processes that are producing the pain.
- Improve the flow of materials and information while reducing waste and cycle time.
- Align accounting and IT Systems with Transformation data requirements.

Quality Evaluation – Management reporting is a critical success factor. Organizations that succeed in effective Lean Six Sigma programs constantly measure their success. They share common success factors, which correlate project success, business commitment and executive support. These factors are:

- A phased implementation
- Clear business Process Ownership and its outcomes
- Data quality and governance
- Leverage on external drivers
- Standardize a information formats for ease of digestion
- Generate Quality Key Performance Indices (KPIs) and apply to improvement of Process, Product, and Service Quality
- Integrate Quality, Strategic and Operational KPIs

The balanced scorecard establishes targets for breakthrough performance not merely to match existing best practices. Many quality programs evaluate their internal process performance against the benchmark best practices and focus as a result of continuous improvement.[48]

Learning Transformation – The goal of Lean Six Sigma is to change traditional ways of doing things to continuously look for ways to reduce variation in Processes, Services and Products, quantitatively. An organization should manage differently after Six Sigma implementation versus before. Process management systems should be developed that document the "what and how" business systems are performed and Six Sigma will be integrated into other key business initiatives. Key elements of Lean Six Sigma being used on a daily basis:

- Continuously working to find better ways of doing things
- Thinking of everything you do as a process
- Recognizing that variation exists in every process and its effects on work
- Working to reduce variation
- Using data to guide your decisions
- Using Lean Six Sigma tools to make your processes more effective and productive.

Sponsors and Champions must continue to ask the right questions, use the DMAIC process, and be genuinely involved in selecting the best projects. The days of "shooting from the hip" must be over and decisions should now be made with the analysis of data.

The organization should continue to grow and learn. More people from all functional areas should get on board and become Green Belts, Black Belts, and Master Black Belts. Lean Six Sigma should, if allowed to become the operating philosophy, change the culture of the company!

The desired end is that Lean Six Sigma becomes such an integral part of the way the organization manages that there is no longer a need for a formal Lean Six Sigma initiative.[49]

---

48   Kaplan and Norton, Strategy Maps, Harvard Business School Press, 2004, Page 93.
49   The Strategy Session, July 4, 2009, Make Lean Six Sigma the Way We Work, Retrieved: 12 Aug 2009.

Flexible Transformation: So, what is the best approach to Transformation implementation? In Meta Planning, you have four options. Quality Transformation is implemented through basic strategies that rely on Executive Management Commitment, buy-in in from the Executive Team and key managers, as well as a thought-out Transformation Plan, Quality expertise, employee training and a commitment to a shared vision. Review, selection, and understanding of the implementation choice should be made prior to your Transformation rollout.

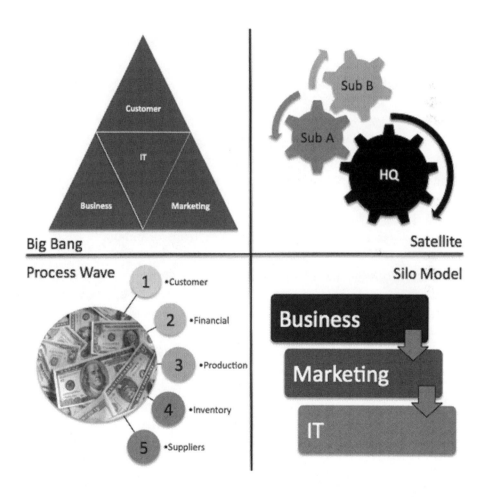

Big Bang – Transformation initiatives often cause a disruption in your normal business activity. The Big Bang approach to Transformation involves your entire Corporation simultaneously. This is taxing to all employees, from executives to front line staff, to engage in remediate waste and inefficiencies in your organization. Additional expertise and temporary resources may be required to fulfill your Transformation initiative.

Satellite – This implementation type gears the Transformation by organizational site. The original organization will be the headquarters, followed by multiple organizations that are incorporated in the Transformation plan. A positive characteristic of this approach limits the disruption of activities to centralized areas and organizations. The use of your core Transformation teams can be leveraged in reply in the satellite organizations.

Process Waves – Process waves identify major swim lanes of internal and external processes. In this situation, the required interfaces between other processes and systems will dictate the implementation of your Transformation teams. Issues regarding the complexity of processes and their entered interdependency with other key processes may become problematic and will require high management visibility to avoid major bottlenecks to Transformation.

Silos Model – Silo Models (Strategic Business Units or Business Units of Business, IT, Marketing) focus on key processes within those commercial models. Although these vertical silos provide clear support of their Owners, cooperation with other silo Owners can be problematic. The opportunity to Transform often opens synergistic improvements between silo Owners' listed interests.

In addition to the choice of approach, the Owner/CEO/Executive Team, need to help formulate the following expectations prior to the implementation of the Transformation initiative and include these deliverables:

- Involve more individual contributors early
- Train and raise awareness of Product, Process and Service Owners, early

- The downside coaching and expertise earlier
- Work on automation and management reporting earlier
- Ensure that accounting will capture and Verify essential data to align and properly calculate tangible benefits
- Give key executives advance notice and concrete deliverables around rollout.
- Be clear and communicate frequently about the rules of Transformation

Process Interlocks: The following end-to-end survey model is constructed to address twelve separate touch points that can extract the Customer experience to what is being brought in through Suppliers and those organizational points you need to know Internally. You can extract valuable information to Verify perceived issues that may be problems in the value of your Products or Services. Quality is a Customer perception; therefore, monitoring that perception will be valuable in clearly understanding shifts in experience, Quality, and satisfaction. The following examples are indicative how surveys could assess Customer perceptions:

- Coaching opportunities at all levels – not just the C-level executives.
- Evaluation of Product and Service value to the Customer
- Customer Satisfaction and Expectations
- Compare your Quality of Service to other competitors your Customers use.
- Identify competitive advantages and opportunities for improvement.

Surveys directed at specific populations will provide insights to your Customers, Suppliers, and Internal perceptions. All queries are important; however, when applied to critical decision-making tasks, those surveys can support initiatives or provide insight to other areas that are considered more important.

1.0 Customer Expectations compared to Customer Perceptions can be examined to better understand a Customer's experience with your services and products.

2.1 Internal Specifications and Requirements compared to Product Quality can be examined to better understand perceptions and gaps in Quality and Requirements.

2.2 Internal Specifications and Requirements compared to Service Delivery can be examined to better understand perceptions and gaps in Quality and Requirements.

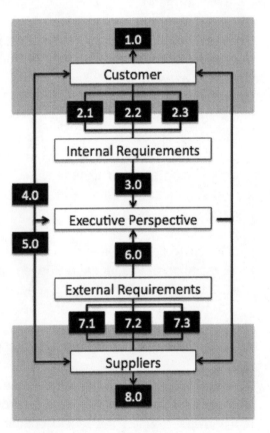

2.3 Internal Specifications and Requirements compared to Process Effectiveness can be examined to better understand perceptions and gaps in Quality and Requirements.

3.0 Executive Perspective of Customer Expectations compared to Internal Specifications and Requirements Perceptions can be examined to better understand expectations and gaps in Quality and Specifications.

4.0 Executive Perspective of Customer Expectations compared to Customer Expectations Perceptions can be examined to better understand perceptions and gaps in Quality and Expectations.

5.0 Executive Perspective of Customer Expectations compared to Supplier Objectives Perceptions can be examined to better understand perceptions and gaps in Quality Requirements and Supplier Objectives.

6.0 Executive Perspective of Customer Expectations compared to External Specifications and Supplier Quality Perceptions can be examined to better understand perceptions and gaps in Quality and Specifications.

7.1 External Specifications and Supplier Quality compared to Product and Material Agreement Perceptions can be examined to better understand perceptions and gaps in Quality and Product and Material defects.

7.2 External Specifications and Supplier Quality compared to Service Quality Agreement Perceptions can be examined to better understand perceptions and gaps in Quality and Service issues or defects.

7.3 External Specifications and Supplier Quality compared to Process Quality Agreement Perceptions can be examined to better understand perceptions and gaps in Quality and Process defects.

8.0 Supplier's Performance compared to Supplier Objectives Perceptions can be examined to better understand the Supplier's problem areas compared to their agreed Service Level Agreement objectives.

Even if you think you know what the problems are or where there are causes of the problems, you must begin with "just the facts" from the beginning. Very few original perceptions of a problem are verified as its true cause. The Washington Monument scenario provides insight to determine why it was disintegrating:

- Why? Use of harsh chemicals
- Why? To clean pigeon poop
- Why so many pigeons? They eat spiders and there are a lot of spiders at Washington Monument

115

- Why so many spiders? They eat gnats and lots of gnats at Washington Monument
- Why so many gnats? They are attracted to the light at dusk.
- Solution: Turn on the lights at a later time.

There can be more than one cause to a problem as well. Avoid following assumptions and remember, you want to drive decision from facts and begin using the Systematic approach of data driven decision making.

A leader needs to view the landscape, holistically, and Meta Planning addresses that need. What happens externally is often as critical as what happens internally. Leadership should look at his or her organization from three high levels: Customer, Internal, and Supplier perspectives. Capturing essential information from your Customers and monitoring your Supplier's Service level agreements are essential. However, you will find situations where data and information are absent. In those situations, apply surveys to provide insight from end-to-end and validate a "best fit" approach or a path for change.

Planning Steps: Let us refine the definition of Meta Planning. Another accurate term for Meta Planning would link planning with execution. In other words, Meta Planning is designed to "plan for changing conditions for transformation deployment." This approach indicates its unique intention: to integrate an entire organization's daily activity with long-term Quality goals. What Meta Planning provides is a planning structure that will bring selected critical business Processes up to the desired level performance and create a "golden thread" for linkage to strategies and visibility. So, what are the benefits of Meta Planning?

- Creates and establishes a process to execute breakthrough ideas and establishes breakthrough objective mind-set.
- Creates commitment to both the direction of Transformation and implementation paths that adequately support the objective.
- Creates collaboration and increases interdepartmental cooperation

- Institutionalizes monthly progress reviews based on Plan-Do-Study-Act (PDSA) Cycles and reviews progress of these plans.
- Augments your current strategic planning system, creates a disciplined implementation system that is responsive and flexible, and changes to plans as required.
- Provides visibility for Leadership to better understand the key problem areas and issues in a company
- Scorecards and Dashboards provide quicker and more accurate feedback loops for Continuous Improvement of key business processes.
- Reinforces the shared vision and provides a common focus throughout the organization and a vehicle for organizational learning.

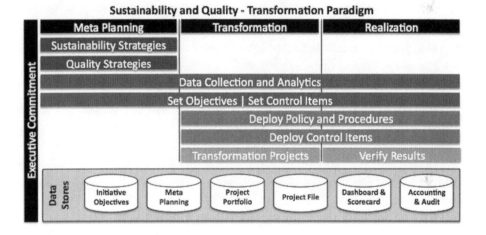

Sustainability and Quality - Transformation Paradigm

1. Choose the Focus: These governing ideas answer three critical questions: "What?" "Why?" and "How?":

- *Vision Is The What* – the picture of the future state the Client seeks to create.
- *Purpose Is The Why* – the organization's answer to the question, "Why do we exist?" The repeated buying behavior of the Customer, your business philosophy, economic, environmental, social, and

technological impact have a larger sense of purpose that surpasses the needs of shareholders and employees.

* *Core Values Answer The How* – How do we want to react, consistent with our Mission, along the path toward achieving our Vision?" The company's values might include integrity, openness, honesty, freedom, equal opportunity, willingness, merit, or loyalty. They describe how the company wants life to be on a day-to-day basis, or for pursuing the Vision.[50]

In addition, the focus of Meta Planning should consider where the organization is now, how you want to develop a for the future and focus on the needs to promote innovation, by:

* Pursue the objectives of Voice of the Client and drive your efforts accordingly
* Illustrate your current state and make it visible to all stakeholders
* Define what the organization wants to be in the future
* Identify what the organization needs to focus on to achieve its vision and goals

2. Align the Organization: In this instance, Meta Planning interfaces with the needs of Strategic Planning. When aligning your organization and your Quality Transformation initiative, you'll be establishing a framework with Measures, Standards, and Targets that are based on negotiated levels that will be incorporated in your finalized three to five-year plan. This alignment will also provide relationship recognition of dependencies and interdependencies in processes.

* Create library of Quality standards
* Develop annual targets with clear Measures of success
* Develop means—how to achieve these targets
* Socialize the targets and means throughout the organization
* Finalize and integrate in your strategic multi-year plan

---

50   Senge, Peter M.; The Fifth Discipline: The Art and Practice of the Learning Organization; Published by Doubleday, 2006; page 208.

To better encapsulate those resources and provide visibility to their performance, portfolio management techniques should be incorporated in the initiative. The ultimate objective of portfolio management is to tame change by providing a proven discipline for delivering value through informed decision making.[51] If you are not using portfolio management techniques before the Transformation, you should be using many of them after its completion. The basis of this Quality standardization also recognizes a need to capture the resources, Processes, products, and services that are in scope for the Transformation. This repository will aid management and refine those critical factors for future success in a post-initiative environment. If executed properly, this decision support System will help drive decision making based on data and will support your new performance culture.

3. Project Transformation: Again, Meta Planning provides structure and implementation of your Transformation based on the Voice of the Client. The model will utilize the DMAIC Roadmap. Interlaced responsibilities from Meta Planning perspectives are included in the DMAIC Roadmap to:

- Mission and Objectives are determined by the Client and documented in the VOC that is addressed in the Define phase of the DMAIC
- In the Analyze phase, the current state analysis and team briefing session records the "what is" state
- In the Improve phase, prepare improvement recommendations in the DMAIC that will transform the process to meet or exceed expectations in the future state
- Determine the control method, based on Quality Evaluation and process monitoring, executed in the Control phase of the DMAIC [accountability is coordinated by IT, Accounting, Silo Owner, Champion and the Transformation Team]

---

51   Durbin, Pat and Doerscher, Terry; Taming Change with Portfolio Management; Greenleaf Book Group Press, 2010, ISBN :978-1-60832-038-7, page 45.

- Initiate Follow-up Audit and other Activities for each project to Verify the generation of tangible benefits

4. Review and Improve: Refinement is a keyword and best practice for both Lean Six Sigma and Meta Planning. Realization of tangible benefits can be accurately Measured after the implementation of the remediation team. Insights into invaluable information they contribute to Profound Knowledge are expected in these areas:

- Diagnose and correct problems as soon as possible and at the level closest to the problem
- Disseminate learning throughout the organization
- Monitor and Improve Results, the plan, and the planning Process
- Recognize and celebrate progress

Transformation Linkages: However, the core of those five initial questions will focus on your enterprise understanding. Those answers centered on your value of importance, creates understanding, as well as, its potential consequences. Additional principles work around these next seven business concepts:

- What is a System?
- What is the System's Value?
- What is an Input?
- What is a Process?
- What is an Output?
- Who is our Supplier?
- What is the Supplier's Value?

In the Transformation phase, we will integrate these process questions and focus effort linking to commitment, defining the problems, measure their impact, analyze the current state and plan for a future state, improve the process with a better solution and control the process to not loose gains or behave outside required limits. The definitive results should be tangible, measured benefits that will contribute to the enterprise effectiveness.

Deliverables for this planning process will be supported and generated by several Lean Six Sigma disciplines and tools (i.e., DFSS, DMAIC, Quality Evaluation, etc.). Following are the three critical components to Hoshi Planning initiatives:

- *Designing Processes for Customer requirements using Design for Six Sigma (DFSS) teams.* DFSS is a robust and Systematic improvement methodology that uses specific Six Sigma tools and metrics to design Products, Services, and Processes that meet Customer requirements from the outset, and that can be produced and delivered at Six Sigma Quality levels.
- *Improving existing Processes using Define, Measure, Analyze, Improve, and Control (DMAIC) Quality teams.* DMAIC is a fact-based, closed-loop; problem-solving methodology that ensures continued Process/Product/Service improvement. It focuses on eliminating unproductive steps, developing and applying new metrics, and using technology to drive improvement.
- *Enterprise-wide Process management using Process teams that work in real time to gauge, monitor, and analyze ongoing business and organizational performance.* The foundation for sustaining Six Sigma improvements over time is the institutionalizing of business improvement through ongoing process management. Process management requires that a company establish a series of Dashboards, metrics, and performance indicators for its core processes through which the top Leadership team can continuously monitor and assess performance. These Dashboards and metrics typically track and monitor a variety of performance indicators, including: leading indicators, results indicators, Customer indicators, and internal indicators (Smith and Blakeslee n.d.).[52]

Apply Lessons Learned: Experience from other Transformation projects provides wisdom and understanding in context to implementing

---

52   Smith, Dick ; Blakeslee, Jerry and Koonce, Richard; Strategic Six Sigma: Best Practices from the Executive Suite, John Wiley and Sons © 2002, Chapter 1.

a Quality Transformation initiative. Your company is not the first company to commit resources, time and management expertise to improve the performance and Quality standards of the company. Please take the following funds from other corporations that have embarked on a Quality Transformation initiative.

- Create a dedicated, fully empowered, cross-functional rollout team
- Don't be afraid to change the entire company at one time
- Get professional help
- Encourage peer-to-peer coaching
- Focus on getting several teams to excellence
- Create a company "esprit de corps"
- Decide early which tools you will use to manage the rollout
- Encourage openness, visibility and transparency
- Insurer top management inclusivity and participation by all employees
- Be patient and expect to make mistakes, learn from them will

Another key Lesson Learned is the apparent need for alignment [Customers, IT, Marketing, Suppliers]. There are several requirements a firm must meet to ensure a successful alignment. First, alignment should be implement after your Sustainability and Quality initiatives are complete. Second, these must survive changes in organization, will have to shift with redirections in business goals and adapt to changes in top Leadership personalities. Alignment guidelines include:

- Show Enhancements to a Business Plan
- Remain Updated as the Business Evolves
- Overcome Obstacles to its Purposes
- Must be Planned, in detail, linking strategies to processes and resources
- Must relate to Measurable and Tangible Benefits

Only Executives who have harmonized their organizations to compete effectively can extract value from Information Technologies. In that arena, computers do certainly have a role, often a leading one, but certainly not one that is decisive. What matters are superb management and people who have the motivation to deliver superior Results. A computer without such commitments is worth only its resale or scrap price, which is not much.[53]

---

53   Strassmann, Paul; The Squandered Computer, The Information Economics Press, 1997, Retrieved: 2 February 2008.

3.3: Transformation

Long-term commitment to new learning and new philosophy is required of any management that seeks Transformation.

~ W. Edwards Deming

Chapter Summary: Business Transformation is a top-down approach to making an organization into a Customer-serving, competitive tool. By nature, this Process encompasses Business Strategies, Transforms Processes, Measures Performance and provides a Continuous Improvement engine that adapts change into Benefits.

Key Points:
- Business Transformation
- Quality Strategies
- Process Transformation
- Quality Evaluation
- Learning Transformation

Business Transformation: "The economists' assumption that long-range, wealth-producing capacity automatically Results from maximizing a large number of short-range consumer benefits carries little intellectual conviction in an era of rapid change and innovation." Drucker was a visionary who clearly understood that "change and innovation" would be continual sources of influence on the free enterprise System, especially with respect to the corporation.[54]

Integrated solutions should be holistic, flexible, and adaptable in order to provide custom solutions that fit your organization's needs. All services should be tailored collaboratively, with the Client, to ensure scope and direction. Services are standardized within an integrated architecture from far-reaching Quality Strategies to Transformation Learning, conducted and implemented through Lean Six Sigma methodology and specific Service Roadmaps. Although results may vary in various business environments, the joint team approach is focused on objectives and goals that are monitored and measured to achieve tangible Results.

Modifying behavior with incentives that improve the Customer experience, also Measure Business Success

- Market share
- New Product penetration
- Productivity improvements
- ROI
- Revenue/profitability increases
- Expense reduction

(handwritten annotations: "Full Books", "author driven / consumer driven", "Success", "Expansion", "Future Books", "marketing", "Electronic book", "Seminar", "Revenue")

---

54   Peter F. Drucker, *The New Realities*, First edition (Harper and Row publishers, 1989).

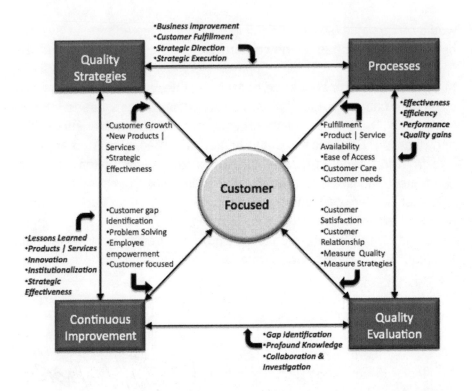

Quality Strategies: *Quality Strategies,* establish a Quality Strategy Initiative and orient your organization down the path of Business Transformation, refresh and integrate Quality into every strategy, verbalize linkage, and emphasize Business Models, Strategy Maps, Process objectives, Performance Measures, and Transformation Learning. Quality Strategies are an organization's framework of defining its planning Process, strategies, objectives, and defining decision-making procedures that affect allocation of its resources to pursue specific commercial paths. This includes timing of the strategy, addressing market barriers, resources needed (i.e., capital and people), technologies required, and benefits (performance, profitability, security, etc.) that such an undertaking could mandate. The strategic time line is usually greater than two years and most commonly falls around five.

Quality Strategies Goals:
- The first step in empowering your employees is through Lean Six Sigma disciplines. Engage all employees in Lean Six Sigma training and reward their efforts when they produce tangible savings, productivity, and efficiencies.
- Identify and assess your projects to determine the size of your Lean Six Sigma effort. Identify and prioritize business impact projects according to anticipated savings, reduction in cycle time and improved throughput.
- Focus on low-hanging fruit and apply Lean principles in reducing waste and other costs.
- True Lean Six Sigma Quality is an elusive goal. Build consensus in your Executive Team and Define and develop Quality for your business.
- Expand the scope of Six Sigma beyond the pilot stage and beyond the group/division level to be consistently applied enterprise wide.
- Align Business, Finance, and IT efforts during the Business Transformation. Charge Finance with a facilitation role and engage all projects. IT solutions remain largely untapped as a response to Business Transformation; so, utilize those talents too.

Map your strategies to your strategic Processes. Lean Six Sigma identifies "disconnects" and "gaps" in strategies by assessing your Quality Strategies that provides focus on Objectives, Process Alignment, and identifies areas of improvement in your Strategic Processes. Where is the focus for that mind-set? Listed below are extensions to those Quality Strategies:

- Strategic impact and Quality as a strategy mind-set
- Process speed, fulfillment, performance, product/Service distribution/ facilitation
- Managerial reporting that increases growth, reduces waste/defects; increases asset performance/turnover
- Measure effectiveness of Continuous Improvement by reducing costs, wastes, defects, or increasing effectiveness, efficiency, performance

Process Transformation: *Process Transformation,* implement your Quality Initiative through Lean Six Sigma's DMAIC Roadmap to provide improvements in Effectiveness, Performance, and Resource Utilization. Covey proclaimed; "An empowered organization is one in which individuals have the knowledge, skill, desire, and opportunity to personally succeed in a way that leads to collective organizational success." Lean Six Sigma empowers people to be more effective in addressing Customers' needs. The ultimate goal is to develop a quick-reacting organization that clearly understands the Customer is the most import stakeholder. By training and expecting excellence, your organization becomes aligned with strategic goals and is flexible to unexpected changes in the marketplace. The success of this approach is based on:

- Long-term Executive Quality Commitment
- Climate of Continuous Improvement focused on the Customer
- Leadership provides direction and sets expectations
- Employees empowered to make changes toward Continuous Improvement
- Incentivizing the behavior your organization needs

Process Goals:
- Apply metrics of DPMO (Defects Per Million Opportunities) across all business Processes, not just manufactured products and parts.
- Implement DMAIC methodologies.
- Integrate Lean Six Sigma terminology into your business vernacular.
- Provide Six Sigma project teams with the necessary data capture and analysis tools.
- Identify Process and project Owners who will accept Ownership of and accountability for the improvement Process.
- Align IT and Financial organizations to remove obstacles that prevent work Processes and data from flowing seamlessly across the organization.
- Must require business impact projects to be formally validated by Finance.

Quality Evaluation: *Quality Evaluation* targets and analyses your Quality Strategy with your existing Balance Scorecard and Quality Dashboards that Measure gains, tangible benefits and Quality metric integration to objectives. This approach creates a total-factor metric base for enterprise-wide productivity.

Quality Evaluation, based on gathered data at the most granular level, provides management business best practice tools for monitoring and decision making. These metric based Dashboards and Scorecards, are designed specifically for your organization and provide your organization effective tools for monitoring the pulse of key activities. The business tools are often linked to services, products, and strategic goals and objectives that Measure and manage success.

In an integrated Quality performance environment; however, measuring only the productivity of workers, whether blue- or white-collar, no longer gives us adequate information about productivity. We need data on total-factor productivity.[55]

Business Transformation Defined – "combination of strategic, Process, organizational change, and technology development focused around one clear vision, resulting in a significant change in the organization and substantial financial benefits."[56] Business Transformation heavily depends on data gathered from your Processes, and interpretation of the data into cause-and-effects and information that validates your progress or regress.

On the importance of measuring progress, Drucker said, "You can only manage what you can Measure." Quality Evaluation tools, integrated with existing Balance Scorecards and External/Internal Dashboards, can be enhanced to offer Quality visibility to existing information for management decision making. Evaluating and measuring your success

---

55   Drucker, Peter F.; The Essential Drucker, 2001 by Peter F. Drucker. HarperCollins publishers, 10 East 53rd St., New York, NY, page 104.
56   Goonan, Brian, "Business Transformation: Doing it Right, Part I," CIO Magazine, February 9, 2005, Retrieved: 30 June 2010.

will promote concrete Results in your Transformation and facilitate your Continuous Improvement Processes across your enterprise.

In this model, Quality Evaluation is the measurement and reporting tool. Any business performance is based on a set of management and analytic Processes that enable the performance of an organization to be managed with a view to achieving one or more preselected goals. Synonyms for "business performance management" include "corporate performance management" and "enterprise performance management."[57] Quality Evaluation has three main activities:

- Selection of goals
- Consolidation of measurement information relevant to an organization's progress against these goals,
- Interventions made by managers in light of this information with a view to improving future performance against these goals

Most recently, technology has allowed the coupling of reporting to Lean Six Sigma methodology. Now, many performance tools allow the end users to use DMAIC Roadmap. This brings with it the benefit of being able to simulate changes to your business Process based on real life data (not assumed knowledge). Also, the coupling of Quality Evaluation to industry methodologies allows users to continually streamline and optimize the Process to ensure that it is attuned to its market need.

A special note regarding interventions: the Process Owners should be responsible for improving the performance. The careful analysis and understanding of the Process or System may be based on how the System is not working to expected levels. Therefore, intervention and obligating who is involved in the Process or System may be the wrong approach. The Process Owner needs to clearly understand, systematically, and learn from each event so it is not repeated in the future.

---

57   Frolick, Mark N.; Thilini R. Ariyachandra (Winter 2006). "Business performance management: one truth" (PDF). Information Systems Management (www.ism-journal.com): Pages 41–48.

For example, reporting may indicate a spike in the data, but careful examination by the Process Owner may indicate only an anomaly, rather than a major trend. Similar to a visit to the dentist, in that you may have a toothache and discomfort, but does it require an immediate root canal? Careful examination could indicate less invasive options.

Issues when implementing a Quality Evaluation program might include:

- *Goal-Alignment Queries* – one must first determine the short- and medium-term purpose of the program. What organizational Mission/Vision does it relate to? A hypothesis needs to be crafted that details how this initiative will eventually improve results/performance (i.e., a strategy map).
- *Baseline Queries* – current information-gathering competency needs assessing. Does the organization have the capability to monitor important sources of information? What data is being collected and how is it being stored? What are the statistical parameters of this data, e.g., how much random variation does it contain? Is this being measured?
- *Customer And Stakeholder Queries* – determine who will benefit from the initiative and who will pay. How will Customer benefits be monitored? What about employees, shareholders, and distribution channel members?
- *Metrics-Related Queries* – information requirements need decomposition into clearly defined metrics. One must decide what metrics to use for each piece of information being gathered.
- *Measurement Methodology-Related Queries* – one should establish a methodology or a procedure to determine the best (or acceptable) way of measuring the required metrics. How frequently will data be collected?
- *Results-Related Queries* – someone should monitor the Quality Evaluation program to ensure that it meets objectives. The program

itself may require adjusting. The program should be tested for accuracy, reliability, and validity.[58]

Learning Transformation: Learning Transformation, manages, captures, and leverages knowledge for reuse, where applicable. Learning Transformation is a specific area of identifying potential areas of refinement or development that could Improve Growth, Performance, or Savings. Learning Transformation (i.e., reducing defects, identifying savings, improving performance, etc.) is fundamental to the success and continuation of your championed Quality initiative. Executives should approach knowledge in modular format for transplantation in other business units. Emphasize the need for collaboration and effectiveness in a Continuous Improvement framework.

Deming was a firm believer that Transformation begins with the individual. It is based on sharing a new vision of the enterprise, perceiving the new role of the individual, and providing a new meaning to life. Once the individual understands that Profound Knowledge will be the basis for Transformation, he will apply those principles into his duties and relating to co-workers and managers. The layout of Profound Knowledge appears here in four parts, all related to each other:

- *Appreciation For A System* – This involves understanding how interactions (i.e., feedback) between the elements of a System can result in internal restrictions that force the System to behave as a single organism that automatically seeks a steady state. It is this steady state that determines the Output of the System rather than the individual elements. Thus it is the structure of the organization rather than the employees, alone, which holds the key to improving the Quality of Output.[59]

---

58   White, Colin; The Next Generation of Business Intelligence: Operational BI; (May 2005); Information Management Magazine. http://www.information-management.com/issues/;_Retrieved: 21 Feb 2010.

59   Deming, W. Edwards. 1993. *The New Economics for Industry, Government, Education,* second edition.

- *Knowledge About Variation* – Once a Process has been brought into a state of statistical Control, it has a definable capability. A Process that is not in statistical Control is not a definable capability: it's performed performance is not predictable.[60]

- *Theory Of Knowledge* – This involves understanding that everything measured consists of both "normal" variation due to the flexibility of the System and of "special causes" that create defects. Quality involves recognizing the difference to eliminate "special causes" while controlling normal variation. Deming taught that making changes in response to "normal" variation would only make the System perform worse. Understanding variation includes the mathematical certainty that variation will normally occur within six standard deviations of the mean.[61]

- *Psychology* – A manager of people needs to understand that all people are different. This is not ranking people. He needs to understand that the performance of anyone is governed largely by the System that he works in, the responsibility of management. A psychologist that possesses even a crude understanding of variation could no longer participate in refinement of a plan for ranking people.[62]

To understand this area Profound Knowledge, getting often illustrated how these four disciplines were interdependent on each other to provide a better picture. One example is that of psychology, in the use of theory a variation, provides understanding as how actions could occur:

- In essence, a teacher did not wish to penalize anyone unjustly, he passed the people that were slightly below passing requirements.

---

60   Deming, W. Edwards; The New Economics for Industry, Government, Education; The MIT Press, 1994; page 99.
61   Deming, W. Edwards. 1993. *The New Economics for Industry, Government, Education,* second edition.
62   Deming, W. Edwards; The New Economics for Industry, Government, Education; The MIT Press, 1994; page 93.

- Statistical calculations than influence predictions were warped by inconsistent figures. The assumptions and interpretations of the statistics lead to confusion, frustration, and wrong decisions.
- Transformation leaders as well as managers involved in Transformation, need to apply psychology to individuals, groups, society to effectively influence change and transform.

Once the individual understands the System of Profound Knowledge, he or she will apply its principles in every kind of relationship with other people. The individual will have a basis for judgment of his or her own decisions and for Transformation of the organizations that the person belongs to. The individual, once transformed, will:

- Set an example
- Be a good listener, but will not compromise
- Continually teach other people
- Help people to pull away from their current practice and beliefs and move into the new philosophy without a feeling of guilt about the past[63]

In recent years, aspects of Profound Knowledge have been incorporated into popular programs and styles emphasizing "collaboration efforts," and this approach has been embraced to foster new behavior in contemporary organization. For a Quality Transformation, principles of Profound Knowledge should be key in your organizational change, institutionalized, and include consideration to bring in external expertise to help modify corporate behavior.

As an extension of Profound Knowledge, Continuous Improvement is the refinement engine to improve fulfillment framework of goods and services to your Customers. Institutionalize your "lessons learned" and integrate those ideas into your innovation Process to further improve

---

63   Deming, W. Edwards; The New Economics for Industry, Government, Education; The MIT Press, 1994; pgs 94-95.

134

Products, Services and Processes. Your goal is to achieve Customer satisfaction by meeting their needs, while attaining these goals:

- Continuous Improvement based on Deming Cycle (PDSA)
- Innovation data feed for Products, Processes and Services
- Provide Control to hold the gains that have been made

Project Choice and Transformation
- Select a project for the project team, from the portfolio of assessed projects that are ranked by priority.
- Select a project team that consists of cross-functional members, that spans all functions upon which the improvement project will have an impact, both direct and indirect.
- Assign a Black Belt as the Team Lead.
- Use financial analysts to confirm and validate estimates.
- Based on the data collected, establish a baseline that confirms with accounting information.
- Establish a metric plan that illustrates improvements that are based on the tangible gains from improvements.
- Institutionalize CXO level reviews, monthly, to illustrate progress of the Transformation, benefits extracted from the organization and Transformation time line. Financial information must be reviewed and linked to each financial analysis previously performed.

Look For Key Wins. Here are some examples:
- Focus on team throughput rather than individual productivity
- Cross functional teams that meet daily
- Focus on simple Processes and encourage common vocabulary
- Prioritize work for every team and assign individual accountability
- Document user stories
- Encourage new estimation methods in addition to standardize methods
- Define organizational roles and document their participation in the project, use RASIC charts
- Automation and Measurement Teams are focused to build flexible, timely analysis with ease of access to the data

- Daily metric reviews with visibility into the progress of the project
- Provide a Weekly Progress Report from every team
- Product, Process, and Service Owners review project progress weekly
- Project completion review should provide Lessons Learned that are both positive and highlight areas for improvement

3.4: Realization

Setting a goal is not the main thing. It is deciding how you will go about achieving it and staying with that plan.

~ Tom Landry

Chapter Summary: Reaping Tangible Benefits must be Measured and Verified to ensure true Realization for the enterprise. That means that Accounting and Auditing must be included and be key players in the Realization.

Key Points:
- Realization
- Governance
- Accountability
- Deming System of Profound Knowledge
- Institutionalization
- Realization Of Tangible Benefits
- Realization Of Intangible Benefits
- Capital Realization
- Post Project Audit
- Quality Evaluation
- Review Products, Services and Processes

Realization: Creating a vision of your future state that fits your needs often takes the perception of the problem and then develops a strategic approach to create a solution based on imagination and out-of-box thinking. The largest wave of change exists today, due to two major influencers: limited energy resources and the "greening" or environmental concerns about our modern way of life and the methods we produce energy. On one hand we must deal with the energy crisis and reallocate the way we use current energies (oil vs. sustainable resources). On the other hand we must also look at renewable alternate energy sources to augment our base to meet the energy needs of today and those of tomorrow. This will be a significant Transformation force for all businesses and governments.

To address these Transformation themes, the client's solution is based on three resources: people, ideas, and technology and those resources are orchestrated to formulate the Transformation Roadmap. Integrated solutions put Executives in Control of the Business Transformation with a customized and collaborative approach that integrates the requirement into the solutions, molds the design, and generates the solutions that effectively harnesses and controls your implementation direction.

Tangible Results are the by-products. The key source of change is from internal changes in your business model. This may be due to internal refinements of Processes, new strategies, Product lines, linkage of strategies to new Systems, or an acquisition that needs to integrated into the corporate structure. Dramatic changes in the external environment may also require modifications or enhancements of current processes (i.e., logistic strategies, objectives and goals may affect policies that are engaged in controlling distribution of goods, review of vendors and services, or even expense reimbursement from your Marketing and Sales personnel). Business requirements will be drivers for Transformation.

- Formally change management plan
- Establish weekly and monthly meetings
- Audit tangible benefits
- Manage Transformation

- Update Communication Plan with tangible benefits
- Validate accountability and reporting accuracy

A well thought out solution is based on best practices and best-in-class models to make a company more competitive, efficient, and profitable. Strategic planning is the most effective management tool for controlling change and instilling Transformation. External influencers often provoke obligatory modifications to your business model (i.e., laws, regulations, competition, globalization, deregulation, etc.). In some cases, change is slow and easy to digest. In others cases, such as the current energy crisis, dramatic and quick changes affect and impact your business and its organization. Proactive management anticipates this possibility and reflects that insight into their plans. An example could be the recognition of Maturity models and what should be considered for the "next step" in Transformation. Strategic planning is a mind-set to embrace change for the benefits to your concern, but this mind-set must conform to a framework in order to be repeatable and consistent.

Governance: Governance should be a twofold responsibility. First, Governance provides visibility of the end-to-end process, how it is interrelated and oversees its effectiveness. Second, Governance should include and manage its processes, including the methods, tools, policies, and standards. This is key information extracted from your Transformation initiative.

In the Realization phase, the Governance Committee needs distance between Silo Owners, Process Leaders and Process Owners and the validation of Tangible Benefits. The Governance Committee needs internal experts from various departments such as: IT, Accounting, Finance, Logistics, Purchasing, and Strategic Planning areas.

Too often we hear that all it takes to be successful is to have an Executive to own the end-to-end processes and we are looking for this Process Owner to carry the following responsibilities:

- Provide Process direction by developing Process vision, strategy, and objectives.
- Develop and implement Process improvement initiatives
- Define the Process and monitor Process performance
- Develop and manage policies and procedures related to the Process
- Ensure Process adoption[64]

Note: end-to-end refers to a streamlined, seamless, and real-time flow of information and linkages across a value chain.

Accountability: Diagrams and e-mail communiqués do not complete your Transformation. It is based on changing the rules, training the participants, and providing incentives for continued progress and proper institutionalization of those changes into best practices, policy, and procedures. Accountability reflects the level of authority and responsibility:

- Process Leader(s) – One or more person(s) who set(s) the strategic direction and objectives related to the identified Process.
- Process Owner – The only person who is responsible to Define, document, and enforce a Process to meet its objectives. In that documentation, strategic maps, lining strategies to key Processes should be clearly understood and documented.
- Process SME(s) – All the people who are participants in the Process that needs to understand their roles and responsibilities and follow the Process properly.

"Once the individual understands the System of Profound Knowledge, he will apply its principles in every kind of relationship with other people. He will have a basis for judgment of his own decisions and for Transformation of the organizations that he belongs to. The individual, once transformed, will:

- Set an example;
- Be a good listener, but will not compromise;

---

64   Bilodeau, Nancy; "Process Ownership and Governance; Paradigm Shift," Sears Holdings Corporation, 8 Jul 2010.

- Continually teach other people; and
- Help people to pull away from their current practices and beliefs and move into the new philosophy without a feeling of guilt about the past."[65]

Deming System of Profound Knowledge: "The prevailing style of management must undergo Transformation. A System cannot understand itself. The Transformation requires a view from outside. The aim of this chapter is to provide an outside view—a lens—that I call a System of Profound Knowledge. It provides a map of theory by which to understand the organizations that we work in.

"The first step is Transformation of the individual. This Transformation is discontinuous. It comes from understanding of the System of Profound Knowledge. The individual, transformed, will perceive new meaning to his life, to events, to numbers, to interactions between people."

Deming advocated that all managers need to have what he called a System of Profound Knowledge, consisting of four parts:

- Appreciation of a System: understanding the overall Processes involving Suppliers, producers, and Customers (or recipients) of goods and services (explained below);
- Knowledge of variation: the range and causes of variation in Quality, and use of statistical sampling in measurements;
- Theory of knowledge: the concepts explaining knowledge and the limits of what can be known (see also: epistemology);
- Knowledge of psychology: concepts of human nature.

Deming explained:

One need not be eminent in any part nor in all four parts in order to understand it and to apply it. The fourteen points for management in industry, education, and government follow naturally as application

---

65   Deming, W. Edwards (1986). Out of the Crisis. MIT Press.

of this outside knowledge, for Transformation from the present style of Western management to one of optimization.

The various segments of the System of Profound Knowledge proposed here cannot be separated. They interact with each other. Thus, knowledge of psychology is incomplete without knowledge of variation.

A manager of people needs to understand that all people are different. This is not ranking people. He needs to understand that the performance of anyone is governed largely by the System that he works in, the responsibility of management. A psychologist that possesses even a crude understanding of variation as will be learned in the experiment with the Red Beads could no longer participate in refinement of a plan for ranking people.[66,67]

The Appreciation of a System involves understanding how interactions (i.e., feedback) between the elements of a System can result in internal restrictions that force the System to behave as a single organism that automatically seeks a steady state. It is this steady state that determines the Output of the System rather than the individual elements. Thus it is the structure of the organization rather than the employees, alone, which holds the key to improving the Quality of Output.

The Knowledge of variation involves understanding that everything measured consists of both "normal" variations due to the flexibility of the System and of "special causes" that create defects. Quality involves recognizing the difference to eliminate "special causes" while controlling normal variation. Deming taught that making changes in response to "normal" variation would only make the System perform worse. Understanding variation includes the mathematical certainty

---

66   Deming, W. Edwards; *The New Economics for Industry, Government, Education*, Second edition (MIT Press, 1993).
67   The Red Beads exercise illustrates to Quality students how variation works in a simple example.

that variation will normally occur within six standard deviations of the mean.[68]

"Massive training is required to instill the courage to break with tradition. Every activity and every job is a part of the process."[69]

Institutionalization: When you implement your Quality Initiative, you will institutionalize Quality best-in-class methodology (Lean Six Sigma) to Control change and promote growth, performance, and savings, LSS will reduce fixed costs to meet or beat trends in the competitive landscape, LSS will leverage innovation to bring faster, better, and cheaper solutions to the marketplace in a timely manner, LSS will effectively manage your resources (Business, Human, IT) and identify, recognize, and mitigate the "Quality talent gap" for creative and knowledge-based specialists.

Every initiative bears different fruit and the mix of the benefits varies. Leveraging Lean and Six Sigma methodologies produces crossover benefits that potentially optimize multiple levels in your organization. Business Transformation recognizes an end-to-end view as to where your success can be harvested. Continuous Strategic Improvement areas of tangible benefits emerge in these groups:

- Customer tangibles
- Innovation tangibles
- HR tangibles
- IT tangibles
- Other business tangibles
- Supplier tangibles

Realization Of Tangible Benefits: Creating a vision of your future state that fits your needs often takes the perception of the problem and then develops a strategic approach to create a solution based on imagination and out-of-box thinking. The largest wave of change exists

68   Deming, W. Edwards (1986). Out of the Crisis. MIT Press.
69   Reilly, Norman B. (1994). Quality: What Makes it Happen? Van Nostrand Reinhold. p. 31. ISBN 0-442-01635-2.

today, due to two major influencers: limited energy resources and the "greening" or environmental concerns about today's modern way of life and the methods we produce energy. On one hand, we must deal with the energy crisis and reallocate the way we use current energies (oil vs. sustainable resources). On the other hand, we must look at renewable alternate energy sources to augment our base to meet the energy needs of today and those of tomorrow. This will be a significant Transformation force for all businesses and governments.

Realization Of Intangible Benefits: "Intangible benefit" is a label often used when knowledge of the benefit cannot be measured in time, money, or any other quantitative way. There are very few truly "Intangible benefits" in many instances people only find it difficult to Measure or that they aren't sure where to begin. Examples include:

- *Increased Timeliness* – This metric suggests a timeliness problem, and you either have to do extra work dealing with delays (time spent answering queries and sorting the issues, which can be measured and a monetary value determined), or you are actually losing clients associated with work. The key is work-hours expended, which can also be linked to monies expended.

- *Information Availability on Employee Engagements* – What is the impact of the lack of information? Does it mean people are not fully utilized (easy to then determine dollar value), or does it mean that management cannot effectively allocate work?

- *Improved Quality of a Process, Service or Product* – other disciplines do not understand that Quality must be measured in a Quality environment. It is customized to reflect those attributes desired by your Customer. Again, this metric can be tied to work-hours, money assets, cycle time, etc.

Capital Realization: Machiavelli wrote: "He who has not first laid his foundations may be able with great ability to lay them afterwards, but they will be laid with trouble to the architect and danger to the building."

Sounds very profound, but what does something written five hundred years ago by an Italian statesman, writer, and political theorist have to do with the Balanced Scorecard? Plenty! Just as a home or building requires a proper foundation to support what lies above, so too does the Balanced Scorecard.[70]

As Norton and Kaplan suggest, three focus areas exist for developing Measures under the Realization perspective:

- Human Capital,
- Information Capital
- Organizational Capital

Together, they focus an organization's skills, knowledge, collective capability to leverage information, and build a foundation for excellence in performance, ensuring success today and tomorrow.

Post Project Audit: Common to both DMAIC and DMADV, a Lean Six Sigma audit compares what was the project's goal, changes made and is then reviewed to determine the effectiveness of that change. Often, this segment considers other potential areas of improvement, whether they were not addressed or may have been out of scope and should be reconsidered.[71]

Process Transformation Mission is to eliminate and Control variation by using empirical, statistical modeling along with methodology to identify, simplify, innovate, or automate your unique needs, Through a structured approach, TMM (Transformation Maturity Model) will provide solutions that will Improve your efficiency, productivity, performance and conceivably increase your profitability. By-products of process evaluation create (i.e., data analysis, process metrics, etc.) data points

---

70   Niven, Paul; "Learning and Growth Perspective"; • EPM Review, Retrieved on: 2 Oct 2010.
71   De Feo, Joseph A.; Barnard, William (2005). *JURAN Institute's Six Sigma Breakthrough and Beyond - Quality Performance Breakthrough Methods*. Tata McGraw-Hill Publishing Company Limited. ISBN 0-07-059881-9.

for process monitoring. This is also an opportunity to enrich and leverage your existing decision-making process.

Lean Six Sigma methodology is designed to search for productivity gaps, weak links and hunts for defects. All of these items can impact your bottom-line Results. Lean Six Sigma also investigates areas for Savings that contribute to your bottom line. Process Transformation utilizes the double-edged sword of Lean and Six Sigma methodologies:

- Independently, Lean methodology includes low cost techniques, on improving an organization's effectiveness. This waste reduction methodology, which provides tools and techniques, often improves productivity and performance in your organization by focusing on what expenditures are actually required to provide Product or Service value to your Customers.
- Likewise, Six Sigma methodology reduces variation in current processes and molds efficiency into new ones. This best practice helps reduce the waste and defects in your processes and helps alignment with Business and IT strategies. It is also a linchpin in the Process Transformation phase that incorporates and ensures Continuous Improvement.

Quality Evaluation, based on gathered data at the most granular level, provides management business best practice tools for monitoring and decision making. These metric based Dashboards and Scorecards, are designed specifically for your organization and provides your organization effective tools for monitoring the pulse of key activities. The business tools are often linked to services, products and strategic goals and objectives that Measure and manage for success. Remember to Measure actual performance and include:

- Measure actual performance.
- Interpret cause and effect
- Identify root cause/record root cause and solution
- Take action on the difference
- Control to hold the gains

Business Transformation Defined – "combination of strategic, Process, organizational change, and technology development focused around one clear vision, resulting in a significant change in the organization and substantial financial benefits."[72]

Quality Evaluation Goals:
- What you Measure makes a difference, but you must be able to Control the variables.
- IT solutions play a key role in performance improvement. Leverage existing Balanced Scorecard and Dashboard data structure.
- Make every employee data-proficient and begin using KPI measurements.
- Establish reporting periods for progress review to ascertain action-able items to regain levels of acceptability.
- Best in Class: Integrate data collection with analysis – connect (potentially disparate) sources of data and establish thresholds and triggers.
- Choose units of Measure existing performance metrics that are Quality metrics and are agreed by all levels of management.
- Set goals that directly tie objectives that address:

  o Minimum/Maximum saving for project selection
  o Minimum/Maximum cycle time saved
  o Minimum/Maximum increase in revenue
  o Minimum/Maximum utilization of resources

- Data for Quality Evaluation should have:

  o Create Data Collection Points
  o Leverage Existing Business Intelligence System (Scorecard, Dashboard)
  o Leverage Existing Collection Points/Sensors,
  o Align With Accounting/Lean Accounting Principles

---

72   Goonan, Brian, "Business Transformation: Doing it Right, Part I," CIO Magazine, February 9, 2005, Retrieved: 30 June 2010

Drucker was quoted on the importance of measuring progress; "You can only manage what you can Measure." Quality Evaluation tools, integrated with existing Balance Scorecards and External/Internal Dashboards, can be enhanced to offer Quality visibility to existing information for management decision making. Evaluation and measuring your success will promote concrete Results in your Transformation and facilitate your Continuous Improvement Processes across your enterprise.

Quality Evaluation is based on Business Intelligence technologies that are probably currently applied in your business environment. Understand that Quality Evaluation is essentially synonymous with effective management tools that is focused on your Quality initiative and should be integrated into your Scorecard, Internal and External Dashboard reporting. In so doing, decision making becomes a 360-degree view, Executive decision making is better informed, impact to your organization is better understood, while encouraging continued investigation, modifications and refinement to business Processes, products and services. What are the benefits to the company or the organizations within the company?

First, Quality Evaluation obligates management to review internal short-term actions and long-term trends that affect the business, its strategies and decide what decisions should be made. Whether these actions and decisions are to invest in various areas for Growth, Quality, Performance, or identification of alternate considerations in other areas where Savings can be made, it will Measure the progress of your Quality Initiative.

Second, Quality Evaluation relies on current tool usage, which obligates management review of the marketplace. Based on your IT data architecture, this external perspective and gleaning understanding for growth in terms of revenue and Product placement reflect the holistic information provided to management's decision-making Process, will further focus on the Customers' needs and satisfaction. Marketing, financial and geographic considerations can determine what type

148

of investment should be made in order to exploit potential long-term opportunities.

Third, due to empowering your employees, do not be surprised by the buy-in from all levels and socialization that better refines Quality Evaluation reporting. External expertise and subject matter expertise can provide additional guidance, direction and refinement, to further promote best practices and to recommend improvements that would be beneficial to your company or organization.

Business executives, middle managers, Information Technology and knowledge workers in both large and small organizations have visibility requirements and specific information needs. Business Intelligence and Performance Management solutions help their companies strategically. They also increase their competitive edge, discover "weak links" and grow their business.

Performance should be based on the effectiveness of your Strategic Planning, Processes and alignment to your objectives and whether you are reaping your desired Results. You need the right tools to Measure success. Leveraging your investment could glean key metrics from your web services and the company activities that could impact your decision-making Process in terms of efficiency, performance, productivity and profitability. This business intelligence helps CXOs and other senior managers understand how effective their strategies perform and they can be applied to their own organizations.

"CIOs expect to invest in business intelligence applications and information consolidation in order to raise enterprise visibility and transparency, particularly around sales and operational performance. These investments are expected to pay extra dividends by responding to new regulatory and financial reporting requirements."[73]

---

73   Gartner Press Release, "Gartner EXP Worldwide Survey of More than 1,500 CIOs Shows IT Spending to Be Flat in 2009," Jan. 14, 2009. 27 May 2010.

The effectiveness of a strategy or a group of integrated strategies is based on the Direction, Objectives, Integration with Strategic Processes and the desired measured outcome. To better improve your planning Quality, and insight, it would be prudent to review and refine your strategic planning methodology on the effectiveness of information flow across your organization. Key drivers include: understanding opportunities and consequences, relationship building form both internal and external stakeholders, Design a decision making Process based on Continuous Improvement and provide visibility that monitors the activity of the organization. Additionally, key advantages include:

- Alignment of an organization around a consistent set of Key Performance Indicators (KPIs) and Metrics
- Quicker, fact-based decision making
- Simplified graphical presentation of KPIs and metrics
- Reliable presentation of information, based on quantitative Measures, data points, etc.
- Combination of multiple data sources (ERP, CRM, Spreadsheets, Budgets...)
- Faster collection and dissemination of information

How can we build a Balanced Scorecard and other Dashboards that translate a strategy into measurements? They must meet three critical principles that enable an organization's Business Intelligence tools to be linked to its strategy:

- Cause-and-effect relationships – If we increase employee training about products, then they will become more knowledgeable about the full range of products they can sell; if employees are more knowledgeable about products, then their sales effectiveness will improve. If their sales effectiveness improves, then the average margins of the products they sell will increase.
- Performance drivers – These generic outcome Measures tend to be lag indicators, such as profitability, market share, Customer satisfaction, Customer retention, and employee skills. The performance

drivers, the lead indicators, are the ones that tend to be unique for a particular business unit.

- Linkage to financials – A Balanced Scorecard must retain a strong emphasis on outcomes, especially financial ones like return-on-capital-employed or economic value-added. Ultimately, causal paths from all the Measures on a scorecard should be linked to financial objectives.

Performance happens out of understanding, knowing where to improve, how to integrate beneficial change that effectively absorbs new methods into your corporate culture. Benefits are realized only when they are sustained and institutionalized in your organization. TMM (Transformation Maturity Model) structures that change, through the use of specialized Roadmaps, for deployment and integrating services into your company that address phases in the development, implementation and provide effective Control of the Transformation.

Business Performance management and/or Management By Objectives, is a set of methodologies and technologies that are combined and utilized so the business can better understand Processes and corporate resources associated with the commercial activity of marketing products and services. Effective use of business intelligence gathers data and applies it in terms of useful information that can be actionable and capable of enhancing business Processes.

- Gather data from Processes and organizations:
- Turn data into information
- Use information to create knowledge
- Utilize knowledge for effective action[74]

Analytics provide historical, current, and predictive views of business operations. Common functions of Business Intelligence technologies are reporting, online analytical Processing, analytics, data mining,

---

74   Gartner Study; "Gartner Reveals Five Business Intelligence Predictions for 2009 and Beyond," January 15, 2009, Retrieved: 24 May 2010.

business performance management, benchmarking, text mining, and predictive analytics. Beginning with data, information is created that will help you better understand Processes and trends. Individually and collectively, you act on that information and build a base of knowledge that will be updated in subsequent cycles of review. Your insights and changes are recorded and provide new data and information that aligns to your business needs and achievement of goals. In order for this to become effective, as a management tool, several business intelligence strategies and techniques are applied to ensure conformity and consistency. Those Business Processes include:

- Data integration
- Information presentation
- Standardized reporting

Review Products, Services and Processes: As previously mentioned, "Change is a constant in business." Perfect example: Every day, when you receive raw material, convert it to finished good, fill an order and ship to your Customer, you are gathering data along points in your internal and external Systems to provide you with insights. *That raw data is a gold mine of a wealth of information! Use it!*

The Financial organization collects transactions, digests, and analyzes various records that track the exchange of monies from the Customer to your organization and stakeholders to payment of your Suppliers. That flow is reported in various management forms, i.e., P/L Statements, General Ledgers and in contemporary terms, Balanced Scorecards and Dashboards.

Quality initiatives are based on principles of data-driven decision making. (If reporting for Quality is nonexistent, then a Quality Dashboard needs to be created and integrated into the Balanced Scorecard.) From a Lean Six Sigma viewpoint that collected data should also reflect the activity, externally, as well as internally.

One of the objectives of the Transformation is based on the constant adjustment to the commercial environment. Your organization needs to be proactive and flex with market responses. Your organization should be dynamic, not static.

Likewise, data realized through activities, instead of transactions, must be transformed into meaningful information to make those adjustments. A Situation Analysis should be carried out in this phase and address these six critical rules:

- Utilize the data and provide a situational diagnosis. Use the effects and retrace what were the root causes. Sort and distinguish important information from "noise."
- Chart the major trends to tell a story. What does a spike indicate or why did a major disconnect materialize?
- Communicate clearly and avoid jargon. Use the language of your Internal Customer. Your insights and analysis should be based on strong data supported views. Avoid unsubstantiated conclusions and biases by maintaining objectivity.
- The KISS method is approved. Keep simplicity in your mind-set and provide straightforward insights. Clear communication is often hard work.
- The objective is to understand the current situation and direction of the journey. It is not a litmus test to determine strategic validation, rather it is a tool to extract best ideas and look for opportunities.
- Drive these insights into Quality Planning, Process Transformation, Quality Evaluation, Continuous Improvement, and Innovation.

Realization and Evaluation
- Include an Audit performance that links to key Quality metrics for three quarters after each project is closed to ensure repeatability and extract areas for improvement.
- Declare a win for each project and reflect actual items in the Realization phase of Transformation.

4.0: Are All Methodologies Alike?

 You can see a lot by just looking.

~ Yogi Berra

Chapter Summary: How does Lean Six Sigma compare with other methodologies? Due to Lean Six Sigma's flexibility, universality, and common statistical techniques, merging with legacy methodologies is almost seamless and many think it is better.

Key Points:
- External Drivers for Change
- Quality Alignment and Flexibility
- No Quality Management
- Toyota Production System | Just-In-Time | Lean Manufacturing
- Quality Management
- Six Sigma
- Total Quality Management
- Business Process Reengineering
- Business Process Management
- Business Process Outsourcing

External Drivers for Change: Today's environmental impact also presents opportunities to Owners or CEOs to transform their companies to be more competitive, Customer sensitive, and incorporate innovation to meet market demands. Don't find your options limited by a reduction in force. Be prudent and consider your immediate key issues: credit, managing change, people issues, culture, and Transformation costs. According to an article from the Economist Intelligence Unit:

- *Current Economy* – The credit crunch and economic slowdown are affecting the way companies act. Business leaders are responding to the economic slowdown by launching more change programs and spending more on them. These initiatives will primarily be driven by the quest for operational efficiency and the need to reduce costs.

- *Transformation Skills* – Successful change management still manages to elude most companies. Despite the fact that change management has been taught at business schools around the world for several decades, companies still struggle to put theory into practice. Fully 58 percent of the survey respondents say that, over the past five years, half or fewer of their change initiatives have been successful. The US fares a lot worse with 75 percent of respondents stating that half or fewer of their change initiatives have been successful.

- *Avoiding Failure* – Failure often comes from companies struggling with people issues. The most frequently cited barrier to success in change management is winning over the hearts and minds of employees at all levels of the organization (51 percent). Other people issues, such as gaining local management buy-in (31 percent) and cultural issues (27 percent), also feature highly as major barriers to successful execution of change. The difficulty is not intransigence: everyone interviewed for the study agreed that employees are willing to be won over. It is how this is done.

- *Cultural Impact* – Culture may seem a smaller challenge in its own right, but it complicates many of the others. Our survey panel ranked cultural issues a distant fifth in terms of difficulties in implementing change successfully. However, interviews with experts indicate that

155

cultural matters can significantly complicate the bigger challenges, such as winning people over.

- *Funding* – Money is not the problem. On average, companies spend just 0.1 percent of annual revenues on change programs and only 8 percent consider a lack of funding an important reason for their failure in the last year. Moreover, the most frequent reason for change programs is cost-cutting, which should improve the bottom line whatever the initial outlay.[75]

Quality Alignment and Flexibility: Most executives would ask how their current environment should be expected to adapt to a Lean Six Sigma initiative. Recognizing that not all situations are similar would have provided six possible approaches to integrating Lean Six Sigma into your current commercial environment. Remember that Lean Six Sigma is a Quality approach and Controls the Variation within a your business environment and provides a change engine to perpetuate that methodology (e.g., Continuous Improvement). Generally speaking, Lean Six Sigma alignment is very flexible, and in many cases, it is easily integrated in your organization.

No Quality Management: In situations where organizations have not been oriented or trained to apply Quality management, introduction to Lean Six Sigma will be much easier, since the employees will not have to go through a process of retraining. This "open-minded approach" will reduce misunderstanding and terminology, which is inherent in Lean Six Sigma and other Quality methodologies. The focus, therefore; will be on the introduction, implementation, and institutionalization of the Lean Six Sigma methodology. In a very broad sense, this situation will provide a broad jump to improvements that would not be hindered by misunderstanding.

---

75   Economist Intelligence Unit, "A Change For The Better - Steps for Successful Business Transformation," May 2008.

Toyota Production System | Just-In-Time | Lean Manufacturing: This scenario provides an entrée to leverage Lean techniques and integrate Six Sigma disciplines and tools. Just-In-Time and Lean Manufacturing are subsets of the Toyota Production System. All of these methodologies are based on the concept of Lean business practices. Additionally, Lean Six Sigma adheres to those principles and easily blends Six Sigma methodology into your current practices. In this context, the focus on training, education, and improvements to your processes will add those tools and qualities that were absent in the Lean Process. Attention to statistical methodology, elimination of variation in your processes, perceiving your processes as part of a business System, and combining those concepts with Continuous Improvement will provide you with more flexibility in terms of Quality Control.

Quality Management: Your organization will be refocusing on the direction of Quality by leveraging Lean Six Sigma ideas in structure. In this context, Quality Management refers to the body of Quality Knowledge that was generally practice prior to 1990. In many cases, sound Quality Management practices are still relevant in today's environment. Introduction to Lean Six Sigma in this environment will provide a major upgrade to techniques, tools, and a holistic System approach to refining your corporate enterprise that is based on familiar concepts and terminology.

Six Sigma: In an organization that utilizes Six Sigma, the training and understanding of Lean concepts provide an additional tool set for improved effectiveness and efficiency. The enterprise will continue with its Six Sigma methodology; however, it will be enhanced by these cost effective alternatives of improving the business environment. Lean's common sense approach to eliminating waste and its techniques and improving Processes will be an apparent enhancement to your current Quality management.

Total Quality Management: Lean Six Sigma's ability to complement existing Quality Management Systems is no exception in this situation. TQM offers many of the qualities that were established by the

157

Fellows and offers a springboard for enhanced changes and improvements. Many of the techniques suggested by Deming, Juran, Ishikawa, Taguchi, and Crosby may already be institutionalized in your organization. These techniques, generally, will not conflict with Lean Six Sigma methodology. In many cases, TQM offers an opportunity for immigration and enrichment. The end result will be an improved Quality Management environment that will utilize best in class and best practices from Lean Six Sigma methodology.

Business Process Reengineering: In the 1990s, Michael Hammer in James Champy published a book entitled: Reengineering the Corporation: A Manifesto for Business Revolution. It described a "clean sheet of paper" concept and published radical redesign ideas of key business Processes as important to market leaders and was essential in aiding failing enterprises. It was seen as a panacea for early pay-off with dramatic improvements in cost Quality and Customer satisfaction.[76] ... Quality improvements seek steady incremental improvement Process performance. Reengineering, as we have seen, seeks breakthroughs, not by enhancing existing Processes, but by discarding them and replacing them with entirely new ones. Reengineering involves, as well, a different approach to change management from that needed by Quality programs. Consequences include:

- Destroys trust between management and employees
- Management had no or little knowledge of old Process
- After employees left or dismissed, knowledge of the Processes left too
- No Input from employees who managed and used Processes
- Employee morale was diminished
- Productivity fell precipitously
- Disgruntled employees become threats
- Cultural values were often abrogated
- New Processes were seldom mapped to strategies

---

76   Hammer and Champy, Reengineering the Corporation, 1993, HarperCollins Publishing, pgs. 48-49.

Business Process Management: Business Process Management (BPM) is a management approach focused on aligning all aspects of an organization with the wants and needs of clients. It is a holistic management approach that promotes business effectiveness and efficiency while striving for innovation, flexibility, and integration with technology. Business Process management attempts to Improve Processes continuously. It could therefore be described as a "Process Optimization Process." It is argued that BPM enables organizations to be more efficient, more effective and more capable of change than a functionally focused, traditional hierarchical management approach.[77]

Business Process management activities can be grouped into five categories: Design, modeling, execution, monitoring, and optimization.

The real issue is that this discipline ignores the business need for Quality requirements and does not emulate DFSS (i.e., DMADV for example) in creating a truly holistic solution. The institutionalization of the Voice of the Client is essential in driving those requirements from strategies to the actual Process level. It is also essential to use the Plan-Do-Study-Act cycle to ensure compliance and understanding prior to, during, and at final implementation of the solution.

Business Process Outsourcing: Business Process Outsourcing (BPO) is a Process outsourcing methodology. Major corporations in the US and Europe are outsourcing their back office operations to India to save costs. For example, employee payroll is maintained in India for their employees worldwide. Although these jobs usually are not directly IT related, their data based orientation often means that they require IT departmental support to be successfully outsourced.[78]

First and foremost, it is not a sage feat to outsource Processes that you have little or no documentation, knowledge, or understanding of. Not

---

77 vom Brocke, J.HKVJH and Rosemann, M. (2010), Handbook on Business Process Management: Strategic Alignment, Governance, People and Culture (International Handbooks on Information Systems) (Vol. 1). Berlin: Springer.
78 BPOIndia.org; FAQ; http://www.bpoindia.org/faq; Retrieved: 22 Feb 2011.

159

only is this problematic in your outsourcing decision, it will continue to haunt you should you reconsider outsourcing itself. Companies have been known to fail simply due to Process bottlenecks or failure not to understand.

Second, you probably don't want to outsource the functions that you rely on for your differentiation. Thinking through the following questions can help you explore the possibilities and narrow the options:

- *Where will we be able to achieve the highest degree of success for the lowest investment?* No matter how much money you put into a project, your core expertise and experience occasionally will fail to improve the delivery of that function.
- *Are we already experts? Are these functions critical to operations? To our strategy?* Many companies have focused on becoming expert at functions that are important but not crucial to them. The result is a distraction of time, money and focus from mission-critical functions.
- *Do we want a scalable business model?* Some traditional companies are entering new business opportunities but are unsure of their needs or how results will take shape.[79]

The basic concepts originating from BPR became the kernels for growth and Business Process Management (BPM) and Business Process Outsourcing (BPO). These alternatives do oblige a standardized approach to Process management and outsourcing; however, none of these methodologies address, nor implement the benefits of a "Quality approach."

Lean Six Sigma can blend with almost any environment. Its flexibility and adherence to Quality standards may be cultural change for your organization. As in previous organizational scenarios, Leadership commitment to Business Transformation will be a critical success factor.

---

79   Furtado, Karen; SMA Strategy Meets Action; "An Increasingly Compelling BPO Value Proposition Raises Questions for Insurers"; August 22, 2010; Retrieved: 22 Feb 2011.

Beware of introducing Quality concepts into an environment that has poor morale or after it has been purged because it may be problematic and, therefore, resistance to change may be very high. From a management viewpoint, the upside to this situation is that, if handled properly, with the right incentives, you can turn the organization around and instill concepts that will produce a performance culture. The downside could be increased distrust of management, added employee or union conflict, sabotage, violence, or workforce fleeing from an out-of-control environment.

5.0: Lean Six Sigma

 In the middle of difficulty lies opportunity.

~ Albert Einstein

Chapter Summary: Learn why Lean Six Sigma is the Best Practices leader in Quality methodology. Learn how Lean eliminates waste and Six Sigma eliminates variation. Learn how these activities move you closer to your Customers' needs.

Key Points:
- Why Your Organization Needs Lean Six Sigma
- Lean Six Sigma Transformation
- Lean Six Sigma Benefits
- Post Project Audit
- Learning Transformation

Why Your Organization Needs Lean Six Sigma: Lean Six Sigma has become the business methodology of choice for the past decade since in provides a dual attack on poor quality. More and more corporations are selecting Lean Six Sigma as the methodology of choice.

- *Provides Flexibility For Sustainable Management* – Lean Six Sigma is a highly sustainable approach. Why? It provides management Control, it is engrained into your culture, provides for flexibility to adjust to your marketplace, and results from quick realization of tangible benefits.

162

- *Lean Six Sigma Links Strategies To Strategic Processes* – By using the Transformation Paradigm, your Business Strategies, initiative objectives and using Lean Six Sigma to link of Products, Services and Processes are then concurrently integrated. As a by-product, this also ensures measurement of strategy effectiveness.

- *Quality Is Seen As An Attribute Of Products And Service* – When combining Sustainability and Quality programs together, the value created for your Customers will be apparent. Your brand image will be enhanced by both initiatives. The Customer will recognize improvement in products and services while recognizing your corporate value to improve and utilize resources wisely. In most cases, you should see rise in profitability and Customer Satisfaction.

- *Focus On A High Performance Business Culture* – Recognizing that Customers are vital to your survival, the constraint of global resources, and increased competition due to globalization, more and more companies are organizations are recognizing that their corporate culture needs to work closer to the marketplace. Lean Six Sigma also provides the philosophy, roadmap and tools to change your organization into a high performance culture.

- *Lean Six Sigma Is Adaptable And Flexible To Its Environment* – The methodology originated in the Manufacturing industry, but its framework provides Quality improvements across other industries, as well. The bias against Lean Six Sigma in other industries is waning and acceptance of the methodology is becoming universal.

- *Lean Adds Tools For Waste Detection In A Sustainability Initiative* – Lean provides techniques to eliminate waste of resources, whether they are time, people or material. In a Sustainability initiative, that is a critical tool to continue elimination in Sustainability processes of unwanted misuse and defects.

- *Six Sigma Provides Control Of Processes* – Six Sigma stands on its own merits, when Sustainability and Quality initiatives are combined, reduction of variation in new processes by nature will improve the quality of products of services. In a sustainable environment where your goal is to extract more variation and then recycle the by-products and cull out non-standard resources, then the methodology again provides effective tools for implementation of Sustainability in Quality paradigm.

- *Immediate Results Produce Tangible Benefits* – The application of Lean Six Sigma usually requires only small windows of execution to materially provide tangible benefits. Lean Six Sigma provides rapid reduction in waste, defects, production time and costs.

Variation Control

The Lean Six Sigma objective is to improve Quality by eliminating variation, removing defects, controlling the process and implementing prudent changes. As part of the methodology, Continuous Improvement is a linchpin for ongoing process control and refinement.

Lean Six Sigma Transformation: Since Lean and Six Sigma are combined into one methodology, identification and removal of non-value added work is tagged as waste and identified for elimination. The eight types of waste discovered by Lean include:

- Wasted human talent – damage to people
- Defects – not right or needs fixing
- Inventory – waiting to be worked
- Overproduction – too much or too early
- Waiting Time – people waiting for material or Process next steps

- Motion – unnecessary human movement
- Transportation – moving people or material or inventory
- Processing Waste – activities that do not add value to the Product or Service we are supposed to be producing.
- Variation – Lean six Sigma provides the tools to keep you processes in control while eliminating swings in variation

The variations in the Processes that produce defects, delays and cycle time bottlenecks are also eliminated in the remediation and application of Lean Six Sigma methodology.

Bill Gates said; "Virtually every company will be going out and empowering their workers with a certain set of tools, and the big difference in how much value is received from that will be how much the company steps back and really thinks through their business processes…thinking through how their business can change, how their project management, their customer feedback, their planning cycles can be quite different than they ever were before."

Lean Six Sigma Empowers People to be more effective in addressing Customers' needs. The ultimate goal is to develop a quick reacting organization that clearly understands the Customer is the most import stakeholder. By training and expecting excellence, your organization becomes aligned with strategic goals and is flexible to unexpected changes in the marketplace. The success of this approach is based on:

- Long-term Executive Quality Commitment
- Climate of Continuous Improvement focused on the Customer
- Leadership provides direction and sets expectations
- Employees empowered to make changes toward Continuous Improvement
- Incentivizing the behavior your organization needs

The Process Transformation Mission is to eliminate and Control variation by using empirical, statistical modeling along with methodology to identify, simplify, innovate or automate your unique needs. Through a structured approach, Transformation Maturity Model (TMM) will provide solutions that will Improve your efficiency, productivity, performance and conceivably increase your profitability. By-products of Process evalua- tion creates (i.e., data analysis, Process metrics, etc.) data points for Process monitoring. This is also an opportunity to enrich and leverage your existing decision making process.

Lean Six Sigma Benefits: A number of benefits are realized when the Lean Six Sigma Process is applied in a Systematic way. All of these examples are tangible rewards. A huge financial payoff is realized within a short period. Some of these benefits include:

- *Decreased Work In Progress* – Bottlenecks are removed and work flows smoothly in the line, thereby reducing in process inventory. Equipment and tools are utilized efficiently with decreased work in progress. There is no wait time.
- *Improved Capacity And Output* – Due to decreased Work-In- Process, more can be produced and shipped.
- *Improved Customer Satisfaction And Process Flow* – On-time ship- ping and on-time delivery of goods will make Customers happy.
- *Improved Inventory Turns* – With decreased work in progress and improved Output, Product will move faster out the door. There will be less inventory of raw material and finished product.
- *Increased Productivity* – Productivity increase is realized when equipment and tools are running at capacity and wastage is reduced.
- *Reduced Cycle Time* – From start to finish, the job can be done within the prescribed time. Waiting is removed from the operation.

Bill Gates recognized the value of Customer relations and recognized that their source of discontent is a good indicator you are not satisfying their needs. He said, "Your most unhappy Customers are your greatest source of learning."

Post Project Audit: Like any complete audit, Six Sigma compares what was the project's change and is reviewed to determine the effec- tiveness of that change. Often, this segment considers other potential areas of improvement, whether they were not addressed or may have been out of scope and should be reconsidered.

Learning Transformation is a specific area of identifying potential areas of refinement or development that could Improve Growth, Performance, or Savings. Learning Transformation (i.e., reducing defects, identifying savings, improving performance, etc.) is fundamental to the success and continuation of your championed Quality initiative.

Therefore, Lean Six Sigma is an investment in your delivery of goods and services to achieve fulfillment to your "satisfied Customer" base. Don't lose your "satisfied Customers"; they are opportunities to learn from. That includes Continuous Improvement as a refinement tool to Improve fulfillment framework of goods and services to your Customers. Your goal is to achieve Customer Satisfaction by meeting their needs.

Learning Goals:
- PDSA: Plan, a way to effect improvement is developed. Do, the plan is carried out, preferably on a small scale. Study, a study takes place between what was predicted and what was observed in the previous step. Act, action is taken on the causal System to effect the desired change.
- Extract team information, in a post-project briefing, as to how solutions can be reapplied to future projects. Create a knowledge database (DB) for future access and reuse of the solution.

5.1: Quality Focused Standards

Quality is the result of a carefully constructed cultural environment. It has to be the fabric of the organization, not part of the fabric.

~ Philip Crosby

Chapter Summary: Quality is the ultimate goal of your Transformation. So, how is Quality measured, what attributes you consider as part of that Quality, what are the Customer preferences and other character-istics to include in formulation for your Quality? Your standards reflect how you define Quality.

Key Points:
- Transformation Initiatives
- Focus on Quality Attributes
- Assess Your Quality Current State
- Determine Quality Metric Parameters

Transformation Initiatives: In today's environment, success can be derived from applied best-in-class solutions. We recognize that your organization has different needs, and approaches must be tailored to fit the stage of growth for the company. Solutions should be fitted with your company's Maturity level, as well as, those bothersome elements you want help to reduce or eliminate. Transformation is controlling business change and repositions your organization to exploit opportunities. It is a change in behavior. The benefit is to increase Growth, Performance or Savings.

Quality of Output is directly dependent upon the commitment of top management and the clear understanding of everyone in the organization. The focus is on what the Customer wants and needs.

Also, it is a commitment of Business and IT resources that creates a holistic Quality program that is successful. Quality is a paradigm of goals and Controls. That paradigm is the quantification of your Customers' perceived attributes that are desired. Therefore, build a relationship with your Customers and understand their needs.

In many organizations, Quality is not a goal; hence, the appearance of lack of discipline reflects their conceptual misunderstanding. Implementation of Quality in strategies, identifying KPIs for Quality objectives, measuring Quality Control within products, services and Processes that are properly managed, only then creates the environment for effective Quality Management.

Focus on Quality Attributes: Many definitions of Quality exist. For decades, Quality has been Defined from various perspectives that consistently produce products and services that Customers want while reducing errors before and after delivery to those Customer. Let us review what the Fellows recognized:

- Quality is variability. ~ Shewhart
- Quality is predictability. ~ Deming
- Quality is fitness for use. ~ Juran
- I cannot use my authority to force them to do what I want them to do. It would not lead to good Quality products. ~ Ohno
- Quality Control starts and ends with training. ~ Ishikawa
- The definition of Quality: the loss imparted to society from the time a non-Quality Product is shipped. ~ Taguchi

- Quality means conformance to requirements. ~ Crosby

More importantly, Quality is not so much an outcome as a never-ending Continuous Improvement Process as it is the Quality of what your company produce. Include these thoughts to establish your unique Quality value proposition:

- Quality is meeting or exceeding your Customers' expectations.
- Quality is not achieved by doing different things. It is achieved by doing things differently.

Assess Your Quality Current State: Define your Customer's view of Quality and then manage to that level. The following list provides some more examples of exactly what Quality might mean.

Product Quality
- Aligned with Customer needs
- Availability of Product or service
- Ease of use
- Ease to maintain
- Flexible for future needs
- Good value at your price point
- Intuitive/easy to understand
- Minimally defective
- Reliability (meets expectations)
- Responsive Service support
- Well documented

Service Quality
- Accessible through various media platforms
- Courteous
- Competent
- Credible
- Good communicators
- Knowledgeable of the Customer profile
- Knowledgeable of products and services sold by their company

170

- Reliable and will fulfill Customer needs in a timely fashion
- Responsive (quick Customer Support and Response)

Determine Quality Metric Parameters: Some of the areas from which top management analysis may gain knowledge by using Quality Evaluation may include:

- Customer-related numbers:
  - o New Customers acquired
  - o Status of existing Customers
  - o Attrition of Customers (including breakup by reason for attrition)
- Turnover generated by segments of the Customers—possibly using demographic filters
- Outstanding balances held by segments of Customers and terms of payment - possibly using demographic filters
- Collection of bad debts within Customer relationships
- Demographic analysis of individuals (potential Customers) applying to become Customers, and the levels of approval, rejections and pending numbers
- Delinquency analysis of Customers behind on payments
- Profitability of Customers by demographic segments and segmentation of Customers by profitability
- Campaign management
- Real-time Dashboard on key operational metrics
- Overall equipment effectiveness
- Click stream analysis on a Web site
- Key Product portfolio trackers
- Marketing-channel analysis
- Sales-data analysis by Product segments
- Call center metrics

The above list more or less describes what a bank might monitor, but could also refer to a telephone company or to a similar service-sector company.

Items of generic importance might include:

- Consistent and correct KPI-related data providing insights into operational aspects of a company
- Timely availability of KPI-related data
- KPIs designed to directly reflect the efficiency and effectiveness of a business
- Information presented in a format that aids decision making for management and decision makers
- Ability to discern patterns or trends from organized information

5.2: Learning and Training

Massive training is required to instill the courage to break with tradition. Every activity and every job is a part of the process.

~ W. Edwards Deming

Chapter Summary: *Changing your corporate culture begins with the individual and training is the catalyst for Savings, Performance and Quality growth. Learning is the output of that change and builds on new ideas and solutions that could further enhance your Quality Culture.*

Key Points:
- Quality Learning
- Learn From Experience
- Lean Six Sigma Training
- Implementation Requirements
- Team Responsibilities

Quality Learning: Lean Six Sigma is an investment in your delivery of goods and services to achieve fulfillment to your "satisfied Customer" base. Don't lose your "satisfied Customers," they are opportunities to learn from. Leverage their needs and experiences. Don't let them wither and fall through the "cracks" (in other words, don't repeat your mistakes). Institutionalize and integrate refinement ideas into your Innovation Process to further improve Products, Services and

Processes. Remember, your goal is to achieve Customer Satisfaction by meeting their needs.

Learning Goals:
- Implement a corporate-wide training program for all employees.
- Identify candidates, with quantitative backgrounds and corporate understanding of Processes, who will be dedicated and trained as Black Belts.
- PDSA is a four-step Process for Quality improvement. In the first step (Plan), a way to effect improvement is developed. In the second step (Do), the plan is carried out, preferably on a small scale. In the third step (Study), a study takes place between what was predicted and what was observed in the previous step. In the last step (Act), action is taken on the causal System to effect the desired change. Extract team information, in a post-project briefing, as to how solutions can be reapplied to future projects.
- Create a knowledge database (DB) for future access and reuse for future solutions.

Learn From Experience: *American manufacturers thought that they had to choose between low cost and high Quality. "Higher-Quality products cost more to manufacture," they thought. "They take longer to assemble, require more expensive materials and components, and entail more extensive Quality Controls." What they didn't consider was all the ways of increasing Quality and lowering costs go hand-in-hand, over time. What they didn't consider was how basic improvements in work Processes could eliminate rework, eliminate Quality inspectors, reduce Customer complaints, lower warranty costs, increase Customer loyalty, and reduce advertising and sales promotion costs.*[80]

Lean Six Sigma Training: A healthy portion of the Six Sigma training involves learning of the theory and the principles behind the

---

80   Senge, Peter M.; The Fifth Discipline: The Art and Practice of the Learning Organization; Published by Doubleday, 2006; page 65.

methodology, i.e., DMAIC cycle. The elements of the DMAIC cycle are explained below.

Define Phase: This phase involves:
- Who are the Customers and what are their needs and expectations?
- Understand the Voice of the Customer issues and transform them into project
- Develop a project team charter (who is doing what, determine project goals, what are the key deliverables, benefits of going the project, costs issues, etc.)
- Gather data from Customers to understand what exactly they want from us (use of Customer surveys, benchmarking data, Quality Function Deployment, etc.)
- What is the Process? Use tool such as high-level Process mapping to map out core Processes

Measure Phase: This phase involves:
- How is the Process Measured and how is it performing?
- Decide what to Measure and how do we Measure it?
- Measure current performance of the Process (Throughput yield, DPMO, capability, etc.)
- Do we have a capable Measurement System?
- What is the variability contributed by the Measurement System to the total variation?

Analyze Phase: This phase involves:
- Identify the root causes of defects or failures
- Understand the data (using simple statistical tools such as scatter plot, histograms, etc.
- Use of simple tools ANOVA, Hypothesis test, Regression analysis, etc. to Analyze the data
- Select the 'vital few' causes from the trivial many for improvement phase

Improve Phase: This phase involves:
- How can the causes of defects or failures be removed?

- Identify the key variables which causes the problem
- Document solution statements
- Test solutions and Measure Results

Control Phase: This phase involves:
- How can the improvements be maintained or sustained?
- Document the new methods
- Select and establish standard Measures to monitor performance

Management operates through various functions, often classified as planning, organizing, leading/motivating, and controlling. Transformation Learning is a specific area of identifying potential areas of refinement or development that could Improve Growth, Performance or Savings. TMM (Transformation Maturity Model) has created a specific process to help enrich your organization and provide you with "refinement engine" to continually Improve your performance.

Insight can be applied to various levels of a corporation and provides knowledge and understanding that can refocus a perception of an issue. Strategically, this could be the realignment with Suppliers, and interpretation of laws and regulations or applying new methodologies and processes to increase production. Again, insight provides how, when, where, who and why efficiencies can be produced and profitability be extracted. We provide that holistic perspective for our clients by conceptualizing your Business Transformation.

Implementation Requirements: One key innovation of Six Sigma involves the "professionalizing" of Quality Management functions. Prior to Six Sigma, Quality Management in practice was largely relegated to the production floor and to statisticians in a separate Quality department. Formal Six Sigma programs borrow martial arts ranking terminology to define a hierarchy (and career path) that cuts across all business functions.

176

Six Sigma identifies several key roles for its successful implementation.

- *Executive Leadership* includes the CEO and other members of top management. They are responsible for setting up a vision for Six Sigma implementation. They also empower the other role holders with the freedom and resources to explore new ideas for breakthrough improvements.
- *Champions* take responsibility for Six Sigma implementation across the organization in an integrated manner. The Executive Leadership draws them from upper management. Champions also act as mentors to Black Belts.
- *Master Black Belts*, identified by champions, act as in-house coaches on Six Sigma. They devote 100 percent of their time to Six Sigma. They assist champions and guide Black Belts and Green Belts. Apart from statistical tasks, they spend their time on ensuring consistent application of Six Sigma across various functions and departments.
- *Black Belts* operate under Master Black Belts to apply Six Sigma methodology to specific projects. They devote 100 percent of their time to Six Sigma. They primarily focus on Six Sigma project execution, whereas Champions and Master Black Belts focus on identifying projects/functions for Six Sigma.
- *Green Belts* are the employees who take up Six Sigma implementation along with their other job responsibilities, operating under the guidance of Black Belts.[81]

In some organizations additional belt colors, such as *Yellow or White Belts*, are used for employees that have basic training in Lean Six Sigma methodology.

Team Responsibilities: Each team should be composed from cross-functional expertise and specialties to bring innovative ideas to teach process solution. The Team Lead should be a certified Lean Six Sigma

---

81   Harry, Mikel; Schroeder, Richard (2000). Six Sigma. Random House, Inc. ISBN 0-385-49437-8.

Black Belt and remainder of the team should include Lean Six Sigma Green Belts or those candidates that plan to pursue certification.

These employee roles are dedicated to the Transformation Initiative. That means if they are assigned from another group, those duties should be transferred to other individuals prior to involvement in the Transformation project. Do not place onerous dual responsibilities on these selected candidates during the remediation.

- Transformation Mission, Voice of the Client, and Project Goals will be the guidelines for each team
- Participation by all team leaders/work team leaders; all staff participate in the project vision, solution creation, task assignment, and timeline
- Performance goals and Quality standards are set by teams and will align with established Quality metrics
- Negotiation techniques should be used effectively to communicate expectations across the organization; back-and-forth conversations are useful and often help assure understanding between the Team and Client
- Engage IT SMEs to provide access to data, information gathering and reporting
- Engage Financial SMEs to validate and sign off tangible benefit calculations that link to accounting practices

5.3: DMAIC

Do not simply cling to your past successes, be willing to change, adopt new ideas and continually review all the different segments of business.

~ Peter Drucker

Chapter Summary: Transformation refurbishes current processes to improve their performance and utilization. Consider the use of DMAIC a "tune-up" for your enterprise.

Key Points:
- Testimonial For DMAIC
- When To Use DMAIC
- Define
- Measure
- Analyze
- Improve
- Control

Special Note: More information is available in Appendix: DMAIC Descriptions.

Testimonial For DMAIC: Six Sigma is as relevant to Business Strategy as it is to Quality Management, but until now the literature has focused on basic Six Sigma philosophy and its implementation and the resulting performance. Little attention has been paid to Six Sigma's relationship to Quality performance. A Six Sigma business strategy framework is proposed that allocates organizational resources to solve critical business problems through Six Sigma methodology. During the business strategy development stage, the organization must develop a Six Sigma organizational culture before prioritizing strategies. Six Sigma Quality approaches should include formation of a steering committee to oversee project management, to implement DMAIC integration, and to Measure Six Sigma Quality and its effects on profitability.[82]

When To Use DMAIC: The DMAIC Roadmap is the primary tool for Lean Six Sigma teams to discover poor Quality, defects, variation, and other deficiencies that would impact you products or services.

- A Product or Process is in existence at your company and one needs to be refined.
- DMAIC is associated with defining a business Process and its applicability.
- DMAIC is used for measuring the current performance of a Business Process.
- In DMAIC, a Business Process is analyzed to find the root cause of a defect or recurring problem.
- In DMAIC, improvements are made in the business Process for eliminating or reducing defects.
- In DMAIC, Control Systems are put in place to keep a check on future performance of a business Process.

Define: In the Define phase, a team clearly identifies the Suppliers, Process Inputs, Process activities, Process Outputs, and Customers; establishes baselines and benchmarks; and sets and agrees upon goals and Measures of success.

During the Define phase, a team and its sponsors reach agreement on what the project is and what it should accomplish. Presuming that a draft

---

82   Cheng, Jung-Lang; Cheng Shiu University, Kaohsiung, Taiwan; 2006, ASQ: Six Sigma Forum Magazine, Vol. 5, No. 4, August 2006, pages 22-28.

of the Project Charter is already in place, the main work in the Define phase is for the project team to complete an analysis of what the project should accomplish and confirm understanding with the sponsor(s).

Measure: During the Measurement phase, the team studies and evaluates relevant measurement Systems to determine if they are capable of measuring key Input variables (raw material characteristics and Process conditions such as temperatures, speeds, pressures, and flow rates) and Output characteristics (Product dimensions, Customer Defined specifications, and Product performance) with the desired precision and accuracy. If they aren't, then the team will work to Improve the related measurement Systems before proceeding with the project.

In the Measure phase, existing Process data is collected, measurement Systems are evaluated, and the Process capability requirements are identified. This phase includes the following steps:

- Determine Process capability.
- Establish measurement method and tools.
- Determine sampling plan to meet goals.
- Collect data.
- Present status report.

Analyze: During the Analysis phase, the team performs graphical and statistical analyses on historical and newly obtained data to develop preliminary hypotheses for improvement. The team identifies "root causes" of problems and "enablers" of poor performance that need to be corrected.

In this phase the Process is evaluated to determine its capability. Process data are analyzed to identify opportunities for improvement and to develop plans for improving the Process. This phase includes the following steps:

- Convert data into information.
- Brainstorming and analysis

- Determine Process capability.
- Develop priority list of parameters.
- Perform root cause analysis.
- Update FMEA.
- Develop improvement plan.
- Present status report.
- Determine path forward.

Improve: In the Improve phase, the team designs and conducts experiments to find the optimal conditions needed to operate the process. Improvement requires change, and the correct changes are determined through statistically designed experiments where Process Inputs or System components are varied and the resulting effects on Process Outputs (related to Quality, cost, and Customer requirements) are observed and measured. If the Results are favorable, Process conditions are changed to these optimal levels.

In the Improve phase, the improvement plan developed in the analyze phase is implemented. The Results are evaluated, conclusions are drawn, and improvements are finalized and tested. After the desired improvements are implemented, the changes to the Process are documented, and new instructions and procedures are developed. This phase includes the following steps:

- Implement improvement plan.
- Perform designed experiment if applicable (Design Of Experiment, DOE).
- Measure improvements.
- Develop conclusions, recommendations, and next steps
- Update documentation.
- Present status report.

Control: The team maintains these optimal conditions during the Control phase where audits and Control Systems sustain the improvements. No project is deemed "completed" until there is sufficient time and evidence to Verify that the desired Results have been obtained and maintained.

In the Control phase, the improvements become institutionalized. The Process changes were documented in the Improve phase. In this phase, Control plans are developed to ensure that the Process continues to be measured and evaluated. This includes implementing Process audit plans, data collection plans, and plans of action for out-of-Control conditions, if they occur. The Control phase includes the following steps:

- Establish Control System for each critical parameter.
- Establish data collection plan.
- Establish out-of-control plan.
- Establish internal audit plan (accounting alignment and verification of benefits).
- Develop and present final report.

5.4: DMADV

To find out what happens when you change something, it is necessary to change it.

~ Unknown

Chapter Summary: Design for Lean Six Sigma, using DMADV, approaches the future state of your processes that improve your enterprise. Designing new Processes, creating requirements entrenched in Lean Six Sigma requirements, will ensure your Quality standards are being met.

Key Points:
- Testimonial For DMADV
- When To Use DMADV
- What is Design for Six Sigma (DFSS)?
- Define
- Measure
- Analyze
- Design
- Verify

Special Note: More information is available in Appendix: DMADV Descriptions.

Testimonial For DMADV: One company that is using Strategic Six Sigma to strengthen its global business operations, build Customer loyalty, and accelerate top-line business growth is Dow Chemical. In recent years, Dow has transformed itself from a "geographically organized and functionally driven company into a global, business-led company with annual sales of over $30 billion," noted Dow president and CEO, Mike Parker. It has also embarked on an aggressive growth campaign, focused both on growing top-line business revenue, and on undertaking strategically significant M and A, one of the most important of which was Dow's recent merger with Union Carbide.

To undergird its growth activities, Parker said Dow built a robust global Information Technology (IT) backbone, and a global enterprise resource planning System to support its business operations. It also instituted use of Strategic Six Sigma to help deploy its strategic blueprint, put in place in 1994. "That blueprint calls for four things," noted Parker:

> First, set the competitive standard, business-by-business. Six Sigma will play a critical role with this by enabling us to become more competitive in everything we do. Second, productivity: Very clearly Six Sigma can play a key role in that because a lot of what we're doing today involves cost savings projects, finding the "hidden factory" (in our operations), and being able to create more capacity out of what we are thinking is a constrained System. Third, value growth: DFSS (is helping us) Design Processes so they can perform at high sigma levels at the beginning, not at three sigma. Fourth, culture change: (Six Sigma is helping us) develop a mind-set and intolerance for waste ... it's going to create breakthrough thought in people as they do their everyday jobs ...[83]

When To Use DMADV: The DMADV methodology, instead of the DMAIC methodology, should be used when:

- A Product or Process is not in existence at your company and one needs to be developed.

---

[83]   Parker, Mike. Interview with Richard Koonce. Midland, MI: PricewaterhouseCoopers, 19 November 2001.

- The existing Product or Process exists and has been optimized (using either DMAIC or not) and still doesn't meet the level of Customer specification or Six Sigma level.
- DMADV helps in defining Customer needs in relation to a Product or service.
- DMADV is used for measuring the Customer needs and specifications.
- In DMADV, a business Process is analyzed for finding options that will help in satisfying the Customer needs and specifications.
- DMADV, an appropriate business model is designed that helps in meeting Customer requirements.
- In DMADV, the suggested business model is put through simulation tests for Verifying efficacy in meeting Customer needs and specifications.

What is Design for Six Sigma (DFSS)? While Six Sigma Process improvement approach leaves the fundamental structure of a Process unchanged, Design for Six Sigma (DFSS) involves changing or redesigning the Process at the early stages of product/Process life cycle. DFSS becomes necessary when:

- The current Process has to be replaced, rather than repaired or just improved,
- The required Quality level cannot be achieved by just improving an existing Process, or
- An opportunity is identified to offer a new Process.
- Breakthrough and new disruptive technologies

Although DFSS takes more effort at the beginning, it will benefit an organization in a long run by designing Six Sigma Quality into products/ Processes. DMADV is a popular methodology since it has the same number of letters as the DMAIC acronym.[84]

---

84   Yang, K. and El-Haik, B., Design for Six Sigma: A Roadmap for Product Development, McGraw-Hill, New York, 2003.

The DMADV project methodology, also known as DFSS ("Design For Six Sigma"), features five phases:

- *Define* Design goals that are consistent with Customer demands and the enterprise strategy. Define the project goals and Customer (internal and external) deliverables.
- *Measure* and identify CTQs (characteristics that are Critical To Quality), Product capabilities, production Process capability, and risks. Remember, Measure and determine Customer needs and specifications.
- *Analyze* to develop and Design alternatives, create a high-level Design and evaluate Design capability to select the best Design.
- *Design* details, optimize the Design, and plan for Design verification. This phase may require simulations.
- *Verify* the Design, set up pilot runs, implement the production Process and hand it over to the Process Owner(s).[85] Verify the Design performance and ability to meet Customer needs

Define: Define Design goals that are consistent with Customer demands and the enterprise strategy. Much like DMAIC, the Define stage is where the end Product or Service is designed based on client's wants or desires.

In the Define phase, a team clearly identifies the Suppliers, Process Inputs, Process activities, Process Outputs, and Customers; establishes baselines and benchmarks; and sets and agrees upon goals and Measures of success.

- The first step in a DFSS project is to establish and maintain a DFSS project team (for both Product/Service and Process) with a shared vision.
- The purpose is to establish and maintain a motivated team.

---

85   De Feo, Joseph A.; Barnard, William (2005). JURAN Institute's Six Sigma Breakthrough and Beyond - Quality Performance Breakthrough Methods. Tata McGraw-Hill Publishing Company Limited. ISBN 0-07-059881-9.

- The success of development activities depends on the performance of this team, which is selected according to the project charter.
- The team should be fully integrated, including internal and external members (Suppliers and Customers).
- Special efforts may be necessary to create a multidiscipline team that collaborates to achieve a Six Sigma-level Design.
- Roles, responsibilities, and resources are best Defined upfront, collaboratively, by all team members. The black belt is the team leader.

During the Define phase, a team and its sponsors reach agreement on what the project is and what it should accomplish. Presuming that a draft of the Project Charter is already in place, the main work in the Define phase is for the project team to complete an analysis of what the project should accomplish and confirm understanding with the sponsor(s).

Measure: Measure and identify CTQs (characteristics that are Critical To Quality), Product capabilities, production Process capability, and risks. Measuring is how you will Process the Product or Service as Defined.

During the Measurement phase, similar to DMAIC, the team studies and evaluates relevant measurement Systems to determine if they are capable of measuring key Input variables (raw material characteristics and Process conditions such as temperatures, speeds, pressures, and flow rates) and Output characteristics (Product dimensions, Customer Defined specifications, and Product performance) with the desired precision and accuracy. If they aren't, then the team will work to Improve the related measurement Systems before proceeding with the project.

Analyze: Analyze to develop and Design alternatives, create a high-level Design and evaluate Design capability to select the best Design. Through analyzing the Process that will result in the end product, areas of improvement and changes are discovered through simulations, not users, so the actual driver never gets to test the Product or Service.

During the Analysis phase, the team performs graphical and statistical analyses on historical and newly obtained data to develop preliminary hypotheses for improvement. The team identifies "root causes" of problems and "enablers" of poor performance that need to be corrected.

Design: Design details, optimize the Design, and plan for Design verification. This phase may require simulations. Here is when DMADV differs from DMAIC. It's clear to the automaker that although the Product or Service will do what it's supposed to do, the Customer doesn't like it. By revisiting the Design based on end user suggestions and Input, the Design can be restructured to please.

In the Design phase, the team Designs and conducts experiments to find the optimal conditions needed to operate the Process. Improvement requires change, and the correct changes are determined through statistically designed experiments where Process Inputs or System components are varied and the resulting effects on Process Outputs (related to Quality, cost, and Customer requirements) are observed and measured. If the Results are favorable, Process conditions are changed to these optimal levels.

Verify: Verify the Design, set up pilot runs, implement the production Process and hand it over to the Process Owner(s). It is important to note that Verification of the new Design must be determined by the end users. If complaints on the uncomfortable Product or Service cease, then the DMADV Process has worked.

Verify stage is focused on a new Product or Process needs to be developed to meet Customer requirements. Additionally, it is used when a Product or Process has been optimized using DMAIC, but is still unable to meet Customer specifications.

6.0: Systems Thinking

To succeed, companies must generate insights, create focus, achieve alignment, and motivate change continuously, in a dynamic cycle of renewal. This cycle is the essence of Strategic Learning.

~ Willie Pietersen; Reinventing Strategy

Chapter Summary: Through Leadership Vision and Direction, he or she foresees the organizational evolution as a destination point of your Business Transformation. Sharing a common Vision for you and your organization will focus on Alignment, Customers, Innovation, Internal Needs, Quality, and provide more flexibility to meet shifting market demands.

Key Points:
- End-to-End Transformation
- Leadership Focus
- When Limiting Deployment
- Profound Knowledge
- Continuous Strategic Improvement

End-to-End Transformation: Lean Six Sigma provides end-to-end remediation of Processes from **S**uppliers, their **I**nput, with focus on the **P**rocess improvement, that drives **O**utput, which your **Customer**s most desire. The brilliance of this methodology is its effectiveness, flexibility and capability to apply structured solutions that create a performance driven culture. It is holistic from the inception of the initiative, through execution and produces measurable Results that are driven by your Executive Team. Since it is constructed on Systems thinking that anticipates future changes to your business environment, additions and modification can also be supported using Lean Six Sigma methodology. Future initiatives can build on top your Quality foundations to expand capabilities that support your Customer needs. Examples include:

- Innovation of Products, Processes and Services
- Alignment of IT with Business Efforts
- Alignment of Suppliers to Your Quality Planning
- Sustainability Initiative
- Strategic Integration of Profound Learning

Leadership Focus: Why choose Lean Six Sigma? If you are a major Owner or CEO, you are daily faced with a number of issues that threaten the existence of your business. The Conference Board published their latest report on the "Top 10 CEO Challenges in 2010." It is no surprise that many of the issues focus on "Business Growth Basics." Some of the top Challenges include:

- *Excellence in Execution* – Lean Six Sigma is a methodology that hones costs, improves Processes, create a mind-set in the employees and management that provides Continuous Improvement for products, services and Processes.
- *Consistent Execution of Strategy by Top Management* – Lean Six Sigma provides additional Control of a "Lean" organization and is able to deliver Customer needs quicker, cheaper and faster.
- *Sustained and Steady Top-Line Growth* – Lean Six Sigma provides a framework to Improve your production and fulfillment Processes and provides tools to start and Improve you innovation efforts. The tandem approach supports Sustainability and increase to growth.
- *Customer Loyalty* – Lean Six Sigma methodology is focused on the Customer and must acknowledge their needs to provide satisfaction and repeat business.

- *Customer Retention* – Lean Six Sigma Quality focus improves your current portfolio and also encourages improvement of Customer touch points in order to Improve their experience.
- *Profit Growth* – Lean Six Sigma is instrumental in reducing waste, defects and variation that directly has a financial impact on profitability.
- *Corporate Reputation for Quality Products/Services* – Lean Six Sigma is focused on Quality. That attribute is a reflection of each of your products or services and the team that provides Quality products and services.
- *Stimulating Innovation* – Lean Six Sigma is specifically designed to capture Design requirements to Improve product, Service or Process enhancements to your portfolios next generation.
- *Creativity* – Lean Six Sigma is limited and focused on creativity regarding Quality application and improvement.
- *Enabling Entrepreneurship* – Lean Six Sigma empowers every employee in your organization to become an effective problem solver and react positively to meet the demands of the marketplace. (The Conference Board n.d.)[86]

When Limiting Deployment: In the absence of Systems thinking, or when Lean Six Sigma concepts are applied in a limited scope, the following symptoms are quite commonly observed:

- Six Sigma is viewed as a Quality improvement tool like others that may not have worked in the past.
- Customers' Critical Criteria are not understood and are not a focus of attention throughout the organization.
- Quality focus and objectives are not clearly Defined or are poorly communicated.
- Executives continually think that Quality has nothing to do with business and profitability.

---

86   The Conference Board, www.conference-board.org, Retrieved: 30 November 2010.

- Measurements (levels and trends) to track operations performance, including Customer Satisfaction, reject rates, rolled yield, COPQ, Design effectiveness, cycle time, inventory levels, employee skills development, and financial performance, are not in place.
- Centralized decision making (executives making the decisions) is the norm.
- Executives are busy fighting fires, making an effort to "look busy," and hassling employees.
- Employees are afraid of management—reluctant to take the initiative to Improve performance—and feel that no one is listening to concerns.[87]

The benefits of implementing Six Sigma are too attractive to overlook. Increased Customer loyalty, more revenues, improved operating margins, higher returns, and increased earnings are all demonstrated outcomes. The question that must be answered is not whether to implement Six Sigma; instead, the question is how to implement Six Sigma to sustain better business performance as part of a whole organizational System.

Profound Knowledge: So, what should a corporation prepare to gain knowledge? "The prevailing style of management must undergo Transformation. A System cannot understand itself. The Transformation requires a view from outside. It provides a map of theory by which to understand the organizations that we work in. Deming advocated that all managers needed to have what he called a System of Profound Knowledge, consisting of four parts:

- *Appreciation Of A System* – understanding the overall Processes involving Suppliers, producers, and Customers (or recipients) of goods and services (explained below);
- *Knowledge Of Variation* – the range and causes of variation in Quality, and use of statistical sampling in measurements;

---

87   Adams, Cary; Praveen Gupta and Charlie Wilson; Six Sigma Deployment; Butterworth-Heinemann © 2003 (311 pages) Citation ISBN:9780750675239.

- *Theory Of Knowledge* – the concepts explaining knowledge and the limits of what can be known (see also: epistemology);
- *Knowledge Of Psychology* – concepts of human nature."[88]

Continuous Strategic Improvement: Oftentimes the "big picture" is lost in the details of everyday analysis, project Transformation, post audit verification, governance activities and other meetings. Communication has been recognized as a key linchpin for success and not this includes your state of company review, including Continuous Strategic Improvement. Sharing a holistic viewpoint that helps visualize progress. It links to your shared vision and values. Continuous Strategic Improvement is an offshoot of your institutionalized Continuous Improvement program and the length of your long-term commitment to Quality. Quarterly reviews and measured effectiveness of your Quality initiative is important not only to the Owner, CEO and Executive Team, but to those who have been engaged in the Transformation, your Transformation teams.

Due to the importance of this concept, which is a measurement of Executive Quality Commitment, this area should be monitored with matrix according to these attributes:

- Continue review to promote Growth, Profitability and Savings
- Base incentives, promotions and professional growth on Lean Six Sigma knowledge and verified Results
- Align organizational effort with strategies and key Processes
- Institutionalize Lean Six Sigma strategies (eliminate variation, timing delays and defects/waste)
- Monitor you Maturity level across proc assess, project management, software development, etc.
- Maintain Executive Commitment to Quality

---

88   Deming, W. Edwards. 1993. *The New Economics for Industry, Government, Education,* second edition.

6.1: Innovation

Innovation distinguishes between a leader and a follower.

~ Steve Jobs

Chapter Summary: After your initial Business Transformation is complete, Leadership should consider making the next investment into Innovation. For Innovation is the change engine to improve Products, Services and Processes.

Key Points:
- Innovative Thinking
- What Drives Innovation?
- Disruptive Innovation Awareness
- Structured Innovation
- Transforming Data into Information
- Data-Driven Innovation

Innovative Thinking: Isaac Asimov once said; "The most exciting phrase to hear in science, the one that heralds discoveries, is not 'Eureka!' but 'Now that's funny….'" Business Transformation is a top-down approach to making an organization into a Customer-serving, competitive tool. By nature, this Process encompasses business strategies, transforms Processes, Measures performance and provides a Continuous Improvement engine that adapts change into benefits. That solid platform provides you options and opportunities to Improve products, Processes and services based on innovation and System thinking.

Transformation is a journey. That journey is based on a forward-thinking approach to discover new and better ways to Improve efficiency, productivity, performance, and profitability. Also, that forward thinking includes an anticipation of changing markets, called Innovation. Let your creativity transform your products and service. Develop that Process to fit your business needs.

Innovation is a tool to enhance wealth, Sustainability and survivability. Innovation is assembled from creativity, ideas, strategies, Processes, and most important the right human elements and a spirit of entrepreneurship. Innovation can be applied to your existing business environment to increase Customer Satisfaction, increase profitability, decrease waste and become more in tune with the marketplace. Innovation is also the vision of new markets and applying creativity and entrepreneurship to increase revenue streams for your company. Today, efficiency and innovation concepts are becoming more linked together and harnessed to provide internal solutions. Those solutions and techniques are also applied to new products and services seen externally in the marketplace. They reflect the Transformation that is being driven by Quality Management, Green Solutions, Energy and Information Technology, as well as, incentives and stimuli created by Government.

Innovation by businesses is achieved in many ways, with much attention now given to formal research and development for "breakthrough innovations." But innovations may be developed by less formal on-the-job modifications of practice, through exchange and combination of professional experience and by many other routes. The more radical and revolutionary innovations tend to emerge from R and D, while more incremental innovations may emerge from practice — but there are many exceptions to each of these trends.

Regarding user innovation, those actually implementing and using technologies and products as part of their normal activities do a great deal of innovation. Sometimes user-innovators may become entrepreneurs, selling their product, they may choose to trade their innovation in exchange for other innovations, or their Suppliers may adopt them. Nowadays, they may also choose to freely reveal their innovations, using methods like open source. In such networks of innovation the users or communities of users can further develop technologies and reinvent their social meaning.

Insight can be applied to various levels of a corporation and provides knowledge and understanding that can refocus a perception of an issue. Strategically, this could be the realignment with Suppliers, and interpretation of laws and regulations or applying new methodologies and Processes to increase production. Again, insight provides how, when, where, who, and why efficiencies can be produced and profitability be extracted. We provide that holistic perspective for our clients by conceptualizing your Business Transformation.

As illustrated below, creative Processes and analysis can be used to stimulate new ideas in four key Quality Strategies:

- *Strategic Innovation* – Adaptation and institutionalization of Transformation improving strategies is an expected outcome. Be prepared to recognize the innovation and how it might impact various strategies promoting or supporting the Product or service.
- *Product Innovation* – New or modified products can inject a new momentum to your revenue stream.
- *Service Innovation* – Services that are new, modified, or new ways of providing Service fulfillment is another key area of innovation.
- *Process Innovation* – Developing new, improving or changing internal Processes for delivery of products or services could increase potential revenue throughput, reduce cost and/or increase profitability and effectiveness.

What Drives Innovation? Like most change elements in business, drivers exist for the change and enhancement of your products, Processes and services. Your type of marketplace will strongly influence your needs, but will fall into these general areas:

- Change for tomorrow's success.
- What are the opportunities, the new conditions, or emerging issues?
- Do they fit you?
- What does the Customer value?[89]

One survey across a large number of manufacturing and services organizations found, ranked in decreasing order of popularity, that Systematic programs of organizational innovation are most frequently driven by:

- Improved Quality
- Creation of new markets
- Extension of the Product range
- Reduced labor costs
- Improved Production Processes
- Reduced materials
- Reduced environmental damage
- Replacement of products/services
- Reduced energy consumption
- Conformance to regulations

---

89   Drucker, Peter; The Five Most Questions You Will Ever Ask About Your Organization, Leader To Leader Institute, Jossey-Bass Publishing, 2008.

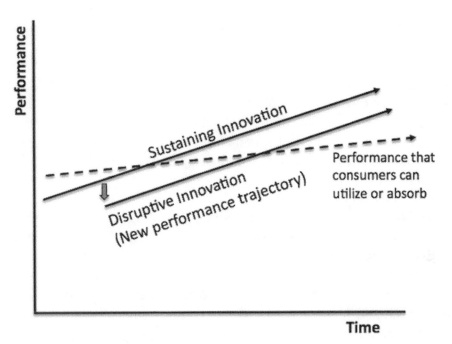

Time

Note: *The Innovator's Solution, (2003) Christensen used the term disruptive innovation because he recognized that few technologies are intrinsically disruptive or sustaining in character. Disruptive innovation is an innovation that disrupts an existing market.*

Disruptive Innovation: In layperson terms, disruptive innovation can be defined as an improvement or advancement that enhances a Service or a Product in a manner that has never been expected by the market. The basic features of disruptive innovation are as follows:

- The disruptive innovation aims at meeting the needs of the upcoming Customers in the market. When the concept is first introduced, this may not be appreciated by the mainstream market but would see a gradual commendation by the budding users of the service, or Product who would value the change that has been brought about in the Product or service.
- The adaptation of the innovation would gradually result in increase of the performance of the Product or Service that has undergone

the innovation. This increase in the performance would steadily result in going beyond the imagination of the mainstream market of the product.

- The responsiveness of the innovation is seen when there is an influencing change perception of the mainstream market about the value of the innovation. With time, the mainstream market would also acknowledge the superiority of the innovation.
- This change in the perception of the mainstream market will result in replacing and disrupting the existing market of the Service or the product.[90]

Lean Six Sigma can be an applied strategy to structure and support for innovation Design, experimentation, proof of concept and final introduction to new products or services. It seeks to improve the Quality of Process Outputs by identifying and removing the causes of defects (errors) and variation in manufacturing and business Processes. It uses a set of Quality Management methods, including statistical methods.

Change is also a constant in business and will always be. In the current business environment, the work we perform, how we do it, where we do it and the Process of actually completing the task is undergoing a significant paradigm shift. That insipid "globalization" is a factual reality and a derivative of the global economy that has emerged; therefore, innovation becomes a strategic tool to promote success and Sustainability.

Structured Innovation: Injecting innovation into projects that can contribute to changing enhanced attributes of Quality to new or existing Processes, Products or Services. Leveraging Lean Six Sigma methodology Controls Transformation into the vision you want in the future. Also, remember that innovation is not necessarily a business paradigm; rather it is better served with participants from business and IT organizations working together.

---

90   Christensen, Clayton M.; The Innovator's Dilemma; Harvard Business School Press, 1997.

Change is a constant in business and will always be. In the current business environment, the work we perform, how we do it, where we do it and the Process of actually completing the task is undergoing a significant paradigm shift. That insipid "globalization" is a factual reality and a derivative of the global economy that has emerged; therefore, innovation becomes a strategic tool to promote success and Sustainability.

Innovation is a tool to enhance wealth, Sustainability, and survivability. Innovation is assembled from creativity, ideas, strategies, Processes, and most important the right human elements and a spirit of entrepreneurship. Innovation can be applied to your existing business environment to increase Customer Satisfaction, increase profitability, decrease waste and become more in tune with the marketplace. Innovation is also the vision of new markets and applying creativity and entrepreneurship to increase revenue streams for your company. Today, efficiency and innovation concepts are becoming more linked together and harnessed to provide internal solutions. Those solutions and techniques are also applied to new products and services seen externally in the marketplace. They reflect the Transformation that is being driven by Quality Management, Green Solutions, Energy and Information Technology, as well as incentives and stimuli created by Government.

Innovation by businesses is achieved in many ways, with much attention now given to formal research and development for "breakthrough innovations." But innovations may be developed by less formal on-the-job modifications of practice, through exchange and combination of professional experience and by many other routes. The more radical and revolutionary innovations tend to emerge from R and D, while more incremental innovations may emerge from practice—but there are many exceptions to each of these trends.

Regarding user innovation, those actually implementing and using technologies and products as part of their normal activities do a great deal of innovation. Sometimes user-innovators may become entrepreneurs, selling their product, they may choose to trade their innovation in exchange for other innovations, or their Suppliers may adopt them.

Nowadays, they may also choose to freely reveal their innovations, using methods like Open Source. In such networks of innovation the users or communities of users can further develop technologies and reinvent their social meaning.

What are the compelling reasons organizations (regardless of their industry) should continually be striving to improve? Simply stated:

- Create compelling new Product and Service offerings,
- Provide Service Quality and value as Defined by Customers,
- Generate attractive returns for shareholders,
- Be the best place to work for employees,
- Operate mutually value-creating partnerships with third-party Suppliers, and
- Act with ethical, social, and environmental responsibility.

Business Transformation also changes how you want to mold the future. Critical success factors for your innovation engine should address these fundamentals:

- Demonstrate Commitment from Top Management – The single most important factor for success is the commitment from to top management. Top management must visibly articulate its value and demonstrate support, even on difficult issues. Visibility on business opportunities
- Architect data captured Results to drive innovation and leverage BI solutions – decision making must rely on the most current infor- mation and an enterprise must be designed to capture that critical information for management reporting.
- Manage innovation as a resource – similar to IT, HR and other cor- porate resources, Innovation should be measured to understand the return on those resources. Innovation is a financial cost, but its Mission is to generate revenues. Don't make innovation a money pit.
- Incentivize people for contributing ideas and knowledge – Behavior rewarded will change the complexion of your corporation and it will

help generate the new ideas to better position your products and services.

- Develop core skills that provide the foundation to innovation – Thinking innovatively is an acquired skill. Make it part of your culture through promotion requirements, sharing ideas, giving credit to people within departments and acknowledging patentable products and services.
- Incorporate innovative Transformation into your strategic initiative – A successful innovation program should impact your strategies, change your business model and promote change in a way that promotes Sustainability and profitability.
- Show Results to the enterprise and communicate successes – Develop a Communication Plan. Externally, publicize your success in the industry and other public mediums. Especially communicate successes in the enterprise newsletters, intranets and other channels.
- Create BI tools for analysis, extraction of trends, Customer needs and price point analysis – Balance Scorecards should reflect your successes. Alternatively, specific BI focus on Innovation would be useful tool to communicate successful completions and benefits.

Transforming Data into Information: "Anyone who stops learning is old, whether at twenty or eighty. Anyone who keeps learning stays young." Henry Ford was quoted to say. So should a corporation learn and gain knowledge?

- Collect Customer data, both internally and externally, to provide better decision making. True
- Manage and leverage knowledge you own. True
- Transform the data into knowledge. True
- Study and correlate relationships from collected data; promote effective use of information, mold into intellectual capital and patent, when possible. True

Data Driven Innovation

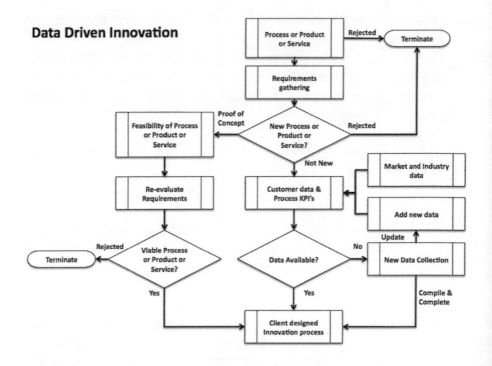

Data-Driven Innovation: Leveraging Lean Six Sigma methodology Controls Transformation into the vision you want in the future. Also, remember that innovation is not necessarily a business paradigm; rather it is better served with participants from business and IT organizations working together.

Data is the foundation to information. Information is the interpretation of the data. Decision making, based on that interpretation, could make a good choice, better. Your company would most likely have unique needs, but the focus for innovation will be how you address your Customer, their needs and wants, and how your innovation Process will be developed to address Transformation of your products and services.

Data-driven innovation is based on the critical elements that are foreseen and ancillary to those products and services you promote. Data elements should be gathered from selected market facing touch points. Sales information could also be drivers that ascertain critical

204

characteristics that Customers want or need. Information gathered in your internal manufacturing Process provide constraints and other valuable variables that would affect production costs. Services promoting a Product or used selectively for services, may narrow or point to potential expansion areas in the market. Distribution channels also provide a gateway to collect data at your point-of-sale.

6.2: IT Alignment

Progress is the activity of today and the assurance of tomorrow.

~ Ralph Waldo Emerson

Chapter Summary: Internally, the Alignment of IT with Business is one of the most significant initiatives on can pursue after your initial Business Transformation. Not only will organizations be coordinated, additionally, Alignment will provide more flexibility to meet the market demands.

Key Points:
- Aligning IT To Your Business Effort
- Business and IT Success Factors
- IT Contribution
- Business Intelligence Trend Grows
- Process Analysis Software
- Alignment Drivers

Aligning IT To Your Business Effort: "Technology is not nature, but man. It's not about tools; it's about how man works. It is equally about how man lives and how man thinks. There is a saying of Alfred Russel Wallace, the co-discoverer, with Charles Darwin, of the theory of evolution: 'Man is the only animal capable of directed in purposeful evolution; he makes tools.' But precisely because technology is an extension of man, basic technological change always both expresses our worldview and, in turn, changes it."[91]

Strategic Six Sigma thinking and business practices will no doubt be of great help to companies as they assess the weakest links in their computer, IT, and telecommunications Systems; as they brainstorm worst-case business scenarios, develop fail-safe disaster recovery plans, and work to ensure the security of airport and airline Customers, tenants of large buildings, and computer and Internet users. All of this has been necessitated as our society comes to grips with operating in a new global environment where Customer care strategies, antiterrorism approaches, and high-tech security planning will all need to be considered within the same strategic business context.[92]

Many issues are not stand-alone problems. They often have a ripple effect on other parts of your organization. We have seven Service solutions to better serve your efforts for Customer support and Satisfaction. We see this as an inter-related business cycle that affects Growth, Performance and Savings.

Business and IT Success Factors: What are Critical Success Factors? Simply, they are linchpins to success! When beginning your journey of Business Transformation, remember that these factors are seldom a small list of factors. As Juran said; "Among those factors to be considered there will usually be the vital few and the trivial many." In this context, consider these guidelines as potential areas to extract Critical Success Factors:

• Top executive management buy-in and responsibilities
• Champion responsible for success and how success will be measured
• Entire enterprise involvement, role and acceptance

---

91   Peter F. Drucker, The New Realities, 1989, Harper and Row publishers, first edition, page 261.
92   Smith, Dick ; Blakeslee, Jerry and Koonce, Richard; Strategic Six Sigma: Best Practices from the Executive Suite, John Wiley and Sons © 2002, Chapter 1.

- IT integration and facilitation
- Modifying behavior with incentives that Improve the Customer experience, Measure Business Success

Joint collaboration and agreement to direction and focus are critical to orchestrate the organization toward goals, objectives and Business Transformation. Maturation of corporations often leads the CXOs to the conclusion that not everyone is heading in the same direction. At this juncture, it is prudent to gather your stakeholders and reassess direction, priorities, external influencers, internal constraints, and reinvigorate the organization. The following diagram illustrates examples that might be identified for remediation.

Lean Six Sigma comes from a heritage of Quality Management and is a reflection of optimizing Lean and Six Sigma principles to benefit the client and their environment. From a Quality approach, Lean Six Sigma, melds well with Toyota Production System, Just In Time, and Lean Manufacturing environments. In addition, it also integrates easily in environments of Quality Management; Total Quality Management and Six Sigma methodologies had been utilized. In many cases, either exact tools or similar tools are utilized in Lean Six Sigma Processes that were previously used in other methodologies. The significant difference is the way those tools are applied in a structured environment in which they are applied. The benefits are real for the client. Being able to leverage prior experience and knowledge will be a springboard in the application and understanding of Lean Six Sigma methodology.

So how does this apply to the future? Lean Six Sigma provides Quality strategies that must be implemented in Marketing, Business, and IT models in order to reap benefits. Again, Lean Six Sigma provides a smoother transition from those disciplines considered to be an engineered approach. Lean Six Sigma provides integrated Process architecture to align those disciplines into a collaborative Lean Six Sigma solution that leverages strengths from each. An example of the success of integrating these two approaches, Quality versus engineered, was demonstrated within General Electric when CMMI complemented Lean Six Sigma and provided a synergistic effect that produce significant savings for that corporation.

Information Technology is becoming increasingly a critical part to most business solutions. The fundamental understanding is that technology supports the business and not the other way around. Therefore, this dictates using technology as a tool to speed up, automate or remove manual time consuming Processes. To incorporate IT's specialties, it must be integrated and address these typical Business-IT issues. That is especially true working higher levels of the Maturity model. Here are some comparison generalities from each approach:

Scope:
- CMMI is specifically designed for the software Design and development.
- DMAIC is a flexible Quality methodology that identifies variation and provides statistical Control.

Focus:
- CMMI is IT project specific and refers to all aspects of the software (Requirements, Design, Integration, Testing, Deployment, Maintenance).
- DMAIC is for a Lean Six Sigma project and focused on improving a Process.

Progress:
- CMMI Progress is assessed by the organizational "Maturity" or Process "capability" in contrast to goals and practices.
- DMAIC Progress is measured by financial measures, time, productivity, efficiency or effectiveness.

Length:
- CMMI varies with complexity, usually promoted to the next level in one to three years.

- DMAIC varies with complexity, projects will take six to eight weeks to complete. Remediation time may take eight or more months based on your Process improvement portfolio.

Process Transformation aligns with those strategies to ensure linkage to Quality and efficiency. Performance solutions provide the analytics for measuring the performance of the organization and the improvement based on standards, specifications and strategic targets. Last, the change engine that continues refinement and improvement is based on Transformation learning, recognizing the influences of the real world and those internal organizational changes and provides your company a means of digesting and adapting to those changing needs. Our services provide a methodology to answer these probing questions:

- Do you have efficient Processes that are aligned to your business strategies?
- Do you have robust Processes in place to incubate new product, Service and business model concepts?
- Are you monitoring the effectiveness of your business intelligence solutions?
- When Customer preferences shift, are you the first to understand and act on this, or do your competitors react more quickly?
- Are you integrating disparate data and Systems to gain new Customer insights?
- Are you Systematically evaluating potential geographic markets?
- Are your leaders thinking and acting globally?
- Are you watching other industries for concepts and business models that could transform your market?
- Do you have access to think tanks, emerging trends and out-of-the-box thinking to provide insight for your business?
- Have you gained insight from current green initiatives that can be applied to your broader corporate social responsibility strategy?

Mapping from your Strategies to your Strategic Processes is critical. Identify "gaps" and "disconnects" in strategies by assessing your Quality Strategies that provides Focus, Objectives, Process Alignment, and identifies areas of improvement in your Culture and Strategic Processes. Accomplish those objectives through best-in-class methodologies and sound state-of-the-art services to provide solutions that are tailored to fit your needs.

Implementation of a Continuous Improvement program (i.e., reducing defects, identifying savings, improving performance, etc.) is fundamental to the success and continuation of your championed Quality initiative. Continuous Improvement is an investment in your delivery of goods and services to achieve fulfillment to your "satisfied Customer" base. Don't lose your opportunities. Don't let them wither and fall through the "cracks" (in other words, don't repeat your mistakes). Institutionalize your "lessons learned."

IT Contribution: An internal opportunity for your Transformation initiative can originate in the relationship between Business and IT. IT integration and facilitation can produce synergistic Results in terms of Productivity, Savings and Quality Improvement. Due to the nature of the evolving IT technology and its potential impact on your internal Processes, Business and IT alignment around those technology drivers can enhance and produce a far-reaching strategies. The following suggestions are examples of how business and technology combined, provide breakthrough strategies that could propel your organization internally, by effective use of utilization of resources, or externally in terms of market value Realization:

- This may be a paradigm shift for Business and IT management, set expectations carefully
- IT should have an active role in business strategy planning
- IT-enabled Business Transformation Initiatives
- Collaboration model required - cannot be driven by IT or business exclusively
- IT needs to understand the business value for deliverables
- Plan tactically (minimize costs and resources), think strategically (automate prudently)

IT Drivers stem from the complexity of infrastructures, data storage requirements and specialized knowledge that is faced with ongoing decrease in value and increase in IT overhead.

Twenty years ago, a new field was born that soon came to be known as "enterprise architecture." The field initially began to address two problems:

- *System complexity*—Organizations were spending more and more money building IT Systems; and
- *Poor business alignment*—Organizations were finding it more and more difficult to keep those increasingly expensive IT Systems aligned with business need.

The bottom line: more cost, less value indicate major problems that need remediation. Examples of these problems include:

- IT Systems that have become unmanageably complex and increasingly costly to maintain.
- IT Systems that are hindering the organization's ability to respond to current, and future, market conditions in a timely and cost-effective manner.
- Mission-critical information that is consistently out-of-date and/or just plain wrong.
- A culture of distrust between the business and technology sides of the organization.[93]

Business Intelligence Trend Grows: Collaborative decision making began to emerge as a new Product category in the early 2000s. That data-driven niche was designed to be combined with existing and stand-alone business intelligence platforms. In 2009, the Gartner Group produced a paper that predicted that 2012 these developments in business intelligence market would emerge:

---

[93]   Sessions, Roger; A Comparison of the Top Four Enterprise-Architecture Methodologies, ObjectWatch, Inc., May 2007.

- Because of lack of information, Processes, and tools, through 2012, more than 35 percent of the top five thousand global companies will regularly fail to make insightful decisions about significant changes in their business and markets.
- By 2012, business units will Control at least 40 percent of the total budget for business intelligence.
- By 2012, one-third of analytic applications applied to business Processes will be delivered through coarse-grained application mashups.[94]

BI technologies provide historical, current, and predictive views of business operations. Common functions of Business Intelligence technologies are reporting, online analytical Processing, analytics, data mining, business performance management, benchmarking, text mining, and predictive analytics.[95]

Beginning with data, information is created that will better help you understand Processes and trends. Individually and collectively, you act on that information and build a base of knowledge that will be updated in subsequent cycles of review. Your insights and changes are recorded and provide new data and information that aligns to your business needs and achievement of goals. In order for this to become effective, as a management tool, several business intelligence strategies and techniques are applied to ensure conformity and consistency. Those business Processes include:

- Data integration:
- Information presentation:
- Standardized reporting:

While focusing on Process refinement, the flow of orders, resources, products and services that are supported and managed benefit from "fine-tuning." Often, improvements to the internal Business Processes

---

94   Gartner Study; "Gartner Reveals Five Business Intelligence Predictions for 2009 and Beyond," January 15, 2009, Retrieved: 24 May 2010.
95   Business Intelligence (BI), Wikipedia, May 2010.

produce bottom line results: Growth, Performance, and Savings. In many cases, external interfaces with vendor Processes can also obtain similar additional benefits. What are the warning signs that Processes are not supporting your organization or impeding the potential efficiencies that could benefit your organization? Here are a few examples:

- Benefits may not be realized in your current Processes
- Bottlenecks hamper services or production
- Progress that was anticipated does not materialize as planned
- A technical solution does not "fit" your environment or your Subject Matter Experts think this is the ONLY solution
- Empirical evidence does not exist or lacks prudent methodology to indicate that your Processes are not performing
- Your SMEs do not how to evaluate your Processes
- Your Processes are not aligned to your strategies

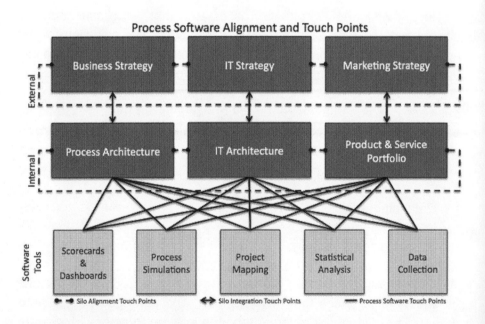

Process Software Alignment and Touch Points

Process Analysis Software: Historically, documentation for Process Improvement required large amounts of man-hours for manual recording a documentation. However, in recent decades, genres of software applications have emerged to address the need to develop and support Transformation Initiatives. These tools provide quicker electronic capabilities that can be easily stored in databases or kept as files for Business, IT and Marketing Processes. These tools present today's contemporary enterprise with tools that provide easy access to information, simulation, mapping and performance of internal and external Processes. These niche tools include:

- *Scorecards and Dashboards* - This form of management reporting often compares the current state Processes and performance to the objectives that are linked to strategic initiatives.
- *Process Simulation Software* - This genre software, provides online simulation of any Process Design, is often utilized in tandem with DFSS methodology to create new Processes based on limitation of variation and other Process requirements.
- *Project Mapping Software* - It is not unusual to discover that strategies are not linked to objectives, let alone Processes that are supposed to facilitate those strategies. That is the reason for the creation of mapping software. This tool maps each strategy to its objective, key Processes, and other resources and outlines the extent of each strategy which then can be Analyzed to better reflect effectiveness.
- *Statistical Analysis* - Many of these tools are either based on mainframe or PC platforms. Increase usage of statistical analysis has created pockets of useful data in many corporations, today. Based on the application of the statistics, their criteria will mandate that I am required data can be extracted from current Process activities. Effectively creating a Quality Dashboard could leverage the data came through the statistical formulation provide information meaningful to Executive Management.
- *Data Collection Tools* - In many cases, especially in corporations that have not used Quality management, data may be sent toward the calculation and verification Process performance, variation, and other Quality Measures. This will be a major critical factor that should be addressed at the beginning of another Process. Then

the collection tools, accumulation of data, storage of data tools to convert data into information will be the data collection objectives.

Alignment Drivers: Specific drivers found in separate layers of your business planning infrastructure, include:

Customer
• Direct impact of the Customer
• Corporate dependence on International Suppliers
• Recertification/rework of goods and services
• Reintroduction of defects, waste and variation
• Communication pitfalls (language, various English definitions, slang, lack of corporate lexicon, lack of industry vocabulary)

Financial
• Country risks (economic stability, exchange rates, crime levels, type of crimes - drug/weapon/terrorism/kidnapping)
• Home office to outsourced location - travel costs
• Retraining for policy and procedures
• Loss of Intellectual capital by theft
• Corporate espionage
• Obligation to create contingency and risk mitigation planning for outsourcing
• Expatriate costs to ensure Quality to products and service; policy and procedures; protect corporate assets

Internal
• Management long distance distractions impacts leader responsibilities
• Technology transfer without Control
• Technological differences (electricity stability, reliable communications, IT standards and protection could be jeopardized, data risk)
• Loss of possible strategic Processes and support Processes
• Communication pitfalls (language various English definitions, slang, lack of corporate lexicon, lack of industry vocabulary)

Learning

- Corporate staff will need to interface effectively in a global organization
- Understood trust between management and employees may be different culturally
- Knowledge, in-house, may be depleted in outsourcing project
- Knowledge levels and expertise (a degree in country X may not be comparable to US college degree, technical expertise by certification is critical, need for testing to validate skills)
- Cultural differences in the outsource host country may have castes Systems, ethnic cliques, or other societal divides that may be contentious
- Cultural differences (holidays, work ethic, work schedule different that your office, corporate rethink of timing and expectations, learn to approach topics with several examples - always validate understanding)

6.3: Supplier Alignment

Let us ask our Suppliers to come and help us to solve our problems.

~ W. Edwards Deming

Chapter Summary: Many times the Suppliers are left out of the Transformation initiatives, like Customers, these stakeholders are strategic and provide a wealth of information that can and often will Improve your efficiency and effectiveness. Take steps for Supplier Alignment and provide a gateway for that flow of Knowledge.

Key Points:
- Aligning Suppliers To Your Business Effort
- Quality Recognition
- From an Outsourcing View

Aligning Suppliers To Your Business Effort: In today's complex world, businesses are confronted with the complexity of the marketplace, as well as, the complexity within their own corporation. The marketplace has become sophisticated in terms of products and services and specific price points, capabilities, and specific applications within the Customers' domain. That includes recognizing that Suppliers are part of the solution and provide your enterprise with commercial opportunities.

Top sales and marketing executives in most corporations will focus on the needs of the Customer or client and perception of the products and services their Corporation creates for the marketplace and ultimately the final consumer. Quality is a key component of those perceived attributes. That perception is channeled through the Process from the marketplace through your organization and ultimately these Suppliers that provide you the raw material and services that differentiate your portfolio from your competitors.

Deming recognized; "It would be better if everyone would work together as a System, with the aim for everybody to win." Clearly, managers attempting Quality Improvement are in some way not fully prepared to go the distance. Any Quality Management visionary needs to fully understand that Business Transformation, based on Lean Six Sigma, is a holistic approach that affects everyone in the organization from end-to-end perspectives. That includes all of your Suppliers of material and services that fulfills your Customers needs. Business Transformation is a long-term commitment that must incorporate Quality strategies, Process Transformation, Quality Evaluation through effective management tools, and implementing a Continuous Improvement process.

In addition, this information can be used to work with Customers and Suppliers to improve their connected processes. Examples of the statistics are the generation of measures on how quickly a Customer order is processed or how many orders were processed in the last month. Traditionally, these measures tend to fit into three categories: cycle time, defect rate and productivity. However, other consideration for developing the Supplier relationship should also consider:

- Lower Cost of Ownership
- Just-In-Time delivery
- High-Quality supply
- New ideas from Suppliers
- Supplier partnerships
- Outsource mature nonstrategic services[96]

---

96   Robert S. Kaplan and David P. Norton, Strategy Maps, Harvard Business School Press, 2004, page 67.

Quality Recognition: Customers recognize that Quality is an important attribute in products and services. Suppliers recognize that Quality can be an important differentiator between their own offerings and those of competitors (Quality differentiation is also called the Quality gap). In the past two decades this Quality gap has been greatly reduced between competitive products and services. This is partly due to the contracting (also called outsourcing) of manufacture to countries like India and China, as well internationalization of trade and competition... Ensure rapid information exchange among manufacturers, Customers, and Suppliers.[97]

"Quality" in a Product or Service with the Supplier puts in. It is what the Customer gets out and is willing to pay for. The Product is not "Quality" because it's hard to make and costs a lot of money, as manufacturers typically believe. That is incompetence. Customers pay only for what is of use to them and gives them value. Nothing else constitutes "Quality."[98] So, where does the Business Transformation begin and where does it end? That depends on whether your Transformation is focused on products, services or both. Look at these examples:

Product-Oriented Transformation
- Client need, client incentive
- Advertising and Marketing
- Web interface
- Brick and Mortar
- Intermediary (Delivery, Warehousing, Distribution Channels, etc.)
- Manufacturing of product
- Product Design
- Suppliers

Service-Oriented Transformation
- Client need, client incentive

---

97   Ghosh, Shantanu and Singh, Monty; The Role of Six Sigma in Outsourced F and A Services; Multi-Process FAO; Magazine Issue: Vol. 3 No. 6 - November 2006/ December 2006; Retrieved: 1 March 2010.
98   Drucker, Ibid, The essential Drucker. Page 172.

- Advertising and Marketing
- Web interface
- Brick and Mortar
- Intermediary (Delivery, Warehousing, Distribution Channels, etc.)
- Manufacturing of Service
- Service Design
- Suppliers

From an Outsourcing View: Look at how Six Sigma discipline can help transform real-life buyers. The Outsourcing contract management team has a "reporting relationship" to the procurement department of the Client firm. As outsourcing Service providers implement multiple Six-Sigma projects across F and A Processes, they deliver business impact to their Customers, some of which include:

- Increasing controllership through Process control, including Sarbanes-Oxley (SOX) compliance;
- Improving Service levels for both internal and external Customers;
- Reducing accounts receivables that can cut funding costs; and
- Timely accounts payable to reduce uncertainty premiums charged by Suppliers.

7.0: Opt for Change

Some painters transform the sun into a yellow spot, others transform a yellow spot into the sun.

 ~ Pablo Picasso

Chapter Summary: Choose wisely and follow a comprehensive and holistic approach that will recognize the Strategies, Process Improvement, Measure progress, develop a Continual Improvement Process, and promote Learning.

Key Points:

- Testimonial for Sustainability
- Sustainability
- Sustainability Transformation
- Corporate Sustainability Examples
- Create Your Quality Ecosystem!
- Quality Transformation
- Commercial Change Drivers
- Crossover Benefits
- Lean Approach
- Six Sigma
- Why Business Alignment?
- Internal Drivers for Change
- Your Decision

With globalization of goods and services, commodity-like pricing will prevail in the global economy. When producing those

consumables, the most significant factor is Quality combined with an effective Sustainability initiative. Reduction in costs will be a strategic tool to be applied in the marketplace in the twenty-first century. Remember:

Survivability = Sustainability + Quality + Continuous Improvement

Or

S! = S + Q + CI

Where; S! = Survivability, S = Sustainability, Q = Quality, CI = Continuous Improvement

Testimonial for Sustainability: Ten years ago this April, struggling under a mountain of debt after deciding to remain independent, Clif Bar and Company made a commitment to Sustainability. At a point when some predicted Clif Bar and Company would disappear in six months, the company proved that going green could get them out of the red.

Starting with a focus on food and agriculture, that environmental commitment grew into a larger business model that moves beyond a triple bottom line to encompass Five Aspirations: Sustaining its Business, its Brands, its People, its Community and the Planet.

"We hope others can learn from our experience, that bringing Sustainability into all parts of the business does not need to be predicated on profitability," said Gary Erickson, Clif Bar and Company founder and co-CEO. "Even amid tough times, we had a bigger vision for the kind of company we wanted to be and the impact we wanted to have on the world around us."

"The foundation of our journey toward Sustainability was our commitment to organic food and farming," said Hammond. "Agriculture has one of the biggest environmental impacts on the planet, profoundly affecting water, wildlife, climate and people's health on a daily basis."

223

In 2010 alone, Clif Bar and Company purchased more than 40 million pounds of organic ingredients—a 25 percent jump over 2009. That increase outpaces the growth in overall organic food sales by a ratio of 5-to-1.1

In 2010, the company helped build the Greensburg Wind Farm project, enabling a Kansas community to rebuild green following a devastating tornado. The Greensburg Wind Farm is now delivering electricity to the regional grid in Kansas and surrounding states. It was recently named "Wind Project of the Year" by RenewableEnergyWorld.com, a leading energy publication, for its community benefits and unique financing model.[99]

Buckminster Fuller was an early environmental activist. In the mid-1960s, he coined the word "spaceship earth" and was keenly aware of the finite resources the planet has to offer. He promoted a principle, "doing more with less." His premise was founded on the concept of resources and waste material from cruder products could be recycled into making more valuable products, increasing the efficiency of the entire Process. Today, this is the underlying foundation of Sustainability initiatives around the globe.

The Brundtland Commission was convened by the United Nations in 1983. The commission was created to address growing concern of "to propose long-term environmental strategies for achieving sustainable development to the year 2000 and beyond" in context "to recommend ways in which concern for the environment may be translated into greater cooperation among developing countries and between countries at different stages of economic and social development and lead to the achievement of common and mutually supportive objectives which take account of the interrelationships between people, resources, environment and development." The concept of Sustainability was coin to

---

99   Sue Hearn, PR Director, Clif Bar and Company Celebrates Decade of Sustainability Progress, April 4, 2011, San Fransicso Chronicle, www.sfgate.com, Retrieved: 8 April 2011

identify "forms of progress that meet the needs of the present without compromising the ability of future generations to meet their needs."

Over the past thirty years, the concept of Sustainability has evolved to reflect perspectives of both the public and private sectors. A public policy view would define Sustainability as the satisfaction of basic economic, social, and security needs now and in the future without undermining the natural resource base and environmental Quality on which life depends. From a business perspective, the goal of Sustainability is to increase long-term shareholder and social value, while decreasing industry's use of materials and reducing negative impacts on the environment.[100]

Sustainability: Social responsibility was a key phase in the 1960s, but waned at the end of twentieth century. Many of those themes continue in the form of Sustainability, but for more holistic reasons: Economical, Environmental and Social. Sustainability is the balancing of the economic, environmental, and social demands in the current state and ensuring the future world government policies do not compromise our future growth. The traditional definition of Sustainability calls for policies and strategies that meet society's present needs without compromising the ability of future generations to meet their own needs.

In a recent study generated 18 April 2011, by KPMG and the Economists Intelligence Unit, globally Sustainability strategies are on the rise; however, the US is lagging behind the competition. Big companies are much more likely to have such strategies: 79 percent of public companies with revenues over $1 billion said they had all-encompassing strategies for corporate Sustainability, compared to 49 percent of private companies with revenues under $500 million.

The study found that creating or finding reliable internal data was the most often cited hurdle in Sustainability reporting, with 78 percent

100   US Environmental Protection Agency, www.epa.gov/sustainability/basicinfo. htm, Last updated on 03/02/2011, Retrieved: 31 March 2011.

saying it was a moderate or major challenge. Meeting the reporting requirements of a variety of stakeholders, and determining meaningful benchmarks for peer-to-peer comparisons, were both cited as moderate or major challenges by 73 percent. Determining what to report on was cited by 65 percent.

Asked to identify the top three benefits from their Sustainability program, the respondents most often chose: better or more efficient business Processes and practices, increased profitability or shareholder value, and the ability to attract or retain new or existing Customers. US executives identified the key business drivers of Sustainability-related business objectives as enhancing brand reputation (37 percent), regulatory or legal compliance (35 percent), reducing costs (34 percent), Product or Service differentiation (24 percent), and increasing profitability and managing Sustainability risks (both 23 percent).[101]

Is there another significant factor for Sustainability? Yes, it is part of measuring the current success of major US corporations. What Does Dow Jones Sustainability North America Index Mean? It is a stock index that captures the top 20 percent of the largest six hundred companies in the Dow Jones Global Index that are based in North America. Companies are evaluated based on both general and industry-specific Sustainability trends by Zurich-based SAM Group, a research firm that surveys thousands of global blue-chip companies each year.[102]

Some key findings from a 2011 survey includes:
- Almost nine in ten (88 percent) experts believe that improving Sustainability performance leads to a stronger brand; only two percent of experts disagree.
- Just over half (55 percent) of experts say that integrating Sustainability into a company's brand image Results in improved Sustainability

101   KPMG and Economist Intelligence Unit, April 2011, Sustainability Strategies On Rise, But Fewer In US, 18 April 2011, www.environmentalleader.com, retrieved 18 April 2011.
102   "Dow Jones Sustainability North America Index"; Investopedia, www.investopedia.com, Retrieved: 31 March 2011.

performance, while two in ten (19 percent) disagree. Corporate experts are more convinced that integrating Sustainability into a company's brand image improves its Sustainability performance.

- Almost three-quarters of experts (73 percent) believe that there will be a great deal more Sustainable Brand Initiatives from companies in the coming year.[103]

Sustainability Transformation =
Economical + Environmental + Social + Technological

Or

$$ST = E_1 + E_2 + S + T$$

Where; ST = Sustainability Transformation, E_1 = Economical, E_2 = Environmental, S = Social, T = Technological

Sustainable Transformation: Today's complex and interwoven environment can, at times, appear chaotic. An increasing number of Owners and Executives are recognizing the importance of formulating complex Transformation strategies into a concise model supported by best practices. This construct also analyzes the benefits of transforming your currently external influences that affect your survivability. Components include:

- *Executive Commitment and Conceptualization* – Support and commitment is the most crucial step in the Transformation initiative. For it is long-term in nature, morphs your culture into an empowered performance organization, it is based on improving your business modes and to efficiently anticipate costly resources.
- *Corporate and Business Unit Strategy* – Planning is the effort and commitment of resources to produce a plan for growth, market

103   GlobeScan SustainAbility, June 8, 2010; "Improving Sustainability Performance Is Key to Enhancing Corporate Brand Image, According to Experts," www.globescan.com; Retrieved: 31 March 2011.

gains, technical effectiveness and increased returns to the shareholders, based on business Integrity, Product and Service Quality, and satisfying the needs of their Customer.

- *Sustainability Initiative* – Based on your long-term strategies for success and growth, this initiative formerly engages your resources into Transformation of business practices that will mold current policy and procedures into a reformed "to be" business environment.
- *Sustainability Transformation* – The engagement of effective solutions that will benefit the long-term and short-term needs of the enterprise on economic, environmental or social aspects.
- *Sustainability Evaluation* – Measurement of resources and other aggregate components that constitute your actual changes in your environment. This is the effectiveness measurement of the initiative.
- *Realization of Tangible Benefits* – Resources, cycle times, costs, growth and other improvement will affect your resources, Processes, and other benefits that can be quantified, especially in terms of money.
- *Long-Term Corporate Financial Performance* – Sharing of information to shareholders, indicated in a statement, that displays measurements of actual Results of an entity's activity over some time period.

Corporate Sustainability Examples: The Business Roundtable recently published "Innovating Sustainability 2011 Report". The Business Roundtable is an association of leading US CEOs that generate $6 trillion in revenue and employ over 13 million people. The following examples indicate their Executive Commitment:

Healthcare – McKesson: McKesson has existed for more than 178 years. So, Sustainability goes hand-in-hand with their goal of building healthier organization that delivers better care to patients. They owe their success to by accuracy, efficiency and continual improvement. With web based analytics technology, they are able to minimize carbon dioxide emissions and related distribution costs. Through data center consolidation, they have reduced annual energy consumption by more than 1.58 million kilowatt hours and reduced carbon dioxide emissions by 1,160 metric tons.

Information Technology – IBM: In 2011, IBM's Sustainability strategies are a reflection of societal, and environmental objectives that are fused into IBM's business approach. That focus is centered on four segments: energy-efficient buildings, next-generation data centers, Smarter Cities, and Smarter Computing.

Insurance – The Hartford Financial Group: the Hartford is celebrating their 200th birthday in 2010. The company has implemented innovation Sustainability strategies that have reduced greenhouse gas emissions, brought "green" products to the market, adopted an environmental investment policy and invested in electric vehicle technology. It has committed to reducing greenhouse as emissions by 15 percent from 2007 to 2017. Hartford's most recent building was built to LEED Silver standard. Since 2009, they have saved a billion sheets of paper from their usage in 2009. They are also the first company to cover electric vehicle charging stations under its homeowner policies.

Manufacturing – Motorola: Has successfully reduced their carbon footprint by 35 percent and their energy use by 28 percent since 2005. They have also increased their purchase of renewable energy by 21 percent worldwide. In addition, Motorola has incorporated their Sustainability strategies into existing business strategies to apply their technologies to reduce Customers run supply chains, logistics and energy grids more efficiently.

Service – Accenture: Skills to Succeed is a strategy to equip 250,000 people globally by 2015. Accenture is also using their Telepresence services to provide 60 international locations to avoid more than 10,000 tons of carbon dioxide from air travel. They have also extended the scope of current strategies to recognize Sustainability, like their global supply chain that reviews the environmental, social, and ethical performance of key suppliers.

Transportation – Union Pacific: Union Pacific has almost reached its 150 anniversary and prides itself owning core resources to connect a nation. In 2010 alone, it reduced diesel fuel by 27 million gallons that improved fuel efficiency by 3 percent. During that time, it increased gross ton freight miles by 8 percent, while reducing fuel emissions. Compared to 2009, it delivered 13 percent more carloads per day while using only 8 percent more train miles.

Create Your Quality Ecosystem! What is a Quality Ecosystem? It is a holistic, end-to-end approach, integrated into your enterprise to create Quality and Excellence. For the past two decades Lean Six Sigma capabilities have been the strategic tool of choice for visibility, Customer relations, refinement, development and institutionalizing Quality. It addresses your most important need to satisfy your Customers. It recognizes your Business Influencers and mitigates their impact. It uses Customer Satisfaction as a Measure of improving that relationship between your company and the marketplace. It considers all Resources, Sales and Profitability to be calculated by Return on Assets, as well as Return on Investment. As your methodology of choice to develop a better enterprise environment, using Lean Six Sigma, your Quality Ecosystem will include:

- Customer focused to meet or exceed needs and expectations for products or services
- Customer Satisfaction is focused on serving the Customer, meeting the needs and fulfillment of products and services in a timely manner
- Business Influencers are recognized and mitigated risks
- Quality Strategies and Initiatives are integrated into existing strategies
- Integration of Lean Six techniques are facilitated and implemented in each business model
- All Process are reviewed, assessed and prioritized
- Specific processes are remediated and conform to business requirements

- Continuous Improvement is implemented to created your ongoing Change Engine
- Quality Evaluation begins with captured data and provides information for effective decision making

Financial stress makes aggressive investment difficult or impossible, but today's financial stress originates in the underinvestment of the past. If you look closely, you also see eroding or declining Quality standards. (by Quality we mean all things that matter to a Customer, such as Product Quality, Service Quality, and delivered reliability). Standards erode, or fail to continually advance with competition, which results in the failure to invest in building capacity to serve Customer needs. Disgruntled Customers then go elsewhere.[104]

Lean Six Sigma enables the enterprise to eliminate waste, defects, and Improve overall Quality when deployed properly. To ensure Quality and keep Customers satisfied, companies also need ways to understand and address the causes of variability. This is Six Sigma's domain. Lean principles help eliminate waste, Six Sigma principles help to institutionalize Quality improvements by continuously identifying the causes of process defects that adversely impact productivity.

A Transformation to a performance-enhancing culture begins in a few short months, that the magnitude of the change that is initiated, the complexity of the organization and the strategic Quality commitment are all factors in determining the length and effort of the major cultural change. Studies indicate that substantial benefits can be generated in terms of revenue growth, employment growth, stock price growth, and net income growth. This is based on the basis of low performance corporate cultures versus performance enhancing cultures. Lean Six Sigma can be a catalyst in your organizational change to a high performance culture.

---

104   Senge, Peter M.; The Fifth Discipline: The Art and Practice of the Learning Organization; Published by Doubleday, 2006; pg. 123.

- A new vision for Quality, performance and growth.
- Managerial actions to restart your systems, policies, business models, communication, and other criteria by which people are recruited and promoted.
- Actions that create a new behavior in the organization.
- Define success and major league behavior and actions to achieve that goal.
- Do not destroy your corporate culture; rather change the norms to fit the new vision and new strategies through shared values and corporate mind-set.

Quality Transformation = Lean + Six Sigma

Or

QT = L + SS
Where; QT = Quality Transformation, L = Lean, SS = Six Sigma

Quality Transformation: "The economists' assumption that long-range, wealth-producing capacity automatically Results from maximizing a large number of short-range consumer benefits carries little intellectual conviction in an era of rapid change and innovation." Drucker was a visionary who clearly understood that "change and innovation" would be continual sources of influence on the free enterprise System, especially with respect to the corporation.[105]

Nancy F. Koehn, an entrepreneurial historian at the Harvard Business School, said Owners commonly look to boost their bottom line by laying off staff. But this isn't always a wise a strategy because it can mean losing out on opportunities to Service new Customers. She warned; "If demand picks up, you can't exploit it because you don't have the resources. It's a really big risk."

---

105   Drucker, Peter F. ; The New Realities, first edition, Harper and Row publishers, 1989, page 170

In general terms, your Transformation could produce major cultural shifts that promote a "performance" and "Quality" based culture that better manages your Customer relationships, decrease costs, encourage "openness without judgment" and promote "lean" concepts while removing variation in your Processes. All of these attributes contribute to:

- Establish a Transformation framework that provides discipline to focus effort on the Transformation you want in your future state.
- Refresh and communicate your Transformation strategy and rely on the "golden thread" to map individual effort to your strategy.
- Cascade and manage strategy and utilize your Balance Scorecard and Dashboards as "early warning Systems," rather than "report cards"
- Improve performance and instill Quality through Lean Six Sigma.
- Manage and leverage your Profound Knowledge.

Drucker said, "The purpose of business is to create and keep a Customer." The Customer is the most important stakeholder in any business model. Without recognizing their importance, you ensure failure. The need of the Customer drives your Sales and Innovation. Timely fulfillment and available of Quality products and services are linchpins to your success. So, the marketplace, your Customer needs, and your organization are major considerations in your Business Transformation approach.

Other research regarding intrinsic value of products and services, by Miles and Snow in 1978, suggested that value comes from choosing Customers and narrowing the operation focus to best serve that market segment; Customer Satisfaction and Loyalty does not, by themselves, create unmatched value. Imagine how Lean Six Sigma can affect fundamental elements of economic and noneconomic characteristics to your Products or Services:

Economic
- Performance *
- Reliability *
- Technology *
- Price *

Noneconomic
- Brand Name
- Styling
- Packaging *
- Appearance

* Areas where Lean Six Sigma methodology can be applied to enhance your products or services.

To illustrate that importance, one recent survey across a large number of manufacturing and services organizations found that the Customers' needs are literally the driving force for change and opportunity. Those responses were ranked in decreasing order of popularity that systematic programs of organizational innovation are most frequently driven by:

- Improved Quality *
- Creation Of New Markets
- Extension Of The Product Range
- Reduced Labor Costs *
- Improved Production Processes *
- Reduced Materials *
- Reduced Environmental Damage *
- Replacement Of Products/Services *
- Reduced Energy Consumption *
- Conformance To Regulations *

* Areas where Lean Six Sigma methodology can be applied to enhance your products or services.

The first, a Customer-led philosophy, is primarily concerned with satisfying Customers' expressed needs, and is typically short term in focus and reactive in nature. The second, a market-oriented philosophy, goes beyond satisfying expressed needs to understanding and satisfying Customers' latent needs and, thus, is longer term in focus and proactive in nature. Based on theory and substantial evidence, the advice to become market-oriented appears sound regardless of the market conditions a business faces.[106]

To ensure a better understanding of your Customer base, gather critical information to further build that relationship, but be sensitive to their privacy. Extraction of germane data elements is critical to retain Customers or entices Prospects to your Product or Service value proposition; however, do not tread on areas that would cause a backlash to your efforts. Take a second look of the Customers' wants and your Company needs:

Commercial Change Drivers: Previously, ten external scenarios or a combination of scenarios that could drive Business Transformation were discussed. Now, consider your options and implications of each as we discuss your next steps.

* Sales Decline
* Management Buyout
* Takeover
* Lack of Internal Skills
* Family Business 'Turmoil'
* Raise Capital
* Exit Strategy
* Delegation or Renegade Action
* Project Based Change
* Third Party Intervention

---

106   Bower, Joseph L., and Clayton M. Christensen. "Disruptive Technologies: Catching the Wave." In *Seeing Differently: Insights on Innovation*, edited by John Seely Brown. Boston, Mass.: Harvard Business School Press, 1997.

Crossover Benefits: Deployment of Lean and Six Sigma methodology along with a Sustainability Transformation initiative by definition should end up in creating a sustainable competitive advantage. In most cases they transform themselves into a high performance organization with a clear direction and execution strategy, ultimately benefiting all stake-holders in the value chain. Organizations taking up Transformation initiatives tune themselves better to an existing market or create a new market. Internally they promote cross-organizational and functional Process improvements by introduction of new processes and automation for optimal performance and operational excellence. Tools to bring to Business Transformation:

- Quality Predecessors and Foundations
- Lean Development
- Six Sigma Development and Innovation
- Process Portfolio, Cataloguing and Simulation[107]

What Customers Want From Companies: Most Customers want a positive experience that is uplifting and hassle free and the purchase of a Product or service, that is easily available, that provides Quality at a reasonable price point, it has a reliable after-purchase Service that easily resolves issues and encourages a relationship with the Customer. The following points also provide the Customers' insight:

- We want companies not to have extensive personal information about us.
- We would be willing to tell some companies what we might like to be informed about.
- We would want companies to reach us only with relevant messages and media at proper times.

---

107   Infosys, "Defining Business Transformation," Hema Prem and George Eby Mathew, May 2006.

- We would want to be able to reach companies easily by phone or e-mail and get a quick response.[108]

What Companies Want From Customers: Companies devour tremendous amounts of information and data to reflect the needs of their Customers. Attention to Products, Processes, and Services relating to their attributes and expectations from their Customers is a significant input to refining and addressing Customer needs. Companies need to walk a fine line between invasive techniques versus Customer privacy. From a company perspective, the following items are often incentives are collecting data:

- We want to know many things about each Customer and prospect.
- We would like to tempt them with offers, including those that they might not have awareness of or initial interest in.
- We would like to reach them in the most cost-effective way regardless of their media preferences.
- We want to reduce the cost of talking with them live on the phone.[109]

What is your Customer's focus? Research, completed by Christensen and Bower in 1996, suggests how Customer power contributes to the failure of leading firms when an industry experiences dramatic changes due to technology, innovation, natural disasters, limiting resources or new trade regulations. In a Customer-led philosophy, is primarily concerned with satisfying Customers' expressed needs, and is typically short term in focus and reactive in nature. Secondly, a market-oriented philosophy, goes beyond satisfying expressed needs to understanding and satisfying Customers' needs; therefore, is longer term in focus and proactive in nature.

---

108   Kottler, Philip; Database Marketing - Marketing Insights from A to Z: 80 Concepts Every Manager Needs to Know; John Wiley and Sons, 2003.
109   Kottler, Philip; Database Marketing - Marketing Insights from A to Z: 80 Concepts Every Manager Needs to Know; John Wiley and Sons, 2003

Companies need to monitor and improve the level of Customer Satisfaction. The higher the Customer Satisfaction is, the higher the retention will be. Here are four facts:

- Acquiring new Customers can cost five to ten times more than the costs involved in satisfying and retaining current Customers.
- The average company loses between 10 and 30 percent of its Customers each year.
- A 5 percent reduction in the Customer defection rate can increase profits by 25 to 85 percent, depending on the industry.
- The Customer profit rate tends to increase over the life of the retained Customer.[110]

Customers are an ongoing and changing relationship. Needs change. Pricing and availability affects the Customer decision-making process. Perceptions manifest into the Customers' value for your products and services. "If you look at Customers in this or a related way, you are likely to take a new view of hiring, training, compensating, and spending on tools to aid the Customer-serving process."[111]

Lean Approach: "Lean manufacturing is a management philosophy that pursues the continuous elimination of waste in all business processes, also known as small and incremental improvement." This sounds familiar with this common definition. Lean's Focus is in these three major areas:

- Efficiency
- Speed
- Flexibility

It is certainly accurate, but we often find that the specific benefits that Lean will have on individual processes and eventually entire companies

---

110   Reichheld, Frederick; *The Loyalty Effect: The Hidden Force Behind Growth, Profits, and Lasting Value*, Boston: Harvard Business School Press, 1996
111   Peters, Tom; "Thriving on Chaos," Alfred A. Knopf, Inc, 1987, page 99

are seldom discussed. Lean is adept and fundamentally addresses these Major Benefits:

- Waste Elimination
- Flow and Pull
- Value Stream

It makes sense that the elimination of waste will result in more efficient operations, but we should consider what are the key enablers:

- *Specify Value* – Value is defined by the ultimate Customers' needs through tools such as value management, Quality function deployment and simulation.
- *Identify and Map the Value Stream* – The value stream identifies all those steps required to make a product. Identifying value stream, the way value is realized, establishes when and how decisions are to be made. The key technique behind value stream is Process mapping for a very specific reason: that of understanding how value is built into the building Product from client's point of view.
- *Flows* – Flows are characterized by time, cost, and value. Resources (labor, material, and construction equipment) and information flows are the basic units of analysis.
- *Pull* – At a strategic level, pull identifies the real need to deliver the Product to the Customer as soon as he or she needs it.
- *Perfection* – To achieve perfection means constantly considering what is being done; how it is being done and harnessing the expertise and knowledge of all those involved in the Processes to improve and change it. With Continuous Improvement done and with waste eliminated along the flow process, perfection is the ultimate sweet reward that companies can achieve.

Lean Quality Management targets eight key areas of waste/defects:

- Eliminates defects
- Reduces inventory
- Reduces labor

239

- Eliminates overproduction
- Reduces space requirements
- Reduces transportation costs
- Eliminates unnecessary human motion
- Eliminates unneeded energy consumption

Six Sigma: Six Sigma is a high-performance management system for executing business strategy. The Six Sigma Management System drives clarity around the business strategy and the metrics that most reflect success with that strategy. It provides the framework to prioritize resources for projects that will improve the metrics, and it leverages leaders who will manage the efforts for rapid, sustainable, and improved business results. Specifically, Six Sigma is a high value approach that focuses on these Major Benefits:

- Variation Elimination
- Statistic Tools
- Reduced Complexity[112]

Additionally, Six Sigma is also a top-down solution to help organizations:

- Effectiveness: Align their business strategy to critical improvement efforts
- Precision: Mobilize teams to attack high impact projects
- Accuracy: Accelerate improved business results
- Visibility: Govern efforts to ensure improvements are sustained.

The following five areas should be Measured to show Dollar benefits:

- *Time* – Practitioners should Measure personnel time needed for a Process before and after improvement. The net savings in time, multiplied by the hourly pay rate for personnel, can count as savings each time the Process is executed. If the Process occurs thousands

---

112   Motorola University; Copyright 1994-2005 Motorola, Inc., http://www.motoro-la.com/Business/US-EN/Motorola+University; Retrieved: 12 September 2010.

of times a month or year, even small savings, if statistically verified, can lead to big benefits.

- *People* – If a new or improved Process needs one person rather than two, or 10, then practitioners can claim those annual wages as project benefits. The people may be transferred elsewhere in the company, but for the Process being improved, they are no longer needed.
- *Inventory* – If a project leads to reductions in inventory, practitioners can claim a one-time benefit, plus the amount saved annually by not carrying that inventory.
- *Errors* – Improving the Quality of a Process will likely lead to a reduction in Customer-reported errors, such as products malfunctioning while under warranty. Practitioners can include in the benefits the cost per error multiplied by the annual amount of reduced errors.
- *Revenue* – If the project leads to a new Product or service, or new sales, practitioners can Measure that revenue and claim it in project benefits.[113]

Why Business Alignment? A methodology is only as good as the people using the methodology. If there is no consensus to your Business Transformation, then a three-legged stool will not stand on one or two legs. It must use all three legs to make it functional, resilient and practical. The CEO and CIO should perform a realistic assessment of the relationship between Business and the internal IT organization. If the relationship does not foster effective collaboration or there is a known alignment challenge then an iterative approach should be considered. Business Benefits from an engaged IT organization will manifest potential growth areas, for example:

- Enabling your IT organization to grow beyond its role as a technology Service provider into a full-fledged business partner
- Higher ROI through innovative and creative concepts delivered by our expert consultants

---

113   Carey, Bryan; "Measuring Six Sigma Financial and Operational Benefits"; isixisgma; http://www.isixsigma.com/; Retrieved: 28 Sep 2010.

- Better operational performance by optimizing business processes based on best practices and enhancing Process governance
- Lower Total Cost of Ownership and more funds for innovation by enhancing your IT strategy and landscape and effectively managing your IT investment

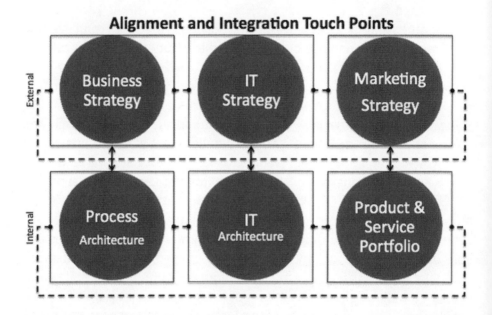

A growing trend in software development is centered around specific applications that produce various artifacts for Process Management and Business Transformation needs. Visualization of effort and tangible benefits are reported on Scorecards and Dashboards. Process documentation and simulation are currently available to support your enterprise needs. In addition, project mapping tools are of currently available to map strategies, objectives to processes. Other statistical tools and data collection technology is also available, currently.

The benefit of this type of technology is focused on the effectiveness of your organization, creating a library source that can be re-utilized, and provide management with ease of access to detailed information. In the not-too-distant future, the software landscape will continue to grow and address these needs in addition to others. It would be wise to keep abreast of technological development in these periods to gain information and knowledge about your enterprise, as well as, have tools that better manage minutia.

Internal Drivers for Change: Most proactive companies elect Business Transformation based on internal issues or external influences that affect the performance of the concern. In today's rapidly changing world, combined with technological catalysts on business information and decision making, once slow business changes are increasing in number and speed.

When grouped by common categories (i.e., Customer, Financial, Internal, Learning, and Transformation) these issues demonstrate contemporary impact across the organization. Application of Lean Six Sigma to these change agents will often remediate their risk and provide benefits in various areas of risk mitigation, cost reduction, asset utilization, and Quality enhancement. In this example, there are various reasons for changing an organization through various methods seeking to realize benefits or lower costs:

Customer
- *Enhanced Innovation* – in this situation, companies who use external knowledge services to provide our supplement limited in-house capacity for Product innovation.
- *Reduce Time-To-Market* – this scenario is based on acceleration of the development are the production of a Product through additional capabilities brought to a Buyer and Supplier.
- *Commoditization* – in today's world of outsourcing there is a trend to standardize business processes, IT processes and services, any application services, which enable to buy at the rise prop, right price that were only thought of available to very large corporations. In today's Internet environment those barriers have declined and price points are available for small and medium-size companies as well.

Financial
- *Cost Savings* – the overall objective of corporation is to lower costs of services to the business. This often involves reducing the scope definition of Quality levels, repricing, not cost restructuring, and renegotiating service-level agreements.
- *Focus The Core Business* – in this situation resources are focused on developing the core business. For example often an organization is outsources their IT support an organization the Spanish specialize on specific IT companies.
- *Cost Restructuring* – often this is the operating leverage to Measure comparable fixed assets and verbal costs across industry. Outsourcing changes the balance of this ratio and offering to move from a fix to a verbal cost in making the cost more predictable.
- *Risk Management* – this is an approach where cost may be mitigated but also risks when outsourcing a large staff. This approach to risk mitigation is shared with the outsourcer in order to reduce or eliminate identified risks.
- *Tax Benefit* – internationally many countries offer tax incentives to move manufacturing operations. This is a temp to counter high corporate taxes within another country.

Internal
- *Improve Quality* – this is achieved in this state change in Quality through contracting out specific services with the new service-level agreement. In this case a direct Service it may be rebuilt to your Customer is negotiated at your originating vendor to improve the Quality of services.
- *Contract* –services will be provided to a publicly binding contract with financial penalties and legal course of action. This is not the case with internal services.
- *Operational Expertise* – this provides access to operational best practices would be too difficult or time consuming to develop in-house. This may be special knowledge or experience that is not in your current organizational structure.

- *Capacity Management* – this is a circumstance where the risk in providing the excess capacity is born on the Supplier and a method of improving capacity management and services through technology.
- *Catalyst For Change* – and organization can use this outsourcing agreement as a catalyst for major step back and that can change the complexion of the organization that cannot be achieved by itself. In this instance the outsourcer becomes a change agent in the process.

Learning and Transformation
- *Knowledge* – this is another area where information, knowledge, can be accessed and package as intellectual property in a wider experience and knowledge for the Customer.

Your Decision: Any corporation can choose only a Sustainability Initiative and improve. Any corporation can choose only a Quality Initiative and improve. Only by combining those two initiatives will you minimize organizational disruption, provide maximum benefits, and implement within the shortest time line and at a lower total investment level. What do you think your shareholders will think? Then, consider this simple formula:

Survivability = Sustainability + Quality + Continuous Improvement

Any Questions?

Appendix: DMAIC Descriptions

Define: In the Define phase, a team clearly identifies the suppliers, process inputs, process activities, process outputs, and Customers; establishes baselines and benchmarks; and sets and agrees upon goals and measures of success.

Focus: The first phase in the DMAIC process is to define the project, develop an improvement project plan, define the process, and evaluate progress. The process includes the following steps:

- Establish purpose and scope for the improvement project.
- Develop improvement project plan, including schedule and resources.
- Develop process map, including key elements and boundaries.
- Conduct a failure modes and effects analysis (FMEA).
- Identify critical parameters.

During the Define phase, a team and its sponsors reach agreement on what the project is and what it should accomplish. Presuming that a draft of the Project Charter is already in place, the main work in the Define phase is for the project team to complete an analysis of what the project should accomplish and confirm understanding with the sponsor(s).

Deliverables: Having identified the improvement project to be carried out, the project needs to be established by carrying out the activities that identifies purpose, problem[s], charter with stakeholders, Voice of the Customer and the accompanying analysis that will be included.

Mission Statement - An understanding of the project's link to corporate objectives, this statement must describe what is going to be done about the problem, i.e., the objective of the improvement project. The mission statement should contain the same variable and unit of measure as does the problem statement.

Problem Statement & Scope - An understanding of the project's link to corporate problem, this statement must describe the problem in specific terms that identify: what is wrong; what is the visible evidence of the problem – the symptoms; how serious is the problem, expressed in quantifiable and measurable terms; how large is the problem – can it be addressed by a single, manageable size improvement project or will it need to be sub-divided into several smaller, manageable projects.

Project Charter - A clear statement of the intended improvement, this statement describes the stakeholders, roles, responsibilities and identifies those items in a grid that is based on identifiable RASIC roles.

Voice of the Customer - A list of what is important to the Customer (VOC). This data is used to identify the quality attributes needed for a supplied component or material to incorporate in the process or product. The VOC is critical for an organization to:

- Decide what products and services to offer
- Identify critical features and specifications for those products and services
- Decide where to focus improvement efforts
- Obtain a baseline measure of Customer satisfaction against which improvement will be measured
- Identify key drivers of Customer satisfaction

Stakeholder Analysis –Identify who are the stakeholders and how do their roles link to RASIC charts. What are their roles and how the collaboration will encompass executives through team members?

Transformation tools:

- Develop project plan, including schedule and resources, including Initial Work Plan or Milestones
- SIPOC Process Map – Prepare a high-level map of the Processes (SIPOC)
- Affinity Diagram - An Affinity & Mind Mapping Diagrams is a combination of special kinds of brainstorming tools to:

  o Gather large numbers of ideas, opinions, or issues are naturally related
  o Identify, for each grouping, a single concept that ties the group together
  o When chaos exists, managing a large volume of ideas, breakthrough thinking is required, broad issues or themes must be identified

- Sign-Off by Team Lead Belt, Project Sponsor and MBB/BB Coach

Measure: During the Measurement phase, the team studies and evaluates relevant measurement systems to determine if they are capable of measuring key input variables (raw material characteristics and process conditions such as temperatures, speeds, pressures, and flow rates) and output characteristics (product dimensions, Customer defined specifications, and product performance) with the desired precision and accuracy. If they aren't, then the team will work to improve the related measurement systems before proceeding with the project.

Focus: In the Measure phase, existing process data is collected, measurement systems are evaluated, and the process capability requirements are identified. This phase includes the following steps:

- Determine process capability.
- Establish measurement method and tools.
- Determine sampling plan to meet goals.
- Collect data.
- Present status report.

Deliverables: Concentrate on the vital few. Juran used the phrase for those sources of error thought to be largely responsible for the problem. It is time consuming to attempt to tackle all possible sources, and the result may not justify the effort. Once the above analysis of the symptoms has been completed, the mission statement should be revisited to confirm that it is still applicable, or to modify it to make it applicable. The results of the analysis may reveal that the problem is somewhat different from the one that was originally described; or that the improvement project is too large and needs to be broken down into more manageable parts.

During this Measure phase, symptoms of the problem that exists are identified and a baseline measurement of current and recent performance is established. Also, a map of how the process that is producing the problem operates is developed. However, the real purpose of this step is to analyze the symptoms and then to confirm, or modify, the mission statement based upon the results of this analysis. In Six Sigma a symptom is defined as the outward, observable evidence of a problem. It is an output of the process that is producing the problem. If a symptom like this occurs on an ongoing basis, it signals a chronic, underlying quality problem that needs to be addressed. To address such a problem, first of all, the symptom needs to be analyzed in the following manner:

- Updated Project Charter and define the boundaries – that is, the scope of the improvement project
- Updated Project Plan
- Prepare an Overarching Value Stream Map, Detailed Process Map, Value Stream Analysis or Value Chain Analysis
- Develop Operational Definitions
- Data Collection Plan and include Baseline Data Collection
- Measure the symptom – provide Failure Modes and Effect Analysis (FMEA)
- Baseline Process Performance and Capability Results
- Sign Off by Team Lead Belt, Project Sponsor, MBB/BB Coach and Resource Manager

Analyze: During the Analysis phase, the team performs graphical and statistical analyses on historical and newly obtained data to develop preliminary hypotheses for improvement. The team identifies "root causes" of problems and "enablers" of poor performance that need to be corrected.

Focus: In this phase the process is evaluated to determine its capability. Process data are analyzed to identify opportunities for improvement and to develop plans for improving the process. This phase includes the following steps:

- Convert data into information.
- Brainstorming and analysis
- Determine process capability.
- Develop priority list of parameters.
- Perform root cause analysis.
- Update FMEA.
- Develop improvement plan.
- Present status report.
- Determine path forward.

Deliverables: During this Analyze step, theories about the causes of the problem are formulated, these theories are tested, and, finally the root causes of the problem are identified.

- Updated Project Charter
- Updated Project Plan
- Updated FMEA
- Regression Analysis, Histograms and/or Scatter Plots
- Cause and Effect Diagram - The project team brainstorms possible theories, documents them, and then organizes them in the form of a cause-and-effect diagram.
- Theory testing - Before any theory can be accepted as true, it must be systematically tested. Any data required to test a particular

theory, that is not available, must first be collected. If the data collected demonstrates that a particular theory is clearly not important, then that theory can be eliminated.

- Root Cause Analysis - Once testing has been completed, the root cause(s) of the problem should be able to be determined. Once found, the removal of the real root cause(s) will sharply reduce or eliminate the problem/deficiency.
- Prioritized Root Causes – Ranking of the causes will be based on the impact to resources, cost, performance and Quality.
- Sign Off by Team Lead Belt and Project Sponsor

Improve: In the Improve phase, the team designs and conducts experiments to find the optimal conditions needed to operate the process. Improvement requires change, and the correct changes are determined through statistically designed experiments where process inputs or system components are varied and the resulting effects on process outputs (related to quality, cost, and Customer requirements) are observed and measured. If the results are favorable, process conditions are changed to these optimal levels.

Focus: In the Improve phase, the improvement plan developed in the analyze phase is implemented. The results are evaluated, conclusions are drawn, and improvements are finalized and tested. After the desired improvements are implemented, the changes to the process are documented, and new instructions and procedures are developed. This phase includes the following steps:

- Implement improvement plan.
- Perform designed experiment if applicable (DOE).
- Measure improvements.
- Develop conclusions, recommendations, and next steps
- Update documentation.
- Present status report.

Deliverables: During this Improve step, several sequential activities are performed.

- Updated Project Charter
- Updated Project Plan
- Prioritized List of Solutions - Alternative improvement methods are evaluated to determine which method will best remove, or reduce the effect of, the root cause(s) of the problem. This evaluation is carried out using a set of evaluation criteria such as cost, impact, cost/benefit ratio, cultural impact, etc.
- "To-Be" Process Map and/or "To-Be " VSM - An improvement method has been selected, the improvement process is designed by confirm that the improvement achieves the project goals; determining the required resources; specify the procedures and the other changes required; assessing human resource requirements to determine whether any training/re-training is required.
- 5S Workplace Organization
- Physical Space Relationship Chart, if applicable
- Culture Plan & Results - Improvement efforts create change in an organization and "cultural resistance" is a natural consequence of change. Therefore, dealing with this potential cultural resistance needs to be factored into the improvement project plan.
- Pilot Plan & Results - It must be proven effective under operating conditions. This could be done with a pilot test; a dry run, which doesn't involve delivery to the Customer; an acceptance test; a simulation
- Implementation Risk Analysis and Mitigation
- Approved Solution and Detailed Implementation Plan - this involves introducing the proposed change to the people that will make it work. This demands: a clear plan; a description of the change; an explanation indicating why the change is necessary; involvement of those affected; the change. The most important parts of implementation, though, are good planning, good preparation, and good cooperation between all of the individuals concerned.
- Sign Off by Team Lead Belt and Project Sponsor

Control: The team maintains these optimal conditions during the Control phase where audits and control systems sustain the improvements. No project is deemed "completed" until there are sufficient time and evidence to verify that the desired results have been obtained and maintained.

Focus: In the Control phase, the improvements become institutionalized. The process changes were documented in the improve phase. In this phase, control plans are developed to ensure that the process continues to be measured and evaluated. This includes implementing process audit plans, data collection plans, and plans of action for out-of-control conditions, if they occur. The Control phase includes the following steps:

- Establish control system for each critical parameter.
- Establish data collection plan.
- Establish out-of-control plan.
- Establish internal audit plan [accounting alignment and verification of benefits].
- Develop and present final report.

Deliverables: During this Control step, controls are put in place to ensure that the gains that have been achieved will continue and the problem will not recur. To do this the following activities need to be carried out.

- Updated Project Charter
- Updated Project Plan
- Design effective quality controls
- Foolproof the improvement
- Measure, Analyze, and Improve Phase Reviews
- Updated/New SOPs & Training Plans
- Plan for Transition to Process Owner
- Process Control/Response Plan & Recurring Report (and/or Visual Controls)

- Project Summary - Control Charts, Control Plan, Reaction Plan and/or Run Charts
- The tools most commonly used in the Control phase are:

  - Control Charts
  - Flow Diagrams
  - Comparative charts (e.g. Pareto Charts)
  - Quality Control Process Chart
  - Standardization

- Detailed Financial & Operational Benefits Estimates
- Sign Off by Project Sponsor, MBB/BB Coach, and Resource Manager

Appendix: DMADV Descriptions

Define: Define design goals that are consistent with Customer demands and the enterprise strategy. Much like DMAIC, the define stage is where the end Product or Service is designed based on client's wants or desires.

Focus: In the Define phase, a team clearly identifies the suppliers, process inputs, process activities, process outputs, and Customers; establishes baselines and benchmarks; and sets and agrees upon goals and measures of success.

- The first step in a DFSS project is to establish and maintain a DFSS project team (for both product/service and process) with a shared vision.
- The purpose is to establish and maintain a motivated team.
- The success of development activities depends on the performance of this team, which is selected according to the project charter.
- The team should be fully integrated, including internal and external members (suppliers and Customers).
- Special efforts may be necessary to create a multidiscipline team that collaborates to achieve a Six Sigma–level design.
- Roles, responsibilities, and resources are best defined upfront, collaboratively, by all team members. The black belt is the team leader.

During the Define phase, a team and its sponsors reach agreement on what the project is and what it should accomplish. Presuming that a draft of the Project Charter is already in place, the main work in the Define phase is for the project team to complete an analysis of what the project should accomplish and confirm understanding with the sponsor(s).

Deliverables: Nine essential tollgate deliverables that must be addressed:

- Problem or opportunity statement
- Goal statement
- Project scope
- Prioritized voice of Customer (VOC) needs and critical-to-quality (CTQ) requirements (i.e., initial DFSS QFD scorecard, benchmarking data, surveys)
- Expected benefits and how improvements are measured
- High-level process map and/or thought map
- Business case or strategic plan
- Timelines – estimated duration of project phases
- Team member names[114]

Measure: Measure and identify CTQs (characteristics that are Critical To Quality), product capabilities, production process capability, and risks. Measuring is how you will process the Product or Service as defined.

Focus: During the Measurement phase, the team studies and evaluates relevant measurement systems to determine if they are capable of measuring key input variables (raw material characteristics and process conditions such as temperatures, speeds, pressures, and flow rates) and output characteristics (product dimensions, Customer defined specifications, and product performance) with the desired precision and accuracy. If they aren't, then the team will work to improve the related measurement systems before proceeding with the project.

---

114   Isixsgima.com; Largest-Breakthrough Innovation Project; Retrieved: 24 Feb 2011

- DFSS projects can be categorized as design or redesign of an entity.
- Customers are fully identified and their needs collected and analyzed.
- The most appropriate set of CTQs metrics are determined in order to measure and evaluate the design.
- The numerical limits and targets for each CTQ are established.

Deliverables: 12 essential tollgate deliverables that should be addressed:

- Identify Customer requirement performance CTQs using system flow-down
- Translate/correlate prioritized VOC requirements into performance CTQs
- Process mapping
- DFSS functional analysis
- Develop initial $Y = F(x)$ transfer functions
- Evaluate current performance metrics
- Use of historic data or develop new data collection plan
- Analysis of the cost of poor quality (COPQ) for existing designs
- Assess product design and/or process design capability
- Define improvement capability targets
- Reassess project scope and finalize charter
- Updated DFSS QFD scorecard with prioritized performance CTQs[115]

Analyze: Analyze to develop and design alternatives, create a high-level design and evaluate design capability to select the best design. Through analyzing the process that will result in the end product, areas of improvement and changes are discovered through simulations, not users, so the actual driver never gets to test the Product or Service.

---

115   Isixsgima.com; Largest-Breakthrough Innovation Project; Retrieved: 24 Feb 2011

Focus: During the Analysis phase, the team performs graphical and statistical analyses on historical and newly obtained data to develop preliminary hypotheses for improvement. The team identifies "root causes" of problems and "enablers" of poor performance that need to be corrected.

- Principles of Design review
- Design for X

Deliverables: 12 essential tollgate deliverables that must be addressed:

- Identify design innovation strategies – applied creativity
- Measurement system analysis
- Estimate design life and assess against reliability requirements
- Identify/prioritize physical design CTQs and correlate to deliver performance CTQs
- Current product/process performance capability studies performed
- Design concept(s) generation (hardware or virtual prototypes)
- Formulate hypotheses regarding design risk, root cause analysis
- Evaluate design risk against Customer requirements for each design concept
- Rationale for the type of statistical analysis used
- Concept design selection that best meets Customer performance CTQs
- Characterize and refine transfer functions
- Updated DFSS QFD scorecard with prioritized physical design CTQs[116]

Design: Design details, optimize the design, and plan for design verification. This phase may require simulations. Here is when DMADV differs from DMAIC. It's clear to the automaker that although the Product or Service will do what it's supposed to do, the Customer doesn't like it. By revisiting the design based on end-user suggestions and input, the design can be restructured to please.

---

116   lsixsgima.com; Largest-Breakthrough Innovation Project; Retrieved: 24 Feb 2011

Focus: In the Design phase, the team designs and conducts experiments to find the optimal conditions needed to operate the process. Improvement requires change, and the correct changes are determined through statistically designed experiments where process inputs or system components are varied and the resulting effects on process outputs (related to quality, cost, and Customer requirements) are observed and measured. If the results are favorable, process conditions are changed to these optimal levels.

- Design of experiments
- Introduction to Simulation for Variance Reduction
- Practical Application of DFSS Scorecards
- FMEA
- Critical Analysis

Deliverables: 10 essential tollgate deliverables that must be addressed:

- Optimize product/process design for robustness
- Design sensitivity analyses complete
- Verification of all transfer functions
- Evaluate design for manufacturability (if applicable)
- Estimate/confirm and allocate tolerances on key product and process characteristics
- Product design specifications translated to process specifications
- Verification/test/analysis to demonstrate design product/process capability meets or exceeds Customer requirements
- Initial product/process design control plan
- Updated DFSS QFD scorecard with prioritized physical design CTQs
- Populated DFSS QFD scorecard with product/process capability data to assess improvement metrics in terms of DPU (defects per unit) and long-term sigma level, minimize design risk and trade-off analysis[117]

117   Isixsgima.com; Largest-Breakthrough Innovation Project; Retrieved: 24 Feb 2011

Verify: Verify the design, set up pilot runs, implement the production process and hand it over to the process owner(s). Verification of the new design must be determined by the end-users. If complaints on the uncomfortable Product or Service cease, then the DMADV process has worked.

Focus: Verify stage is focused on a new product or process needs to be developed to meet Customer requirements. Additionally, it is used when a product or process has been optimized using DMAIC, but is still unable to meet Customer specifications.

Deliverables: Eight essential tollgate deliverables that must be addressed:

- Document optimized design solution methods that drove design decisions throughout DFSS project
- Document results and financial benefits that product/process design improvements have been achieved
- Finalize DFSS QFD scorecard summary to verify that defect and sigma levels of all product/process characteristics meet Customer CTQs
- Final product/process design control plan
- Evaluate replication opportunities across company organization
- Communicate product/process design guidelines and DFSS score-card results to project team
- Final DFSS project report summarizing findings
- Project close out, team reward and recognition[118]

---

118   Isixsgima.com; Largest-Breakthrough Innovation Project; Retrieved: 24 Feb 2011

Appendix: Acronym Descriptions

Acronym and Description

BB - Black Belt
BT - Business Transformation
C&P - Cost and Performance
CBR - Critical Business Requirement
CCR - Critical Customer Requirement
CEO - Chief Executive Officer
CFO - Chief Financial Officer
CIO - Chief Information Officer
CMO - Chief Marketing Officer
COO - Chief Operating Officer
COPQ - Cost of Poor Quality
CPI - Continuous Process Improvement
CSO - Chief Sales Officer
CTO - Chief Technology Officer
CTQ - Critical To Quality
CXOs - Executive Team members: CEO, CFO, CIO, COO, CTO, etc.
DMAMV - Define, Measure, Analyze, Design and Verify
DMAIC - Define, Measure, Analyze, Improve and Control
DOE - Design Of Experiment
DPMO - Defects Per Million Opportunities
EIT - Enterprise Integration Team
EPIT - Enterprise Process Improvement Team
FMC - Financial Management and Comptroller
GB - Green Belt
KB - Knowledge Base
KPA - Key Process Areas

KPI - Key Performance Indicators
LSS - Lean Six Sigma
MBB - Master Black Belt
PM - Project Manager
PMO - Program Management Office
POC - Point of Concept
RASIC - Responsible, Accountable, Support, Informed, Consulted
RCE - Readiness Core Enterprise
RM - Resource Manager
ROI - Return on Investment
SME - Subject Matter Expert
SOP - Standard Operating Procedure
SQL - Sigma Quality Level
SWOT - Strengths, Weaknesses, Opportunities, Threats analysis
TMM - Transformation Maturity Model
VOC - Voice of the Customer

Appendix: Lexicon

Affinity diagram. A management tool for organizing information (usually gathered during a brainstorming activity).

Alignment. Actions to ensure that a process or activity supports the organization's strategy, goals and objectives.

Assessment. A systematic evaluation process of collecting and analyzing data to determine the current, historical or projected compliance of an organization to a standard. For measurement; See Measurement, and for metrics, See Metrics.

Black Belt (BB). Full-time team leader responsible for implementing process improvement projects—DMAIC or DMADV—within a business to drive up Customer satisfaction and productivity levels.

Business process. Those activities that, collectively, combine to create a business's product(s) or service(s). A true business process functions to fulfill the business's mission and objectives.

Business Transformation [BT]. Change Management strategy aims to align People, Process and Technology initiatives more closely with its business strategy and vision. In turn this helps to support and innovate new business strategies.

Business Transformation Initiative. Improvements to an Enterprise's business processes resulting in better effectiveness, efficiency or alignment with Enterprise priorities.

Cause and Effect diagram. A tool for analyzing process dispersion. It is also referred to as the "Ishikawa diagram," because Kaoru Ishikawa developed it, and the "fishbone diagram," because the complete diagram resembles a fish skeleton. The diagram illustrates the main causes and sub causes leading to an effect (symptom). The cause and effect diagram is one of the "seven tools of quality" (see listing).

Champion. A business leader or senior manager who ensures resources are available for training and projects, and who is involved in

263

periodic project reviews; also an executive who supports and addresses Six Sigma organizational issues.

Change agent: An individual from within or outside an organization who facilitates change in the organization; might be the initiator of the change effort, but not necessarily.

Charter. A written commitment approved by management stating the scope of authority for an improvement project or team.

Checklist. A tool for ensuring all important steps or actions in an operation have been taken. Checklists contain items important or relevant to an issue or situation. Checklists are often confused with check sheets (see listing).

Company Culture. A system of values, beliefs and behaviors inherent in a company. To optimize business performance, top management must define and create the necessary culture.

Continuous Process Improvement. Continuous Process Improvement is a strategic approach for developing a culture of continuous improvement in the areas of reliability, process cycle times, costs in terms of less total resource consumption, quality, and productivity.

Cost of Poor Quality (COPQ): The costs associated with providing poor quality products or services.

Critical To Quality: CTQs are the internal critical quality parameters that relate to the wants and needs of the Customer.

Cultural resistance: A form of resistance based on opposition to the possible social and organizational consequences associated with change.

Customer satisfaction. The result of delivering a product or service that meets Customer requirements.

Data. A set of collected facts. There are two basic kinds of numerical data. measured or variable data, such as "16 ounces," "4 miles" and "0.75 inches;" and counted or attribute data, such as "162 defects."

Defect. A product's or service's nonfulfillment of an intended requirement or reasonable expectation for use, including safety considerations.

Deming cycle. The Deming cycle is another term for the Plan-Do-Study-Act cycle. **DMADV.** A data driven quality strategy for designing products and processes, it is an integral part of a Six Sigma quality initiative. It consists of five interconnected phases. Define, Measure, Analyze, Design And Verify.

Design Of Experiments (DOE). is the design of any information-gathering exercises where variation is present. In statistics, these terms are usually used for controlled experiments.

DMAIC. A data driven quality strategy for improving processes and an integral part of a Six Sigma quality initiative. DMAIC is an acronym for define, measure, analyze, improve and control. A Six Sigma improvement methodology. Define, Measure, Analyze, Improve, Control.

Effect. The result of an action being taken; the expected or predicted impact when an action is to be taken or is proposed. The result produced by a particular cause – e.g., the result achieved by a specific action. Sometimes expressed as the "response variable," represented by "Y," with the cause, or independent variable, represented by "X."

Effectiveness. The state of having produced a desired effect. A measurable quality representing the ability (i.e., of a particular product, process, service, system, operation, enterprise, etc.) to achieve a particular objective or obtain a particular desired result.

End-to-End. the end of one object in contact lengthwise with the end of another object; from first to last; "the play was excellent end-to-end"; specifically, commercial linkage through processes in an enterprise from the Suppliers to the Customer.

Enterprise management. The management of the Enterprise's business operations through the application of philosophies and practices that focus on achieving the objectives of the organization as a whole, rather than merely furthering the parochial interests of individual components.

Effect: The result of an action being taken; the expected or predicted impact when an action is to be taken or is proposed.

Effectiveness: The state of having produced a decided on or desired effect.

Efficiency: The ratio of the output to the total input in a process.

Efficient: A term describing a process that operates effectively while consuming minimal resources (such as labor and time).

Efficiency Measures. Effective programs not only accomplish their outcome performance goals, they strive to improve their efficiency by achieving or accomplishing more benefits for a given amount of resources.

Eighty-twenty (80-20) rule. A term referring to the Pareto principle, which was first defined by J. M. Juran in 1950. The principle suggests most effects come from relatively few causes; that is, 80% of the effects come from 20% of the possible causes. Also see "Pareto chart."

External Customers. Recipients of products, services or processes supported by your organization; may include product lines, services, logistics or intellectual capital.

Green Belt (GB). An employee who has been trained in the Six Sigma improvement method and will lead a process improvement or quality improvement team as part of his or her full-time job.

Hawthorne effect: The concept that every change results (initially, at least) in increased productivity.

Integrated Management System. Currently, the Enterprise management structure is composed of numerous focused management systems tailored to functional areas (resourcing, logistics, finance, human resources, etc). The Enterprise's Integrated Management System is envisioned to be a holistic and integrated set of management processes intended to align decision making with enterprise strategy and guidance.

Internal Customers. Recipients of a product, service, etc., from within an organization; may include individual employees and/or entire teams or departments.

Ishikawa Diagram. Also known as a "fishbone diagram," a "cause and effect diagram," or a "cause and effect technique," the Ishikawa diagram is used to analyze cause and effect; named for diagram inventor Kaoru Ishikawa.

Key Performance Indicator (KPI). A statistical measure of how well an organization is doing in a particular area. A KPI could measure a company's financial performance or how it is holding up against Customer requirements.

Key process. A major system level process that supports the mission and satisfies major consumer requirements. Successful companies have operational and managerial processes that allow them to deliver value in a way they can successfully repeat and increase in scale.

These may include such recurrent tasks as training, development, manufacturing, budgeting, planning, sales and service. Key processes also include a company's rules, metrics and norms.

Key Resources The key resources (or assets) are the people, technology, products, facilities, equipment and brand required to deliver the value proposition to the targeted Customer.

Knowledge Base: Computer Science The part of an expert system that contains the facts and rules needed to solve problems. A collection of facts and rules for problem solving.

Lean. A methodology to improve processes with an emphasis on the reduction of waste, based on the eight wastes: 1. overproduction ahead of demand; 2. waiting for the next process, worker, material or equipment; 3. unnecessary transport of materials (for example, between functional areas of facilities, or to or from a stockroom or warehouse); 4. over-processing of parts due to poor tool and product design; 5. inventories more than the absolute minimum; 6. unnecessary movement by employees during the course of their work (such as to look for parts, tools, prints or help); 7. production of defective parts; 8. underutilization of employees' brainpower, skills, experience and talents.

Lean Six Sigma. A quality improvement concept designed to reduce waste and process cycle time. Producing the maximum sellable products or services at the lowest operational cost while optimizing inventory levels.

Life-cycle Management. A management process applied throughout the life (systems development, production, delivery, sustainment, and disposal) of a system or commodity (human capital, materiel, readiness, services, and infrastructure) that bases all programmatic decisions on the anticipated mission-related and economic benefits (cost, schedule, performance, risk, and supportability) derived over the life of that system.

Management. Management is linked with leadership, just as doctrine, systems, processes, facilities, and equipment are connected with the people who use them.

Master Black Belt (MBB). An MBB is qualified to teach other Six Sigma facilitators the methods, tools and applications in all functions and levels of the company and is a resource for using statistical process control in processes.

Measurement. The strategic plan features declarative statements also known as strategic goals, which state what the agency wants to accomplish in terms of outcomes or results. Each strategic goal is supported by performance goals – performance measures with time-specific targets. Managers are encouraged to frequently compare actual results of performance measures against their time-specific targets and previous levels of performance to assess progress towards meeting strategic goals.

Metric. A numeric measurement or formula for monitoring control in a process, goal, objective that monitors compliance or effectiveness. Metrics are used to assess and adjust operations and business strategies. Metrics are indicators that measure and assess progress in achieving desired outcomes. Desired outcomes may include decreasing costs, increasing performance, and reducing cycle time in order to improve support to the Customer.

Muda. Japanese word for waste; any activity that consumes resources but creates no value for the Customer.

Objective. A specific statement of a desired short-term condition or achievement; includes measurable end results to be accomplished by specific teams or individuals within time limits.

Outcome measures. Outcome measure refers to an assessment of the results of a program activity compared to its intended purpose.

Out-of-control process: A process in which the statistical measure being evaluated is not in a state of statistical control.

Output measures. Outputs refer to the internal activities of a program (such as the products and services delivered).

Pareto chart. A graphical tool for ranking causes from most significant to least significant. It is based on the Pareto principle, which was first defined by Joseph M. Juran in 1950.

Partnership/alliance. Both a strategy and a formal relationship between a supplier and a Customer that engenders cooperation for the benefit of both parties.

Poka-yoke: Japanese term that means mistake proofing. A poka-yoke device is one that prevents incorrect parts from being made or assembled or easily identifies a flaw or error.

Program. The term may describe an agency's mission, functions, activities, services, projects, and processes, and is defined as an organized set of activities directed toward a common purpose or goal that an entity undertakes or proposes to carry out its responsibilities.

Performance goal. A performance goal comprises a performance measure with targets and timeframes. Performance measures. Indicators, statistics, or metrics used to gauge program performance.

Process. Sequence of interdependent and linked procedures that, at every stage, consume one or more resources (employee time, energy, machines, money) to convert inputs (data, material, parts, etc.) into outputs. These outputs then serve as inputs for the next stage until a known goal or end result is reached.

Project Charter: A written declaration of the purpose and expected result of the project. An effective statement of aim follows the SMART format (S=specific, including the process boundaries; M=measurable & measured; A=agreed upon by the manager & his/her supervisor; R=Realistic, yet stretch; T=time specific, results to be achieved by a defined date).

Quality. A subjective term for which each person or sector has its own definition. In technical usage, quality can have two meanings. 1. the characteristics of a product or service that bear on its ability to satisfy stated or implied needs; 2. a product or service free of deficiencies.

Reliability. The probability of a product's performing its intended function under stated conditions without failure for a given period of time.

Repeatability. The variation in measurements obtained when one measurement device is used several times by the same person to measure the same characteristic on the same product.

Reproducibility. The variation in measurements made by different people using the same measuring device to measure the same characteristic on the same product.

Requirements. The ability of an item to perform a required function under stated conditions for a stated period of time.

Resource utilization. Using a resource in a way that increases throughput.

Results. The effects that an organization obtains at the conclusion of a time period.

Root cause. A factor that caused a nonconformance and should be permanently eliminated through process improvement.

Stakeholder. Any individual, group or organization that will have a significant impact on or will be significantly impacted by the quality of a specific product or service.

Standard. The metric, specification, gauge, statement, category, segment, grouping, behavior, event or physical product sample against which the outputs of a process are compared and declared acceptable or unacceptable.

Strategic goal or strategic objective. Statement of aim or purpose included in a strategic plan. Strategic goals should be used to group multiple program outcome goals. Each program outcome goal should relate to and in the aggregate be sufficient to influence the strategic goals or objectives and their performance measures.

Strategic planning. The process an organization uses to envision its future and develop the appropriate strategies, goals, objectives and action plans.

SWOT. (Strengths, Weaknesses, Opportunities, Threats analysis) A strategic technique used to assess what an organization is facing.

Stretch goals: A set of goals designed to position an organization to meet future requirements.

Target. Quantifiable or otherwise measurable characteristic that tells how well or at what level a program aspires to perform.

Total Quality Management (TQM): TQM is based on all members of an organization participating in improving processes, products, services and the culture in which they work.

Transformation. A process of profound and radical change that orients an organization in a new direction and takes it to an entirely different level of effectiveness.

Value proposition. An analysis and quantified review of the benefits, costs, and value that an organization can deliver to Customers. It is also a positioning of value, where Value = Benefits – Cost (cost includes risk).

Voice of the Customer [VOC]. Requirements and expectations of Customers relative to products or services, as documented and disseminated to the providing organization's members.

Waste. Any activity that consumes resources and produces no added value to the product or service a Customer receives. Also known as muda.

Zero defects. A performance standard and method Philip B. Crosby developed; states that if people commit themselves to watching details and avoiding errors, they can move closer to the goal of zero defects.

Appendix: Key Points

Bibliography

Andel, Tom. *"Lean & Six Sigma Traps to Avoid".* 2007.

Antony, Jiju. *"Pros and cons of Six Sigma: an academic perspective".* Edited by: http://web.archive.org/

Bower, Joseph L., and Clayton M. Christensen. *"Disruptive Technologies: Catching the Wave".* Edited by Edited by John Seely Brown. Boston, Mass.: Harvard Business School Press,, 1997.

BusinessDictionary.com. Edited by http://www.businessdictionary.com/definition/process.html.

CEO Advisor Blog. This entry was posted on October 6, 2010. This source provide the original 10 key issues that motivates change in a business.

De Feo, Joseph A. and Barnard, William. *JURAN Institute's Six Sigma Breakthrough and Beyond - Quality Performance Breakthrough Methods.* Tata McGraw-Hill Publishing Company Limited, 2005.

Deming, W. Edwards. *Out of the Crisis.* MIT Press, 1986.

Deming, W. Edwards. *The New Economics for Industry, Government, Education.* MIT Press, 1993.

Deming, W.Edwards. *Out of the Crisis.* 1986.

DiBasio, Darcie. *"How to Define a Process".* Series: International Conference on Software Quality, October 4-6 1999. Edited by American Society for Quality. Translated by http://asq.org/qic/display-item/index.html?item=13826. Vols. Vol. 9, No. 0. Cambridge, MA, 1999.

Dr. Deming's Management Training. W. Edwards Deming Institute.

Drucker, Peter F. *The New Realities.* First edition. Harper & Row publishers, 1989.

Economist Intelligence Unit. *"A Change For The Better - Steps for Successful Business Transformation".* May 2008.

Gartner. *"Gartner EXP Worldwide Survey of More than 1,500 CIOs Shows IT Spending to Be Flat in 2009".* Gartner Press Release,, Jan. 14, 2009.

Gartner. *"Gartner Reveals Five Business Intelligence Predictions for 2009 and Beyond".* Gartner Study, January 15, 2009.

Goldratt, Eliyahu M. *What is this thing called Theory of Constraints a how should it be implemented.* North River Press, 1990.

Goonan, Brian. *"Business Transformation: Doing it Right, Part I,"* CIO Magazine, February 9, 2005.

Hayler, Rowland and Nichols, Michael D. *How Leading Companies Are Driving Results Using Lean, Six Sigma, and Process Management.* 2007.

Infosys. *"Defining Business Transformation".* May 2006.

Keck, Paul R. *"Why Quality Fails?",*. 1995.

Kotler, Philip. *Database Marketing - Marketing Insights from A to Z: 80 Concepts Every Manager Needs to Know.* John Wiley & Sons, 2003.

Lean Six Sigma. *Areas where Lean Six Sigma methodology can be applied to enhance your products or services.*

Marks, Dr. Mitchell Lee. *"In With The New".* Wall Street Journal, May 24, 2010,.

Motorola, Inc. *Six Sigma Methodology.* http://www.motorola.com/ Business/. Motorola University, Copyright 1994-2005.

Palmer, Jonathan. *"Change Management in Practice: Why Does Change Fail?".* 2008.

Peters, Tom. *"Thriving on Chaos".* Alfred A. Knopf, Inc,, 1987.

PMHUT.COM. *"Six Sigma vs. Total Quality Management". http://www. pmhut.com/six-sigma-vs-total-quality-management. Retrieved April 19, 2010.* Source: "Six Sigma vs. Total Quality Management". http://www. pmhut.com/six-sigma-vs-total-quality-management.

Prem, Hema & George Eby Mathew. *"Defining Business Transformation",.* Infosys, May 2006.

Prem, Hema & Mathew, George Eby. *"Defining Business Transformation".* Infosys, May 2006.

Reichheld, Frederick. *The Loyalty Effect: The Hidden Force Behind Growth, Profits, and Lasting Value.* Boston: Harvard Business School Press, 1996.

Reilly, Norman B. *Quality: What Makes it Happen?* Van Nostrand Reinhold, 1994.

Schuler, Dr. A. J. *"Overcoming Resistance to Change: Top Ten Reasons for Change Resistance"*. 2003.

Smith, Dick, and Jerry and Koonce, Richard Blakeslee. *Strategic Six Sigma: Best Practices from the Executive Suite.* John Wiley & Sons © 2002.

Stein, Philip. *"Effective Measurement of Business Performance"*. ASQ Annual Quality Congress proceedings, May 1998.

Strassmann, Paul. *The Squandered Computer.* The Information Economics Press,, 1997.

Strategos-International. *Toyota Production System and Lean Manufacturing.*

Taguchi, Genichi. *Design Of Experiments (DOE) is the design of any information-gathering exercises where variation is present. In statistics, these terms are usually used for controlled experiments.*

The Conference Board. www.conference-board.org.

Willetts, David. Willetts is a qualified accountant (FCMA) and provides special financial and management support to business owners. 2010.

Womack, James P., Daniel T. Jones, and Daniel Roos. *The Machine That Changed the World.* 1990.

Wurtzel, Marvin. *"Reasons for Six Sigma Deployment Failures"*. Friday June 13, 2008.

9509623R0019

Made in the USA
Charleston, SC
19 September 2011